G000293037

TOWN PLANS

3rd edition August 2003

© Automobile Association Developments Limited 2003

Original edition printed 1997

Ordnance Survey® This product includes mapping data licensed from Ordnance Survey® with the permission of the Controller of Her Majesty's Stationery Office. © Crown copyright 2003. All rights reserved. Licence number 399221.

Published by AA Publishing (a trading name of Automobile Association Developments Limited, whose registered office is Millstream, Maidenhead Road, Windsor, Berkshire SL4 5GD. Registered number 1878835).

Mapping produced by the Cartographic Department of The Automobile Association. (A01776).

ISBN 0 7495 3906 2 (wire bound)

A CIP catalogue record for this book is available from The British Library.

Printed in Italy by G. Canale. & S.P.A., Torino.

The contents of this atlas are believed to be correct at the time of the latest revision. However, the publishers cannot be held responsible for loss occasioned to any person acting or refraining from action as a result of any material in this atlas, nor for any errors, omissions or changes in such material. This does not affect your statutory rights. The publishers would welcome information to correct any errors or omissions and to keep this atlas up to date. Please write to the Cartographic Editor, Publishing Division, The Automobile Association, Fanum House, Basing View, Basingstoke, Hampshire RG21 4EA.

Atlas contents

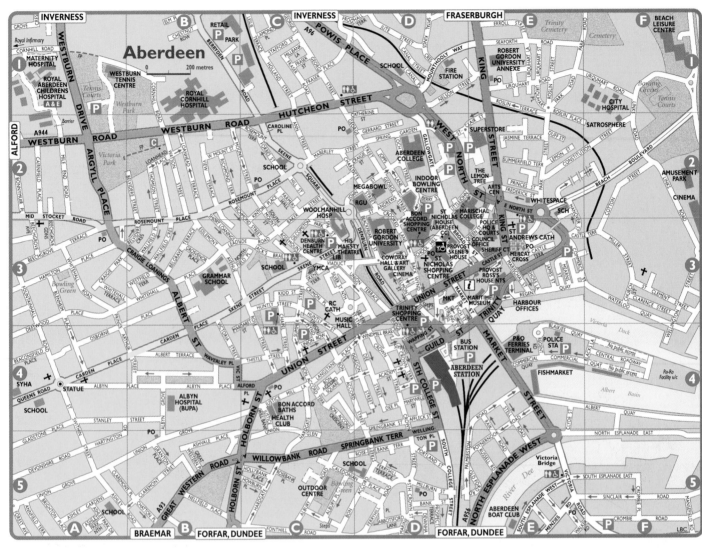

Aberdeen

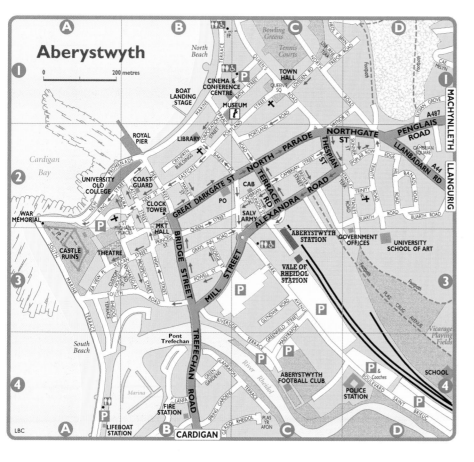

Aberystwyth

Basingstoke

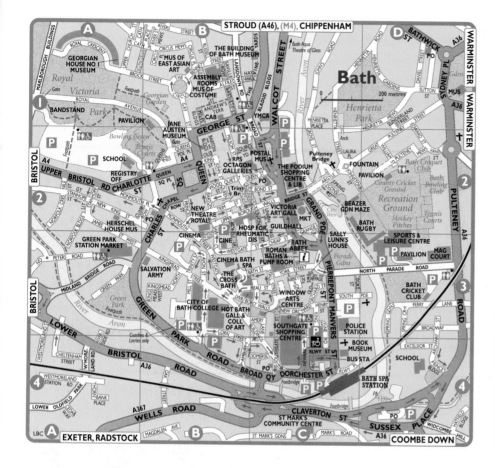

Bath

C3	Abbey Square	A3	Lower Bristol Road
B1	Alfred Street	A4	Lower Oldfield Park
B4	Ambury	C3	Manvers Street
C2	Argyle Street	A3	Midland Bridge Road
B3	Avon Street	B3	Mill Street
B2	Barton Street	B2	Milsom Street
B3	Bath Street	A2	Monmouth Place
C3	Beau Street	B2	Monmouth Street
B1	Bennett Street	B2	New Bond Street
C1	Bladud Buildings	A2	New King Street
B2	Bridewell Lane	C3	New Orchard Street
C2	Bridge Street	D3	North Parade Road
B4	Broad Quay	B4	Oak Street
C2	Broad Street	C3	Old Orchard Street
D3	Broadway	C3	Pierrepont Street
A1	Brock Street	B2	Princes Street
B2	Chapel Row	D2	Pulteney Road
B3	Charles Street	B2	Queen Square
A2	Charlotte Street	B2	Queen Square Place
C3	Cheap Street	B2	Queen Street
B1	Circus Mews	B2	Queens Parade Place
C4	Claverton Street	B2	Quiet Street
B3	Corn Street	C4	Railway Street
C4	Dorchester Street	A1	Royal Avenue
D2	Edward Street	A1	Royal Crescent
D3	Ferry Lane	B1	Russell Street
B1	Gay Street	C1	St John's Road
B1	George Street	B2	Saw Close
C2	Grand Parade	C3	South Parade
C2	Grange Grove	C4	Southgate Street
D2	Great Pulteney Street	C3	Stall Street
A2	Great Stanhope Street	D4	Sussex Place
A3	Green Park	D1	Sydney Place
B3	Green Park Road	B1	The Circus
B2	Green Street	C1	The Vineyards
C2	Grove Street	B2	Trim Street
D1	Henrietta Gardens	C2	Union Passage
D1	Henrietta Mews	C2	Union Street
C1	Henrietta Road	B2	Upper Borough Walls
C1	Henrietta Street	A2	Upper Bristol Road
C3	Henry Street	A1	Upper Church Street
A2	James Street West	C1	Walcot Street
B2	John Street	B4	Wells Road
B3	Kingsmead North	B3	Westgate Buildings
B3	Kingsmead Street	B3	Westgate Street
B1	Lansdown Road	A4	Westmoreland Road
A2	Little Stanhope Street	B2	Wood Street
B3	Lower Borough Walls	C3	York Street

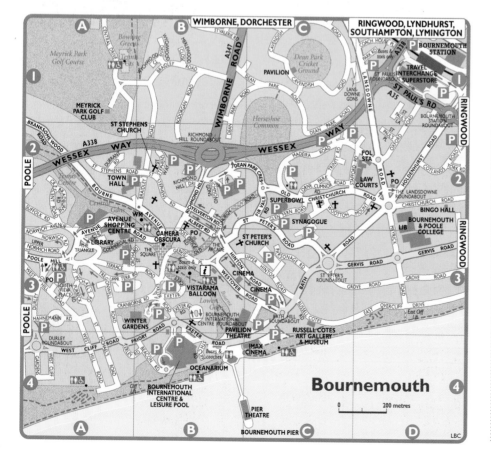

Bournemouth

B2	Albert Road	C3	Parsonage Road
A3	Avenue Lane	A3	Poole Hill
A3	Avenue Road	B3	Post Office Road
C3	Bath Road	B4	Priory Road
B4	Beacon Road	A3	Purbeck Road
B1	Bodorgan Road	B2	Richmond Gardens
A2	Bourne Avenue	B2	Richmond Hill
A2	Bradburne Road	B2	Richmond Hill Drive
B2	Braidley Road	C3	Russell Cotes Road
A2	Branksome Wood Road	A3	St Michael's Road
C1	Cavendish Road	D1	St Paul's Lane
A1	Central Drive	D2	St Paul's Place
D2	Christchurch Road	D1	St Paul's Road
D1	Coach House Place	C2	St Peter's Road
A3	Commercial Road	A2	St Stephens Road
C2	Cumnor Road	B2	St Stephens Way
D2	Cotlands Road	B1	St Valerie Road
A3	Cranborne Road	B4	South Cliff Road
A2	Crescent Road	A3	South View Place
B2	Dean Park Crescent	C2	Stafford Road
C1	Dean Park Road	A3	Suffolk Road
A3	Durley Road	A3	Terrace Road
A2	Durrant Road	B3	The Arcade
D3	East Overcliff Drive	B3	The Square
B3	Exeter Crescent	A3	The Triangle
B3	Exeter Park Road	A3	Tregonwell Road
B3	Exeter Road	C2	Trinity Road
C2	Fir Vale Road	C3	Upper Hinton Road
B3	Gervis Place	A3	Upper Norwich Road
D3	Gervis Road	A3	Upper Terrace Road
C2	Glen Fern Road	A2	Wessex Way
D3	Grove Road	A4	West Cliff Gardens
A3	Hahnemann Road	A4	West Cliff Road
B3	Hinton Road	A3	West Hill Road
D2	Holdenhurst Road	B3	Westover Road
A4	Kerley Road	B1	Wimborne Road
C1	Lansdowne Gardens	C2	Wootton Mount
D1	Lansdowne Road	B1	Wychwood Close
C2	Lorne Park Road	B1	Wychwood Drive
C2	Madeira Road	B2	Yelverton Road
B1	Merlewood Close	D2	York Road
D3	Meyrick Road		
A3	Norwich Avenue		
A3	Norwich Road		
B3	Old Christchurch Road		
A3	Orchard Street		
D2	Oxford Road		
D1	Park Road		

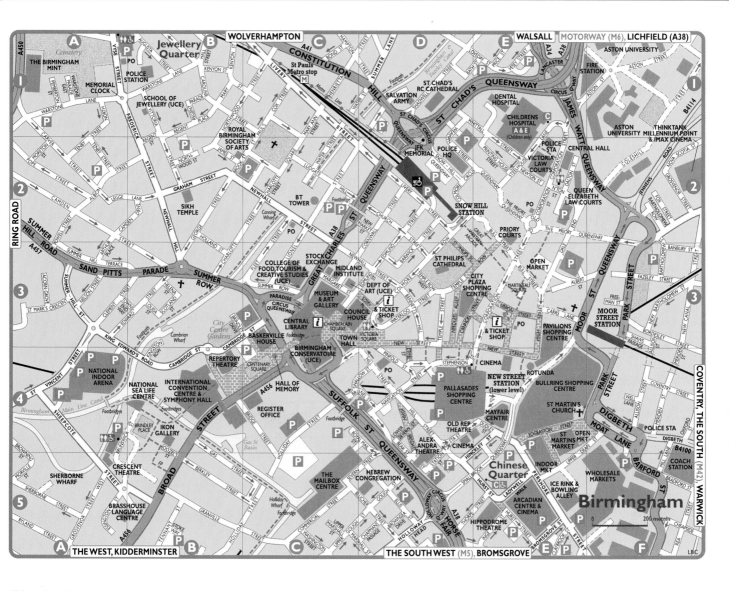

Birmingham

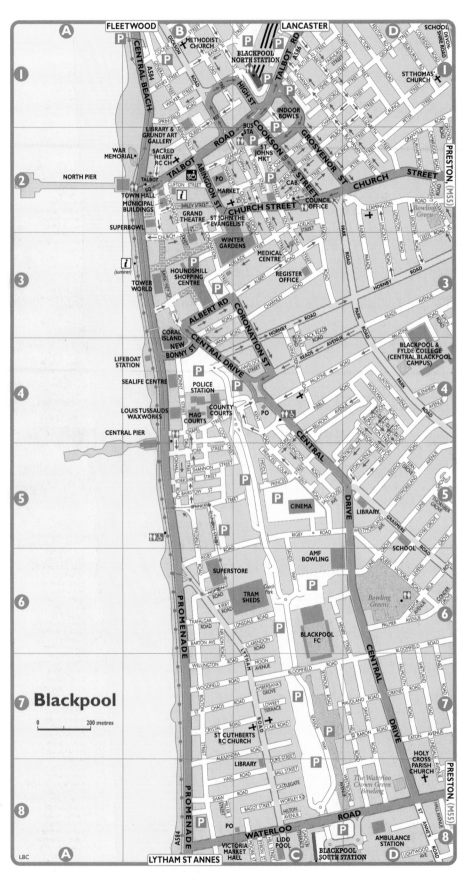

Blackpool

Bradford

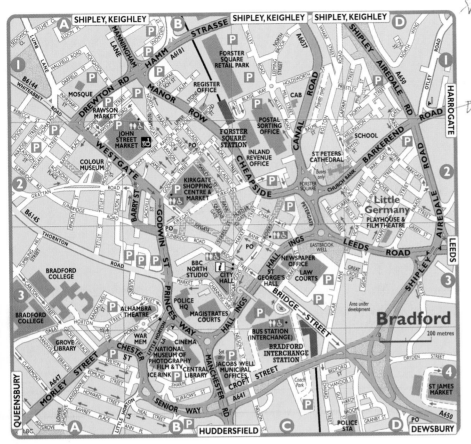

B2	Bank Street
D2	Barkerend Road
B2	Barry Street
C2	Bolton Road
B3	Bridge Street
C3	Broadway
D2	Burnett Street
C2	Canal Road
D1	Captain Street
A3	Carlton Street
B3	Channing Way
D3	Chapel Street
C2	Charles Street
C2	Cheapside
A4	Chester Street
C2	Church Bank
A4	Claremont
C4	Croft Street
C2	Currer Street
B2	Dale Street
A1	Darfield Street
B2	Darley Street
C3	Drake Street
A1	Drewton Road
D4	Dryden Street
B2	Duke Street
D3	East Parade
A4	Edmund Street
C4	Edward Street
C2	Forster Square
B2	Godwin Street
B1	Grammar School Street
A2	Grattan Road
A3	Great Horton Street
C4	Guy Street
C3	Hall Ings
A1	Hallfield Road
B1	Hamm Strasse
C1	Holdsworth Street
A1	Houghton Place
A4	Howard Street
B3	Ivegate
B2	James Street
B2	John Street
B2	Kirkgate
D3	Leeds Road
B4	Little Horton Lane
A1	Lumb Lane

B4	Manchester Road
B1	Manningham Lane
A4	Mannville Terrace
B1	Manor Row
C3	Market Street
A4	Morley Street
B4	Neal Street
C4	Nelson Street
B3	Norfolk Gardens
C1	North Brook Street
B1	North Parade
D1	North Street
B1	Northgate
D1	Otley Road
D2	Peckover Street
C2	Petergate
B2	Piccadilly
B3	Princes Way
A2	Providence Street
B3	Quebec Street
B2	Rawson Place
A2	Rawson Road
B2	Rawson Square
C1	St Blaise Way
A2	St Thomas Road
B1	Salem Street
A4	Sawrey Place
B4	Senior Way
B4	Sharpe Street
D3	Shipley Airedale Road
A2	Simes Street
A2	Stott Hill
A2	Sunbridge Road
A3	Tetley Street
A3	Thornton Road
A3	Tumbling Hill Street
B3	Tyrrel Street
D2	Upper Parkgate
B2	Upper Piccadilly
C1	Valley Road
C3	Vicar Lane
C2	Well Street
D2	Wellington Street
A2	Westgate
C1	Wharf Street
A1	Whiteabbey Road
A2	Wigan Street
A4	Wilton Street

Brighton

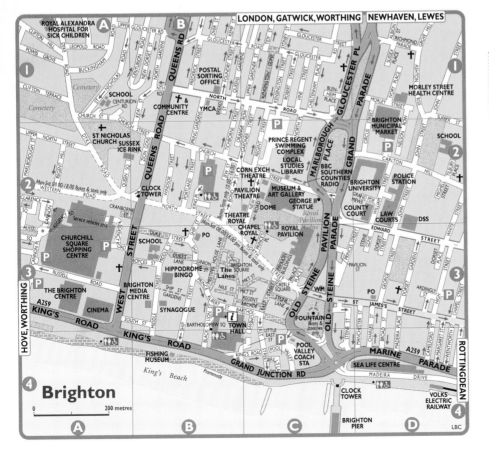

D1	Ashton Rise
B3	Bartholomew Square
B3	Bartholomews
B4	Black Lion Street
C1	Blenheim Place
B2	Bond Street
B3	Brighton Square
D4	Broad Street
A1	Buckingham Road
D4	Camelford Street
A3	Cannon Place
D2	Carlton Hill
C3	Castle Square
B1	Centurion Road
D4	Charles Street
C1	Cheltenham Place
A1	Church Street
D2	Circus Street
A1	Clifton Terrace
D3	Dorset Gardens
B3	Duke Street
B3	Duke's Lane
A1	Dyke Road
C4	East Street
D3	Edward Street
B1	Foundry Street
B1	Frederick Street
C2	Gardner Street
D3	George Street
C1	Gloucester Place
B1	Gloucester Road
C1	Gloucester Street
B4	Grand Junction Road
C2	Grand Parade
D3	High Street
D1	Ivory Place
D2	John Street
C1	Kensington Gardens
C1	Kensington Street
B1	Kew Street
A3	King's Road
A1	Leopold Road
C4	Little East Street
D4	Madeira Drive
D4	Madeira Place
D4	Manchester Street
D4	Margaret Street
D4	Marine Parade

C3	Market Street
C2	Marlborough Place
B3	Meeting House Lane
B3	Middle Street
D1	Morley Street
B1	New Dorset Street
C2	New Road
B1	North Gardens
B1	North Road
B2	North Street
C3	Old Steine
C3	Palace Place
C3	Pavilion Buildings
C3	Pavilion Parade
C4	Pool Valley
B2	Portland Street
A1	Powis Grove
B3	Prince Albert Street
C3	Prince's Place
C3	Princes Street
A2	Queen Square
B1	Queens Gardens
B2	Queens Road
A2	Regency Road
C3	Regent Arcade
A2	Regent Hill
C2	Regent Street
C1	Robert Street
A3	Russell Road
D3	St James's Street
A1	St Nicholas Road
B3	Ship Street
B3	Ship Street Gardens
B2	Spring Gardens
C3	Steine Lane
C4	Steine Street
B2	Tichborne Street
B3	Union Street
C1	Upper Gardner Street
A1	Upper Gloucester Road
A2	Upper North Street
C1	Vine Street
D4	Wentworth Street
A3	West Street
A2	Western Road
D3	White Street
D2	William Street
B2	Windsor Street

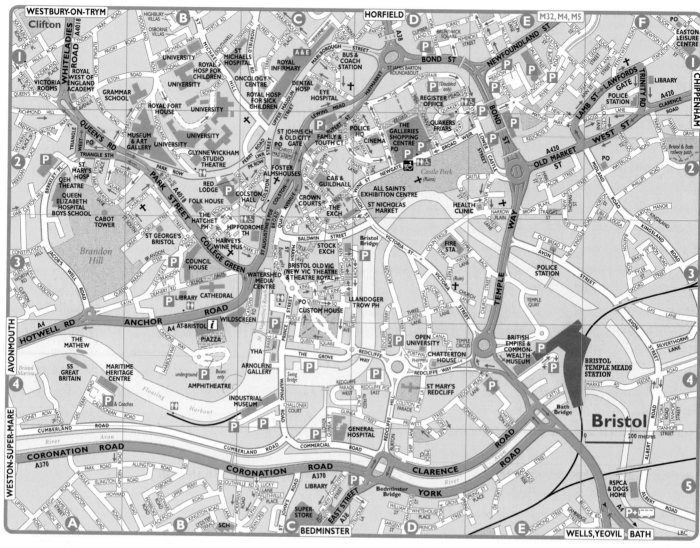

Bristol

Brixham

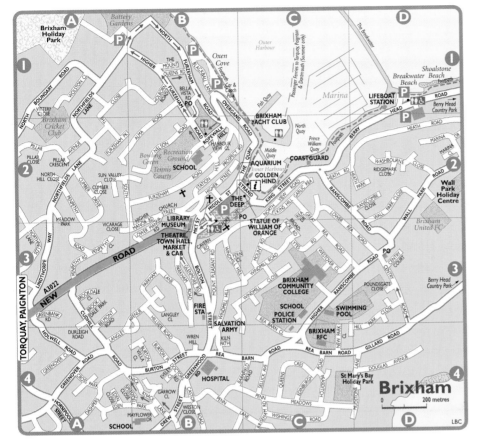

B2	Alma Road
B4	Barnfield Road
B1	Bella Vista Road
D2	Berry Head Road
B1	Blackball Lane
B3	Bolton Street
C4	Briseham Road
C3	Broadacre Road
B4	Burton Street
B4	Castor Road
B3	Cavern Road
D3	Centry Court
D3	Centry Road
B2	Church Street
A4	Cross Park
A3	Cudhill Road
A2	Cumber Drive
A4	Dashpers
B4	Doctors Road
D4	Douglas Avenue
B4	Drew Street
A4	Eden Park
C4	Edinburgh Road
C2	Elkins Hill
B2	Fore Street
A2	Furzeham Park
C2	Garlic Rea
D4	Gillard Road
B3	Glenmore Road
C2	Great Rea Road
A3	Greenbank Road
A4	Greenover Road
B4	Greenwood Road
B2	Harbour View Close
D2	Heath Park
C2	Heath Road
B1	Higher Furzeham Road
B3	Higher Manor Road
C3	Higher Ranscombe Road
B2	Higher Street
D4	Hill Park Close
B3	Hillside Road
B1	Holborn Road
A4	Holwell Road
A4	Horsepool Street
C2	King Street
B4	Knick Knack Lane
A4	Langley Avenue

A3	Lindthorpe Way
B3	Lower Manor Road
C2	Lower Rea Road
C3	Lytes Road
D2	Marina Drive
B3	Market Street
B2	Middle Street
B3	Mount Pleasant Road
C3	Mount Road
D4	Mudstone Lane
B2	Nelson Road
C4	New Park Close
A3	New Road
A1	North Boundary Road
B1	North Furzeham Road
C2	North View Road
A3	Northfields Lane
B1	Overgang Road
B3	Parkham Lane
B3	Parkham Road
C4	Peasditch
B4	Penn Lane
C4	Penn Meadows
A2	Penpethy Road
A2	Pillar Avenue
B2	Prospect Road
C4	Queens Crescent
B1	Queens Road
C2	Ranscombe Road
C3	Rea Barn Close
B4	Rea Barn Road
B2	Ropewalk Hill
C4	Sellick Avenue
A2	South Furzeham Road
B2	Station Hill
C2	Strand
A1	The Close
B1	The Mount
C2	The Quay
D2	Wall Park Close
D3	Wall Park Road
D2	Washbourne Close
C3	Westover Close
C3	Windmill Close
B3	Windmill Hill
C3	Windmill Road
C4	Wishings Road
A1	Wolston Close

Canterbury

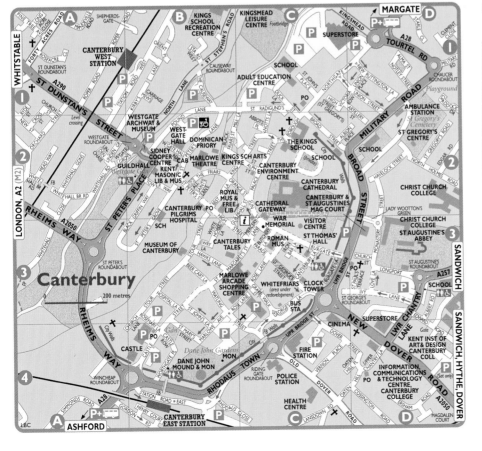

D1	Artillery Street
B3	Beer Cart Lane
B2	Best Lane
B2	Black Griffin Way
B2	Blackfriars Street
D2	Broad Street
C3	Burgate
C3	Butchery Lane
C3	Canterbury Lane
B4	Castle Row
B4	Castle Street
D3	Church Street
A2	Cross Street
C4	Dover Street
C1	Duck Lane
D4	Edward Road
A1	Forty Acres Road
C3	George's Lane
A4	Gordon Road
C3	Gravel Walk
B3	Guildhall Street
D2	Havelock Street
B3	Hawks Lane
B2	High Street
B3	Hospital Lane
C3	Iron Bar Lane
D3	Ivy Lane
B3	Jewry Lane
B2	King Street
C1	Kingsmead Road
B1	Kirby's Lane
C4	Lansdown Road
A2	Linden Grove
D3	Longport
C3	Lower Bridge Street
D4	Lower Chantry Lane
B4	Marlowe Avenue
C3	Mercery Lane
D2	Military Road
B2	Mill Lane
D3	Monastery Street
D4	New Dover Road
D1	New Ruttington Lane
A2	New Street
D2	North Holmes Road
B1	North Lane
C1	Northgate
D1	Notley Street

C4	Oaten Hill
C4	Old Dover Road
B2	Orange Street
A2	Orchard Street
C2	Palace Street
C3	Parade
B2	Pound Lane
A3	Rheims Way
B4	Rhodaus Town
A1	Roper Road
B3	Rose Lane
A1	Roseacre Close
B3	Rosemary Lane
C2	St Alphege Street
A1	St Dunstan's Street
C3	St George's Street
B3	St John's Lane
C1	St John's Place
B3	St Margaret's Street
B4	St Mary's Street
B3	St Peter's Grove
B2	St Peter's Lane
A2	St Peter's Place
B2	St Peter's Street
C1	St Radigund's Street
B1	St Stephen's Road
A4	Simmonds Road
B4	Station Road East
A1	Station Road West
B3	Stour Street
C2	Sun Street
B1	The Causeway
C2	The Borough
B2	The Friars
D1	Tourtel Road
B2	Tower Way
D1	Union Street
C4	Upper Bridge Street
D4	Upper Chantry Lane
C4	Vernon Place
C1	Victoria Row
B3	Watling Street
A2	Westgate Grove
A3	Whitehall Close
A2	Whitehall Gardens
A2	Whitehall Road
B4	Worthgate Place

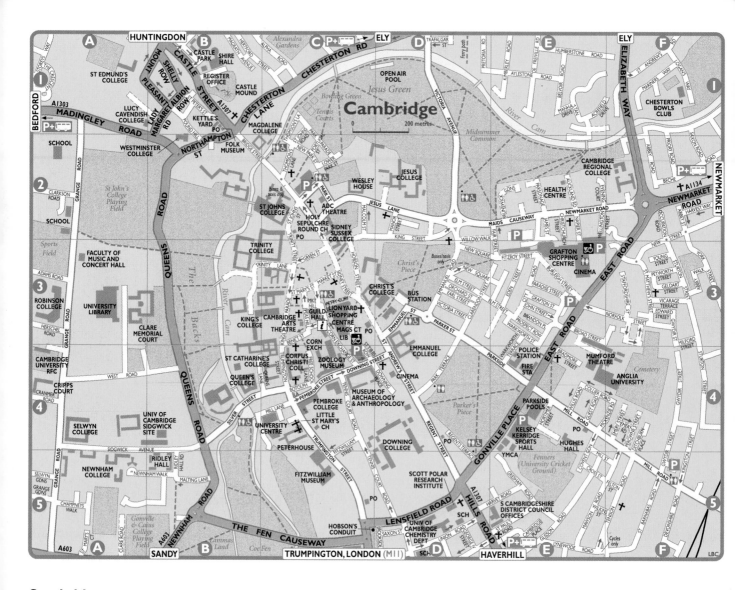

Cambridge

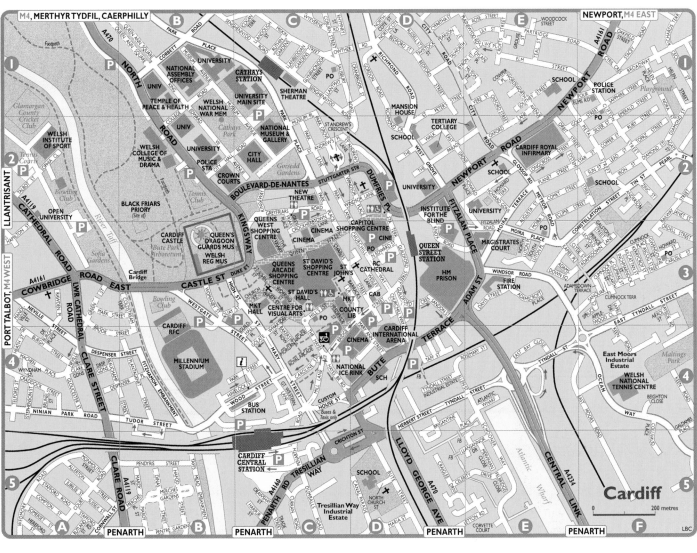

Cardiff

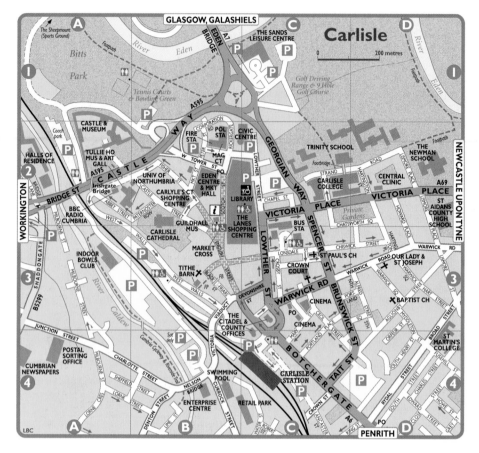

Carlisle

A2	Abbey Street	C3	Mary Street
D3	Aglionby Street	A3	Milbourne Street
D3	Alfred Street North	D3	Myddleton Street
D3	Alfred Street South	B4	Nelson Bridge
B3	Blackfriars Street	D4	Orfeur Street
C4	Botchergate	B2	Paternoster Row
A2	Bridge Lane	B2	Peter Street
A2	Bridge Street	C4	Portland Place
D3	Broad Street	D3	Portland Square
C3	Brunswick Street	B2	Rickergate
B2	Castle Street	C4	Robert Street
A2	Castle Way	D4	Rydal Street
C3	Cecil Street	B2	Scotch Street
C2	Chapel Street	A3	Shaddongate
D4	Charles Street	B4	Sheffield Street
A4	Charlotte Street	D4	South Henry Street
C2	Chatsworth Square	D4	South Street
C3	Chiswick Street	C3	Spencer Street
D4	Close Street	C2	Strand Road
B2	Corporation Road	C4	Tait Street
C3	Crosby Street	C4	Victoria Place
C4	Crown Street	B4	Victoria Viaduct
B4	Currock Street	C3	Warwick Road
B4	Denton Street	D3	Warwick Square
C3	Devonshire Street	C4	Water Street
B1	Eden Bridge	B2	West Tower Street
D4	Edward Street	A2	West Walls
B3	English Street		
B2	Fisher Street		
D4	Fusehill Street		
C2	Georgian Way		
D4	Grey Street		
D3	Hart Street		
D3	Hartington Place		
D2	Hartington Street		
D2	Howard Place		
D4	Howe Street		
A4	Junction Street		
D4	King Street		
C4	Lancaster Street		
B4	Lime Street		
D2	Lismore Place		
D3	Lismore Street		
C3	Lonsdale Street		
A4	Lorne Crescent		
A4	Lorne Street		
C2	Lowther Street		
B2	Market Street		

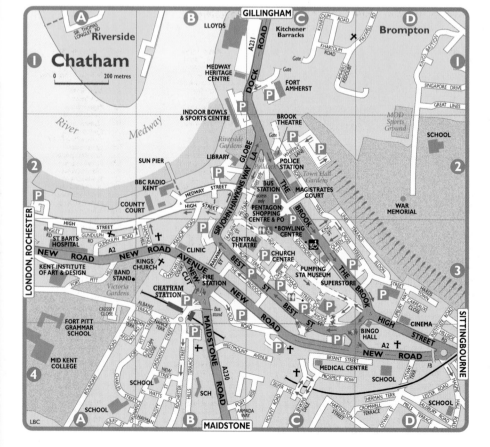

Chatham

A4	Afghan Road	A3	New Road
B3	Albany Terrace	A3	New Road Avenue
C1	Amherst Redoubt	B4	New Street
B4	Armada Way	B3	Old Road
B3	Best Street	B4	Ordnance Street
A3	Bingley Road	B3	Ordnance Terrace
A4	Boundary Road	D4	Otway Street
C4	Bryant Street	D4	Otway Terrace
D3	Carpeaux Close	B4	Pagitt Street
A4	Charles Street	A4	Perry Street
B3	Chartwell Court	B4	Port Rise
B4	Chilham Close	C4	Prospect Row
C3	Clover Street	C3	Queen Street
A3	Cressey Close	B3	Railway Street
D4	Cromwell Terrace	C3	Rhode Street
C3	Cross Street	C3	Richard Street
C1	Dock Road	B4	Rochester Street
D3	Eldon Street	B3	Rome Terrace
A3	Fort Pitt Hill	C2	Rope Walk
A4	Fort Pitt Street	D4	Salisbury Road
C2	Globe Lane	C4	Silver Hill
D1	Great Lines	D1	Singapore Drive
A3	Gundulph Road	B2	Sir John Hawkins Way
B3	Hamond Hill	A1	Sir Thomas Longley Road
D3	Hards Town	C3	Solomons Road
C4	Hartington Street	C2	The Brook
B4	Hayman Street	B3	The Paddock
D4	Herman Terrace	D3	Upbury Way
A3	High Street	B4	Watts Street
B4	Hills Terrace	B4	Westmount Avenue
D4	Hillside Road	C2	Whiffin's Lane
D4	Institute Road		
C4	Jenkins Dale		
C1	Khartoum Road		
C3	King Street		
D1	Kings Bastion		
D4	Lester Road		
C2	Lines Terrace		
A3	Lumsden Terrace		
D4	Magpie Hall Road		
B3	Maidstone Road		
B3	Manor Road		
D1	Maxwell Road		
B2	Medway Street		
B2	Military Road		
D4	Mills Terrace		
C4	Mount Road		
B3	New Cut		

Cheltenham

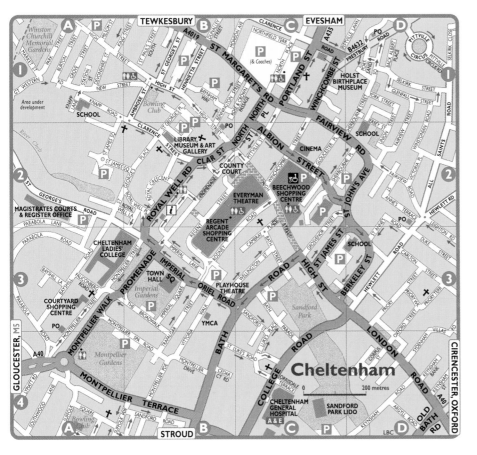

C2	Albion Street	A2	Parabola Lane
D2	All Saints Road	A3	Parabola Road
B1	Ambrose Street	A1	Park Street
D1	Back Albert Place	D1	Pittville Circus
C3	Bath Parade	D1	Pittville Circus Road
B4	Bath Road	D1	Pittville Lawn
C3	Bath Street	C2	Pittville Street
B1	Baynham Way	D1	Portland Square
A3	Bayshill Road	C1	Portland Street
B1	Bennington Street	D1	Prestbury Road
D3	Berkeley Street	D3	Priory Street
A1	Burton Street	D3	Priory Terrace
C3	Cambray Place	D3	Priory Walk
D3	Carlton Street	B3	Promenade
C1	Clarence Road	B3	Regent Street
B2	Clarence Street	B3	Rodney Road
C4	College Road	B2	Royal Crescent
A1	Devonshire Street	B2	Royal Well Place
D3	Duke Street	B2	Royal Well Road
C2	Fairview Road	D3	St Anne's Road
D2	Fairview Street	D2	St Anne's Terrace
A3	Fauconberg Road	B2	St George's Place
D1	Glenfall Street	A2	St George's Road
C2	Gloucester Place	B1	St George's Street
A1	Great Western Road	A2	St James Square
C3	Grosvenor Street	C3	St James Street
A1	Grove Street	D2	St John's Avenue
B1	Henrietta Street	C4	St Luke's Place
D3	Hewlett Road	C4	St Luke's Road
A1	High Street	B1	St Margaret's Road
B3	Imperial Lane	B1	St Paul's Street South
B3	Imperial Square	B4	Sandford Road
D4	Keynsham Road	C3	Sandford Street
A1	Knapp Road	D1	Selkirk Street
D4	London Road	C2	Sherbourne Place
B1	Monson Avenue	D1	Sherbourne Street
B4	Montpellier Drive	A4	Southwood Lane
B4	Montpellier Parade	A4	Suffolk Square
A3	Montpellier Spa Road	D4	Sydenham Villas Road
A3	Montpellier Street	B3	The Broadwalk
A4	Montpellier Terrace	B3	Trafalgar Street
A4	Montpellier Walk	D2	Union Street
A1	New Street	D2	Victoria Place
C1	North Place	B4	Vittoria Walk
C2	North Street	C3	Wellington Street
C1	Northfield Terrace	C1	Winchcombe Street
B3	Oriel Road	D2	Winstonian Road
D3	Oxford Street	D1	York Street

Chester

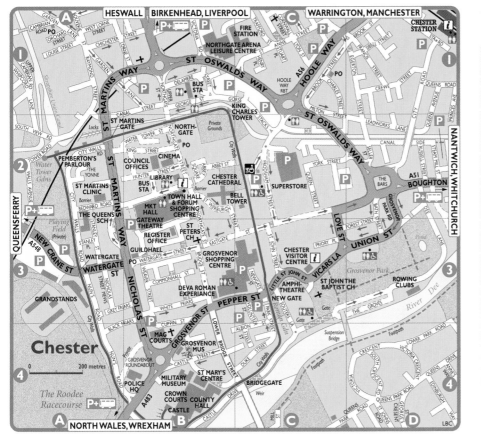

B2	Abbey Square	A3	New Crane Street
B2	Abbey Street	C3	Newgate Street
C4	Albion Street	B3	Nicholas Street
D2	Bath Street	A3	Nicholas Street Mews
A2	Bedward Road	B2	Northgate Street
A4	Black Friars	A3	Nun's Road
D2	Boughton	C3	Park Street
B3	Bridge Street	B3	Pepper Street
C1	Brook Street	C2	Queen Street
B4	Bunce Street	D2	Queens Avenue
D2	Canal Side	D4	Queens Drive
B1	Canal Street	D4	Queens Park Road
B4	Castle Drive	D1	Queens Road
B4	Castle Street	A1	Raymond Street
C1	Charles Street	D2	Russell Street
A1	Chichester Street	C1	St Anne Street
D1	City Road	C3	St John Street
A2	City Walls Road	A2	St Martins Way
B3	Commonhall Street	B1	St Oswalds Way
D1	Crewe Street	B2	St Werburgh Street
B3	Cuppin Street	D2	Seller Street
D2	Dee Lane	D1	Sibell Street
B1	Delamere Street	C3	Souters Lane
C4	Duke Street	D4	South Crescent Road
B3	Eastgate Street	A2	South View Road
D4	Edinburgh Way	A3	Stanley Street
D1	Egerton Street	D1	Station Road
D3	Forest Street	D2	Steam Mill Street
D1	Francis Street	C4	Steele Street
C2	Frodsham Street	C1	Stuart Place
A1	Garden Lane	D2	The Bars
B1	George Street	D3	The Groves
C1	Gorse Stacks	A2	Tower Road
A3	Grey Friars	C1	Trafford Street
D2	Grosvenor Park Road	D3	Union Street
B4	Grosvenor Street	B1	Upper Northgate Street
C1	Hoole Way	C3	Vicars Lane
B2	Hunter Street	D4	Victoria Crescent
B2	King Street	B1	Victoria Road
D2	Leadworks Lane	C3	Volunteer Street
C3	Little St John Street	A2	Walls Avenue
B1	Lorne Street	B2	Water Tower Street
A1	Louise Street	A3	Watergate Street
C3	Love Street	B3	Weaver Street
B4	Lower Bridge Street	A1	West Lorne Street
D4	Lower Park Road	A1	Whipcord Lane
C1	Lyon Street	B3	White Friars
C1	Milton Street	C2	York Street

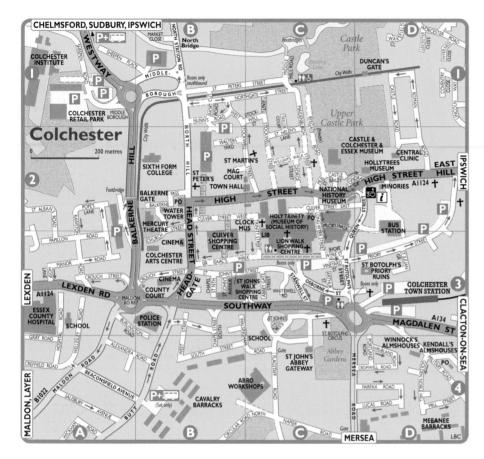

Colchester

C3	Abbey Gate Street
A4	Alexandra Road
C3	Arthur Street
A2	Balkerne Hill
B2	Balkerne Passage
A4	Beaconsfield Avenue
A3	Burlington Road
A4	Butt Road
C2	Castle Bailey
D1	Castle Road
B3	Chapel Street North
B3	Chapel Street South
B3	Church Street
B4	Circular Road North
D1	Coventry Close
C2	Cowdray Crescent
A4	Creffield Road
D4	Cromwell Road
B3	Crouch Street
C2	Culver Street East
B2	Culver Street West
D2	East Hill
C2	East Stockwell Street
D4	Fairfax Road
C4	Flagstaff Road
C2	George Street
D4	Golden Noble Hill
A4	Gray Road
B2	Head Street
B3	Headgate
B2	High Street
A3	Hospital Lane
A4	Hospital Road
D1	Inverness Close
D1	Leicester Close
A3	Lexden Road
D1	Lincoln Way
C2	Long Wyre Street
D4	Lucas Road
D3	Magdalen Street
C1	Maidenburgh Street
A4	Maldon Road
A3	Manor Road
C4	Mersea Road
C1	Middle Mill Road
B1	Middleborough
D4	Military Road
D4	Mill Street

C2	Museum Street
C4	Napier Road
B2	North Hill
B1	North Station Road
B1	Northgate Street
B1	Nunn's Road
C3	Osborne Street
A3	Papillon Road
A2	Pope's Lane
D4	Portland Road
D3	Priory Street
C2	Priory Walk
C3	Queen Street
A2	Rawston Road
D1	Roman Road
C2	Ryegate Road
A2	St Alban's Road
C3	St Botolph's Street
C2	St Helen's Lane
B3	St John's Avenue
C3	St John's Green
B3	St John's Street
D3	St Julian Grove
B1	St Peters Street
A4	Salisbury Avenue
A1	Sheepen Place
A1	Sheepen Road
B1	Short Cut Road
C3	Short Wyre Street
D4	Shrubland Road
B3	Sir Isaac's Walk
B4	South Street
B3	Southway
C3	Stanwell Street
C1	Stockwell Street
C1	Taylor Court
C2	Trinity Street
C3	Vineyard Street
D1	Wakefield Close
B3	Walsingham Road
B2	Walters Yard
A4	Wellesley Road
B1	West Stockwell Street
B4	West Street
A1	Westway
A4	Wickham Road
C2	William's Walk
D1	Worcester Road

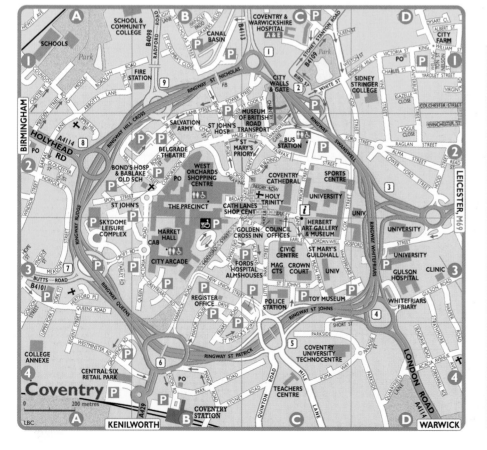

Coventry

A1	Abbotts Lane
D4	Acacia Avenue
D2	Alma Street
A2	Barras Lane
C2	Bayley Lane
C1	Bird Street
B1	Bishop Street
B2	Bond Street
B2	Broadgate
B2	Burges
A3	Butts Road
D1	Canterbury Street
C2	Chantry Place
B2	Chapel Street
D1	Charles Street
D1	Colchester Street
C1	Cook Street
B2	Corporation Street
A1	Coundon Road
D1	Cox Street
A3	Croft Road
B2	Cross Cheaping
C3	Earl Street
B4	Eaton Road
C2	Fairfax Street
D2	Ford Street
B4	Friars Road
D3	Gosford Street
B3	Greyfriars Lane
B3	Greyfriars Road
A4	Grosvenor Road
D3	Gulson Road
B2	Hales Street
C3	Hay Lane
B3	Hertford Street
C3	High Street
A2	Hill Street
A2	Holyhead Road
D2	Hood Street
C3	Jordan Well
D1	King William Street
B1	Lamb Street
C3	Little Park Street
D4	London Road
D2	Lower Ford Street
B3	Manor House Drive
B4	Manor Road
A3	Meadow Street

A2	Meriden Street
A1	Middleborough Road
C4	Mile Lane
C3	Much Park Street
C2	New Buildings
B3	New Union Street
A2	Norfolk Street
B4	Park Road
C4	Parkside
D1	Primrose Hill Street
C2	Priory Row
C2	Priory Street
C4	Puma Way
D4	Quarryfield Lane
B3	Queen Victoria Road
A3	Queens Road
C4	Quinton Road
B1	Radford Road
D2	Raglan Street
A4	Regent Street
A2	Ringway Hill Cross
A3	Ringway Queens
A3	Ringway Rudge
C3	Ringway St Johns
B1	Ringway St Nicholas
B4	Ringway St Patrick
D3	Ringway Swanswell
D3	Ringway Whitefriars
C3	St John's Street
B1	St Nicholas Street
B4	St Patrick's Road
C3	Salt Lane
B1	Silver Street
A2	Spon Street
B4	Stoney Road
C1	Stoney Stanton Road
D4	Strathmore Avenue
C2	Swanswell Gate
B1	Tower Street
C2	Trinity Street
B2	Upper Well Street
D1	Victoria Street
D1	Vine Street
B3	Warwick Road
A4	Westminster Road
C1	White Street
C3	Whitefriars Street
D1	Yardley Street

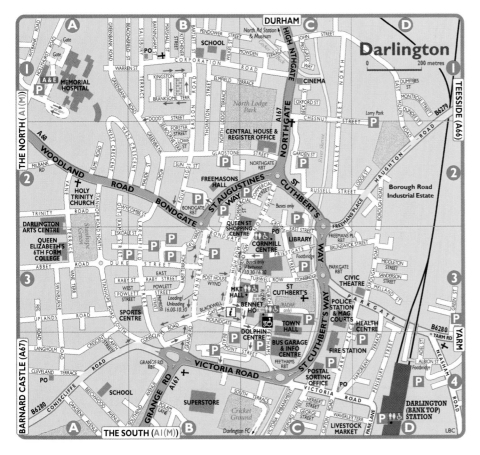

Darlington

A3	Abbey Road	B3	Larchfield Street
D4	Albion Street	BI	Marshall Street
BI	Barningham Street	B2	Maude Street
BI	Bartlett Street	D3	Melland Street
AI	Beaconsfield Street	CI	Mowden Terrace
B4	Beaumont Street	D4	Neasham Road
CI	Beck Street	BI	North Lodge Terrace
C4	Bedford Street	C2	Northgate
A4	Beechwood Avenue	A4	Oakdene Avenue
B3	Blackwell Gate	A2	Outram Street
B2	Bondgate	CI	Oxford Street
D3	Borough Road	D4	Park Lane
BI	Branksome Terrace	C4	Park Place
C3	Brunswick Street	D3	Parkgate
CI	Chesnut Street	BI	Pendower Street
C3	Church Row	D4	Pensbury Street
A4	Cleveland Terrace	B3	Post House Wynd
C4	Clifton Road	B3	Powlett Street
B2	Commercial Street	C3	Prebend Row
A4	Coniscliffe Road	C3	Priestgate
BI	Corporation Road	B3	Raby Terrace
C2	Crown Street	C2	Russell Street
BI	Dodd's Street	B2	St Augustines Way
A3	Duke Street	C4	St Cuthbert's Way
BI	Easson Road	BI	Salisbury Terrace
DI	East Mount Road	B3	Salt Yard
B3	East Raby Street	B2	Selbourne Terrace
C3	East Street	B3	Skinnergate
BI	Elmfield Terrace	C4	South Terrace
A3	Eskdale Street	B4	Southend Avenue
C4	Feethams	A2	Stanhope Road North
B2	Forster Street	A3	Stanhope Road South
B2	Four Riggs	C3	Stonebridge
C2	Freemans Place	A3	Swinburne Road
C2	Garden Street	BI	Thornton Street
B2	Gladstone Street	A2	Trinity Road
B4	Grange Road	C3	Tubwell Row
AI	Greenbank Road	A3	Uplands Road
D4	Hargreave Terrace	C2	Valley Street North
D2	Haughton Road	A2	Vane Terrace
CI	High Northgate	C4	Victoria Embankment
B3	High Row	B4	Victoria Road
AI	Hollyhurst Road	C4	Waverley Terrace
B3	Houndgate	A2	West Crescent
CI	John Street	BI	Wilkes Street
BI	Kingston Street	A2	Woodland Road
BI	Kitchener Street	A2	Wycombe Street
A4	Langholm Crescent	D4	Yarm Road

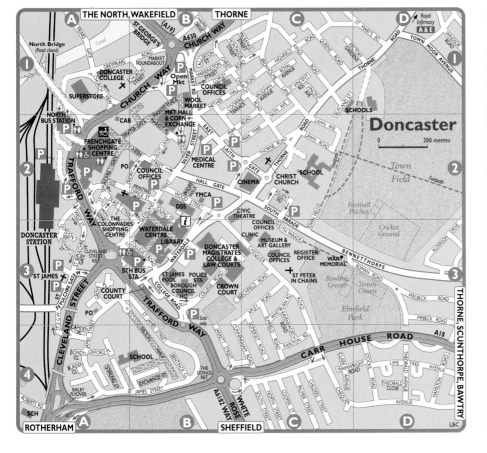

Doncaster

D3	Alderson Drive	BI	Montague Street
BI	Allerton Street	BI	Nether Hall Road
C3	Apley Road	C4	North Street
A2	Baxter Gate	A4	Oxford Place
C3	Beechfield Road	C4	Palmer Street
C3	Bennetthorpe	B2	Park Road
B4	Bentinck Close	B2	Park Terrace
A4	Bond Close	B2	Printing Office Street
CI	Broxholme Lane	B2	Priory Place
A4	Camden Place	CI	Queens Road
C4	Carr House Road	C4	Rainton Road
C4	Chequer Avenue	C3	Ravensworth Road
C3	Chequer Road	DI	Rectory Gardens
C4	Childers Street	C2	Regent Square
BI	Christ Church Road	A4	Roberts Road
AI	Church View	D3	Roman Road
BI	Church Way	CI	Royal Avenue
C4	Clark Avenue	CI	Rutland Street
A4	Cleveland Street	A4	St James Street
B3	College Road	DI	St Mary's Road
C4	Cooper Street	A2	St Sepulchre Gate
BI	Coopers Terrace	A3	St Sepulchre Gate West
BI	Copley Road	CI	St Vincent Avenue
B4	Cunningham Road	CI	St Vincent Road
A2	Duke Street	B2	Scot Lane
B2	East Laith Gate	B2	Silver Street
C3	Elmfield Road	C4	Somerset Road
B4	Exchange Street	C2	South Parade
D3	Firbeck Road	C4	South Street
AI	Friars Gate	A2	Spring Gardens
CI	Glyn Avenue	A4	Stirling Street
A3	Gordon Street	A3	Stewart Street
AI	Greyfriars Road	D4	Stockil Road
A3	Grove Place	D4	Theobald Avenue
B2	Hall Gate	C2	Thorne Road
D4	Hamilton Road	C3	Town Fields
BI	Harrington Street	DI	Town Moor Avenue
B2	High Street	A2	Trafford Way
CI	Highfield Road	CI	Vaughan Avenue
B4	Jarrett Street	C4	Wainwright Road
CI	Kings Road	B3	Waterdale
C2	Lawn Avenue	D3	Welbeck Road
C2	Lawn Road	A2	West Street
D4	Lime Tree Avenue	C3	Whitburn Road
BI	Market Place	B4	White Rose Way
BI	Market Road	DI	Windsor Road
CI	Milbanke Street	B2	Wood Street
B4	Milton Walk	B2	Young Street

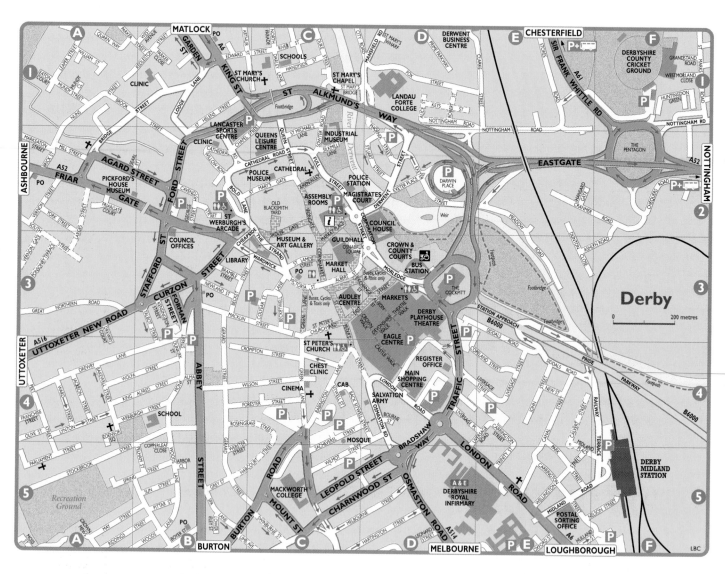

Derby

Dover

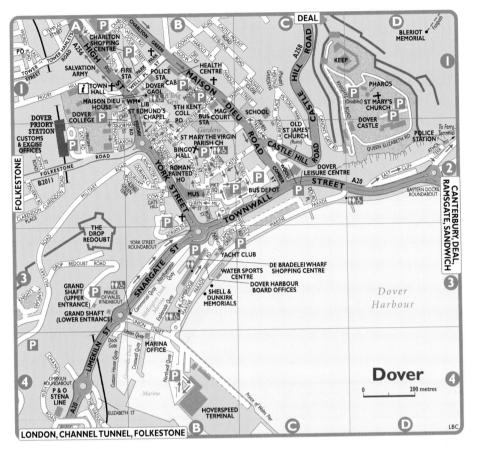

B3 Adrian Street	B2 Market Square
C2 Ashen Tree Lane	A3 Military Road
D2 Athol Terrace	B2 Mill Lane
B2 Bench Street	B3 New Bridge
B2 Biggin Street	B2 New Street
B2 Bowling Green Terrace	A2 Norman Street
B3 Cambridge Road	B1 Park Place
B3 Camden Crescent	B1 Park Street
B2 Cannon Street	B1 Pencester Road
C2 Canon's Gate Road	A2 Priory Gate Road
C2 Castle Hill Road	A1 Priory Hill
B1 Castle Mount Road	B2 Priory Road
B2 Castle Street	B2 Priory Street
A4 Channel View Road	D2 Queen Elizabeth Road
B1 Charlton Green	B2 Queen Street
B2 Church Street	B2 Queens Gardens
A2 Clarendon Place	C2 Russell Street
A2 Clarendon Road	A2 St John's Road
B2 Cowgate Hill	A2 Saxon Street
A1 Crafford Street	B3 Snargate Street
B1 Dour Street	B2 Stem Brook
C2 Douro Place	C1 Taswell Close
A3 Drop Redoubt Road	C1 Taswell Street
B2 Durham Close	A1 Templar Street
B2 Durham Hill	B1 The Paddock
D2 East Cliff	A4 The Viaduct
A1 East Street	A1 Tower Hamlets Road
A1 Effingham Crescent	A1 Tower Street
A2 Effingham Street	C2 Townwall Street
A4 Elizabeth Street	B3 Union Street
A2 Folkestone Road	C1 Victoria Park
B1 Godwyne Close	C2 Wellesley Road
B1 Godwyne Road	A1 Widred Road
B1 Harold Street	A1 Wood Street
C1 Heritage Gardens	C2 Woolcomber Street
B1 Hewitt Road	B2 Worthington Street
A1 High Street	B2 York Street
B2 King Street	
C1 Knights Road	
A3 Knights Templars	
B1 Ladywell	
B2 Lancaster Road	
C2 Laureston Place	
B1 Leyburne Road	
A4 Limekiln Street	
B1 Maison Dieu Road	
A2 Malvern Road	
B3 Marine Parade	

Dundee

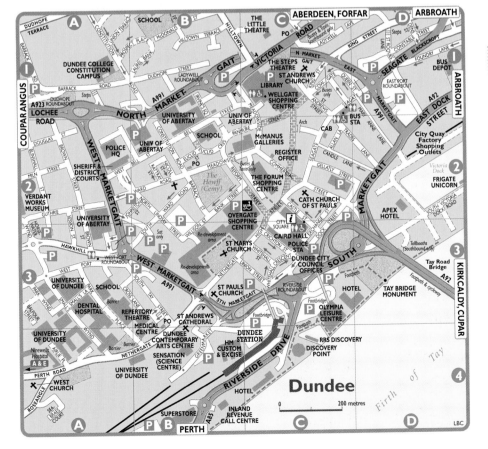

A4 Airlie Place	B2 Nicoll Street
C2 Allan Lane	B2 North Lindsay Street
A3 Balfour Street	B1 North Marketgait
B2 Bank Street	C2 Panmure Street
A1 Barrack Road	A3 Park Place
B2 Barrack Street	A3 Park Wynd
B2 Bell Street	A4 Perth Road
D1 Blackscroft	A1 Prospect Place
A2 Blinshall Street	C1 Queen Street
A2 Brown Street	B2 Rattray Street
C2 Candle Lane	B2 Reform Street
C2 Castle Street	B4 Riverside Drive
C2 Commercial Street	A4 Roseangle
D1 Constable Street	C1 St Andrews Street
A1 Constitution Road	D1 St Roques Lane
C1 Cowgate	A4 Seabraes Court
C3 Crichton Street	C2 Seagate
A3 Cross Lane	A3 Session Street
D1 Dens Road	A3 Small's Lane
C3 Dock Street	A3 Small's Wynd
A2 Douglas Street	C3 South Marketgait
B1 Dudhope Street	B3 South Tay Street
A1 Dudhope Terrace	D2 South Victoria Dock Road
D1 East Dock Street	B3 South Ward Road
D1 East Marketgait	C2 Trades Lane
B2 Euclid Crescent	C3 Union Street
B2 Euclid Street	A1 Union Terrace
C3 Exchange Street	A1 Victoria Road
D1 Foundry Lane	B2 Ward Road
C2 Gellatly Street	A2 West Bell Street
B4 Greenmarket	A2 West Marketgait
A2 Guthrie Street	A3 West Port
A3 Hawkhill	C3 Whitehall Crescent
C3 High Street	C3 Whitehall Street
B1 Hilltown	B3 Willison Street
B1 Hilltown Terrace	
A3 Horsewater Wynd	
B1 Irvine's Square	
A2 Johnston Street	
C1 King Street	
C1 Ladywell Avenue	
B1 Laurel Bank	
A1 Lochee Road	
D1 Mary Anne Lane	
B1 McDonald Street	
B2 Meadowside	
A2 Miln Street	
A4 Nethergate	

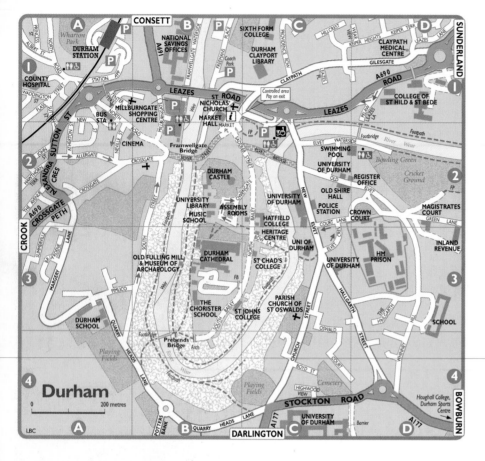

Durham

A1	Albert Street		B2	Silver Street
A2	Alexandra Crescent		B3	South Bailey
A2	Allergate		B3	South Street
A2	Atherton Street		A1	Station Approach
C3	Bow Lane		C4	Stockton Road
C4	Boyd Street		A3	Summerville
A3	Briardene		A2	Sutton Street
C4	Church Street		A1	Tenter Terrace
C1	Claypath		A2	The Avenue
C2	Court Lane		D3	The Hallgarth
A2	Crossgate		A1	Waddington Street
A2	Crossgate Peth		D1	Wear View
C2	Elvet Bridge		D4	Whinney Hill
C3	Elvet Crescent			
C2	Elvet Waterside			
A1	Flass Street			
B1	Framwellgate Waterside			
B1	Freemans Place			
D1	Gilesgate			
D2	Green Lane			
C3	Hallgarth Street			
A2	Hawthorn Terrace			
C4	Highwood View			
C1	Hillcrest			
A2	John Street			
D1	Keiper Heights			
D1	Keiper Terrace			
D1	Leazes Lane			
C1	Leazes Place			
B1	Leazes Road			
A3	Margery Lane			
B2	Market Place			
B1	Millburngate			
A2	Neville Street			
C2	New Elvet			
A1	New Street			
C3	North Bailey			
A1	North Road			
C2	Old Elvet			
C3	Oswald Court			
C2	Owengate			
D1	Pelaw Leazes Lane			
A3	Pimlico			
B4	Potters Bank			
A1	Princess Street			
C1	Providence Row			
A3	Quarry Heads Lane			
B2	Saddler Street			

Eastbourne

A3	Arlington Road		C4	Lascelles Terrace
B2	Ashford Road		D1	Latimer Road
B1	Ashford Square		B1	Leaf Road
A1	Bedford Grove		B3	Lismore Road
C1	Belmore Road		B2	Longstone Road
A4	Blackwater Road		B3	Lushington Lane
B3	Bolton Road		B3	Lushington Road
C1	Bourne Street		D2	Marine Parade
B3	Burlington Place		D1	Marine Road
C3	Burlington Road		B2	Mark Lane
A3	Camden Road		A3	Meads Road
A1	Carew Road		C1	Melbourne Road
A4	Carlisle Road		C1	New Road
C1	Cavendish Avenue		C2	North Street
B1	Cavendish Bridge		A3	Old Orchard Road
C1	Cavendish Place		A4	Old Wish Road
C2	Ceylon Place		C2	Pevensey Road
B3	Chiswick Place		C2	Queens Gardens
B3	College Road		D1	Royal Parade
B1	Commercial Road		A1	St Anne's Road
B4	Compton Street		D1	St Aubyn's Road
B3	Connaught Road		A2	St Leonard's Road
B3	Cornfield Lane		A3	Saffrons Road
B2	Cornfield Road		D1	Seaside
B3	Cornfield Terrace		C2	Seaside Road
B3	Devonshire Place		A3	South Street
C1	Dursley Road		A2	Southfields Road
C2	Elms Avenue		B3	Spencer Road
C2	Elms Road		A2	Station Parade
A1	Enys Road		B2	Station Street
A1	Eversfield Road		B1	Susans Road
A3	Furness Road		C1	Sydney Road
B3	Gildredge Road		B2	Terminus Road
C4	Grand Parade		A2	The Avenue
A3	Grange Road		C2	Tideswell Road
A4	Granville Road		C3	Trinity Place
A4	Grassington Road		B3	Trinity Trees
A3	Grove Road		B1	Upper Avenue
B3	Hardwick Road		A1	Upperton Gardens
A2	Hartfield Road		A2	Upperton Road
C3	Hartington Place		A3	West Street
C4	Howard Square		A2	West Terrace
B3	Hyde Gardens		A2	Wharf Road
A3	Hyde Road		C1	Willowfield Road
A2	Ivy Terrace		B4	Wilmington Gardens
B2	Junction Road		B4	Wilmington Square
B4	King Edward's Parade		B3	Wish Road
C2	Langney Road		A3	York Road

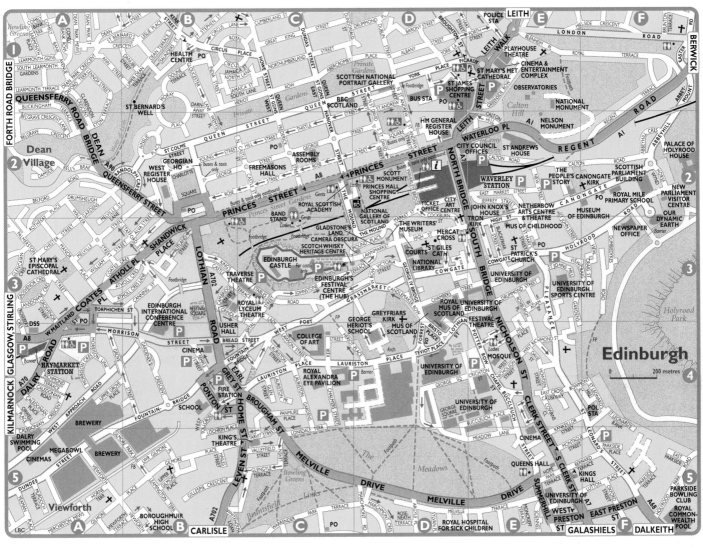

Edinburgh

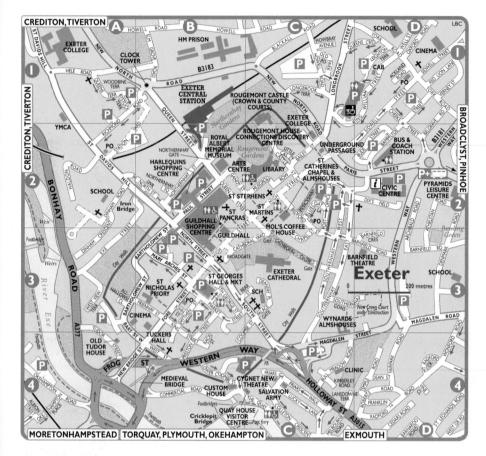

Exeter

D3 Archibald Road	C1 Longbrook Street
D2 Athelstan Road	C1 Longbrook Terrace
C2 Bailey Street	B4 Lower Coombe Street
D2 Bampflyde Street	B2 Lower North Street
D3 Barnfield Road	C4 Lucky Lane
A3 Bartholomew Street	D3 Magdalen Road
B3 Bartholomew Street East	C4 Magdalen Street
A3 Bartholomew Street West	B3 Market Street
C2 Bedford Street	B3 Mary Arches Street
D2 Belgrave Road	C4 Melbourne Road
C1 Blackall Road	C2 Musgrove Row
C2 Bluecoat Lane	A4 New Bridge Street
A2 Bonhay Road	A1 New North Road
B3 Broadgate	B3 North Street
D2 Bude Street	B2 Northernhay Street
C4 Bull Meadow Road	A4 Okehampton Road
C2 Castle Street	D1 Oxford Road
C3 Cathedral Close	C3 Palace Gate
B3 Cathedral Yard	C2 Paris Street
C3 Chapel Street	B2 Paul Street
D1 Cheeke Street	C2 Post Office Lane
C4 Colleton Crescent	B4 Preston Street
B4 Commercial Road	C2 Princesway
B4 Coombe Street	B1 Queen Street
D4 Dean Street	A1 Queens Terrace
C3 Deanery Place	D4 Radford Road
D3 Denmark Road	D1 Red Lion Lane
A3 Dinham Crescent	A2 Richmond Road
A2 Dinham Road	D4 Roberts Road
D2 Dix's Field	A2 St Davids Hill
B1 Elm Grove Road	D4 St Leonards Road
A3 Exe Street	D1 Sidwell Street
D4 Fairpark Road	B3 Smythen Street
B3 Fore Street	B3 South George Street
C4 Friars Walk	C3 South Street
B3 Frienhay Street	C3 Southernhay East
A4 Frog Street	C3 Southernhay Gardens
B2 Gandy Street	C3 Southernhay West
A2 Haldon Road	A2 Station Yard
A1 Hele Road	D4 Temple Road
B3 High Street	C4 The Quay
C4 Holloway Street	A4 Tudor Street
B1 Howell Road	B4 West Street
B3 John Street	A3 West View Terrace
B3 King Street	B4 Western Way
D1 King William Road	D3 Western Way
D1 Leighton Terrace	D4 Wonford Road
C2 Little Castle Street	D1 York Road

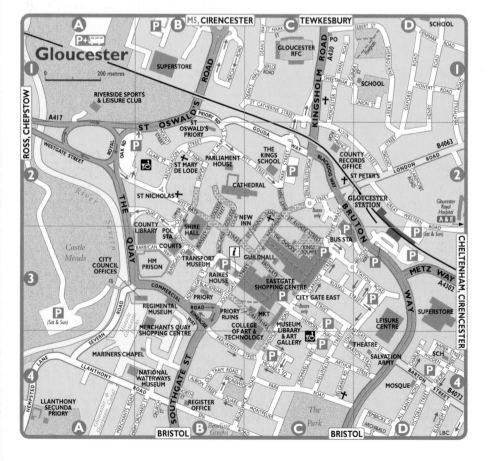

Gloucester

B4 Albion Street	C2 Market Parade
D4 All Saints Road	A4 Merchants Road
C2 Alvin Street	B1 Mercia Road
B2 Archdeacon Street	D3 Metz Way
C4 Arthur Street	C4 Montpelier
B3 Barbican Road	B2 Mount Street
B3 Barbican Way	D4 Napier Street
D4 Barton Street	B4 North Street
C4 Belgrave Road	C2 Northgate Street
B3 Berkeley Street	B4 Old Tram Road
C2 Blackdog Way	D1 Oxford Road
B3 Blackfriars	D2 Oxford Street
D4 Blenheim Road	C4 Park Road
C4 Brunswick Road	C2 Park Street
B4 Brunswick Square	B4 Parliament Street
D3 Bruton Way	D4 Pembroke Street
B3 Bull Lane	C2 Pitt Street
B2 Clare Street	B1 Priory Road
D2 Claremont Road	B2 Quay Street
C2 Clarence Row	A2 Royal Oak Road
C3 Clarence Street	C3 Russell Street
B2 College Court	C2 St Aldate Street
B2 College Street	C1 St Catherine Street
B3 Commercial Road	C2 St John's Lane
C4 Cromwell Street	C1 St Mark Street
C1 Dean's Walk	B2 St Mary's Square
C1 Dean's Way	B2 St Mary's Street
D1 Denmark Road	C4 St Michael's Square
C3 Eastgate Street	B2 St Oswald's Road
C2 Gouda Way	D1 Sebert Street
D2 Great Western Road	C1 Serlo Road
C3 Greyfriars	A4 Severn Road
C1 Guinea Street	D1 Sherbourne Street
C3 Hampden Way	D4 Sinope Street
C2 Hare Lane	B3 Southgate Street
D1 Heathville Road	B4 Spa Road
A4 Hempsted Lane	D3 Station Road
D1 Henry Road	C1 Swan Road
B4 High Orchard Street	C1 Sweetbriar Street
D1 Honyatt Road	C3 The Oxbode
B3 Kimbrose Way	A2 The Quay
C4 Kings Barton Street	D1 Union Street
C3 Kings Square	B2 Upper Quay Street
C1 Kingsholm Road	D4 Victoria Street
B3 Ladybellgate Street	C4 Wellington Street
A4 Llanthony Road	B2 Westgate Street
D2 London Road	D4 Widden Street
B3 Longsmith Street	C1 Worcester Street

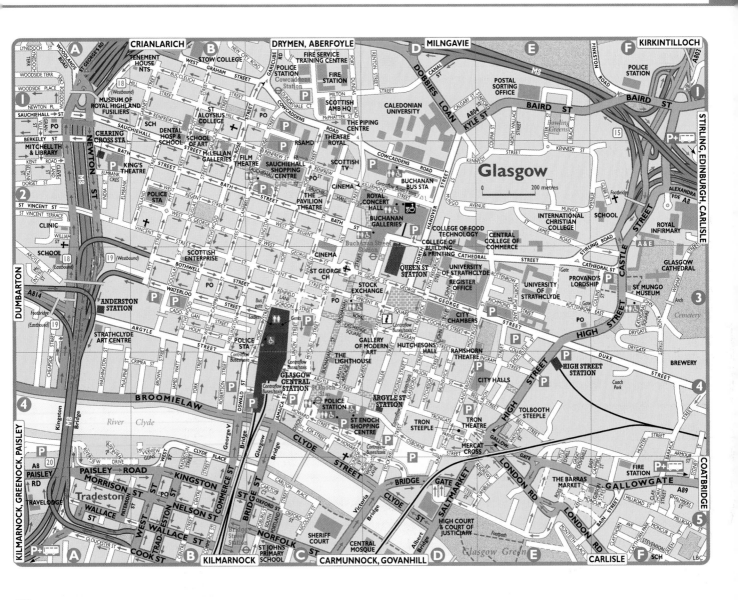

Glasgow

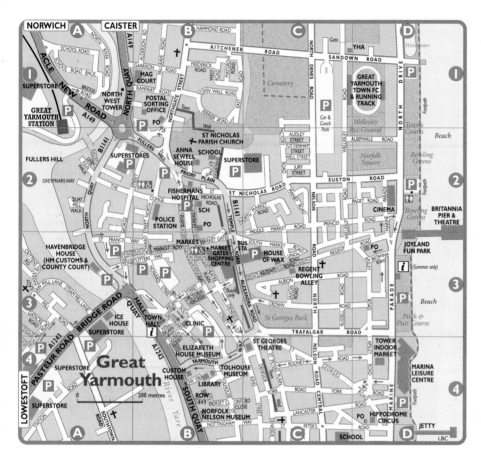

Great Yarmouth

A1	Acle New Road	A2	North Quay
D2	Albemarle Road	A1	North River Road
C3	Albion Road	B1	Northgate Street
B1	Alderson Road	B4	Nottingham Way
C3	Alexandra Road	B4	Orford Close
D3	Apsley Road	D2	Paget Road
C2	Audley Street	B1	Palgrave Road
A1	Bridge Road	A4	Pasteur Road
A3	Bridge Road	C2	Princes Road
D3	Britannia Road	B2	Priory Gardens
A3	Crittens Road	B2	Priory Plain
C3	Crown Road	A2	Quay Mill Walk
B3	Deneside	B4	Queen Street
B4	Dorset Close	B1	Rampart Road
B1	East Road	C3	Regent Road
C2	Euston Road	B3	Regent Street
C2	Factory Road	C4	Rodney Road
B1	Ferrier Road	B4	Row 106
B1	Frederick Road	C3	Russell Road
B2	Fullers Hill	A3	St Francis Way
B1	Garrison Road	C4	St Georges Road
A2	George Street	B2	St Nicholas Road
B3	Greyfriars Way	C4	St Peter's Road
B3	Hall Plain	C4	St Peters Plain
B3	Hall Quay	C1	Sandown Road
B1	Hammond Road	A3	Saw Mill Lane
A3	High Mill Road	C3	Saxon Road
B3	Howard Street North	A1	School Road
B3	Howard Street South	C3	South Market Road
C2	Jury Street	B4	South Quay
B3	King Street	A4	Southtown Road
B1	Kitchener Road	A4	Station Road
A3	Lady Haven Road	A3	Steam Mill Lane
C4	Lancaster Road	A3	Stonecutters Way
A2	Lime Kiln Walk	B2	Temple Road
C2	Manby Road	A2	The Conge
D4	Marine Parade	B3	Theatre Plain
B3	Market Gates	B4	Tolhouse Street
B2	Market Place	C2	Tottenham Street
B3	Market Row	B1	Town Wall Road
B1	Maygrove Road	C3	Trafalgar Road
C2	Middle Market Road	C3	Union Road
A3	Mill Road	B3	Victoria Arcade
C4	Nelson Road Central	C2	Well Street
C2	Nelson Road North	C2	Wellesley Road
C1	North Denes Road	B1	West Road
D1	North Drive	B4	Yarmouth Way
C2	North Market Road	C4	York Road

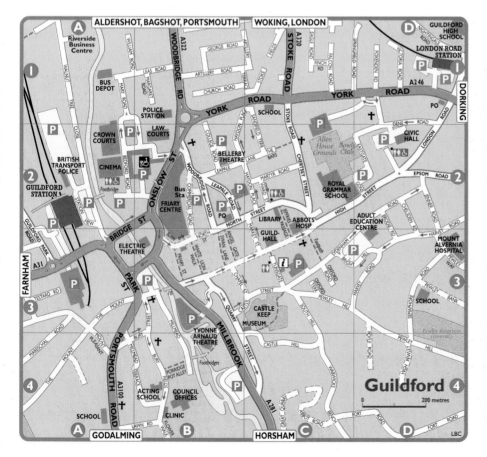

Guildford

C4	Abbot Road	B3	Millmead
B3	Angel Gate	B4	Millmead Terrace
B1	Artillery Road	A4	Mount Pleasant
B1	Artillery Terrace	D1	Nightingale Road
A2	Bedford Road	B3	North Street
A3	Bridge Street	B2	Onslow Street
C3	Bright Hill	C3	Oxford Road
D2	Brodie Road	C3	Oxford Terrace
B4	Bury Fields	A3	Park Street
B4	Bury Street	D3	Pewley Bank
C4	Castle Hill	C3	Pewley Hill
C3	Castle Street	D3	Pewley Way
B3	Chapel Street	B4	Porridge Pot Alley
D2	Chelsden Road	A4	Portsmouth Road
C2	Chertsey Street	D4	Poyle Road
B1	Church Road	B3	Quarry Street
B2	College Road	C1	Sandfield Terrace
B2	Commercial Road	D3	Semaphore Road
D1	Dene Road	C3	South Hill
C1	Eagle Road	D1	Springfield Road
D2	Eastgate Gardens	A2	Station View
D2	Epsom Road	C1	Stoke Fields
C1	Falcon Road	C1	Stoke Road
C1	Finch Road	B3	Swan Lane
B4	Flower Walk	C3	Sydenham Road
D4	Fort Road	A3	Testard Road
D1	Foxenden Road	C2	The Bars
B3	Friary Street	A4	The Mount
B1	George Road	C3	Tunsgate
C4	Great Quarry	D1	Victoria Road
A3	Guildford Park Road	A1	Walnut Tree Close
D3	Harvey Road	C2	Ward Street
B2	Haydon Place	C4	Warwicks Bench
D4	High Pewley	B3	White Lion Walk
C2	High Street	A1	William Road
C2	Jeffries Passage	B1	Woodbridge Road
D2	Jenner Road	B1	York Road
B4	Lawn Road		
B2	Leapale Lane		
B2	Leapale Road		
B1	Leas Road		
D2	London Road		
A4	Mareschal Road		
B1	Margaret Road		
C2	Market Street		
C2	Martyr Road		
A1	Mary Road		
B4	Millbrook		

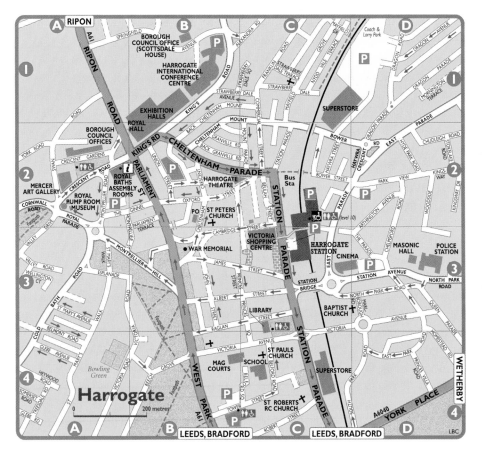

Harrogate

B3	Albert Street	D1	Mornington Terrace
C1	Alexandra Road	C2	Mount Parade
D2	Arthington Avenue	D3	North Park Road
B1	Back Cheltenham Mount	C1	Nydd Vale Terrace
B2	Back Granville Road	B2	Oxford Street
B4	Beech Grove	D2	Park View
C4	Belford Road	B2	Parliament Street
C4	Belford Square	B2	Parliament Terrace
A4	Belmont Road	C3	Princes Square
C2	Beulah Street	B3	Princes Street
C2	Bower Road	D4	Princes Villa Road
C2	Bower Street	D3	Queen Parade
B3	Cambridge Street	B3	Raglan Street
D3	Chelmsford Road	A1	Ripon Road
B2	Cheltenham Crescent	C4	Robert Street
B2	Cheltenham Mount	A2	Royal Parade
B2	Cheltenham Parade	A3	St Mary's Avenue
D2	Chudleigh Road	A4	St Mary's Walk
A3	Cold Bath Road	A4	Somerset Road
C1	Commercial Street	D4	South Park Road
A2	Cornwall Road	A1	Springfield Avenue
A2	Crescent Gardens	D3	Station Avenue
A2	Crescent Road	C3	Station Bridge
D1	Dragon Avenue	C2	Station Parade
D2	Dragon Parade	D2	Stonelake Road
D1	Dragon Road	C1	Strawberry Dale
C3	East Parade	B1	Strawberry Dale Avenue
D4	East Park Road	C1	Strawberry Dale Square
A3	Esplanade	C1	Strawberry Dale Terrace
C1	Franklin Road	A2	Swan Road
A4	Glebe Avenue	A2	The Ginnel
A4	Glebe Road	D3	The Parade
B2	Granville Road	B4	Tower Street
D2	Haywra Crescent	A4	Treesdale Road
C2	Haywra Street	B2	Union Street
A4	Heywood Road	A3	Valley Drive
D4	Homestead Road	A3	Valley Road
D2	Hyde Park Road	B4	Victoria Avenue
B3	James Street	A4	Victoria Road
B3	John Street	A3	Wellington Court
B2	King's Road	B4	West Park
D2	Kingsway	D2	Woodside
D2	Kingsway Drive	D4	York Place
D3	Marlborough Road	A2	York Road
C1	Mayfield Grove		
A3	Montpellier Hill		
A2	Montpellier Road		
A2	Montpellier Street		

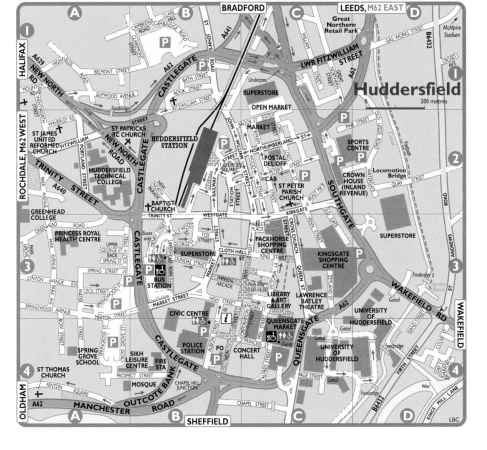

Huddersfield

B4	Albion Street	A3	Merton Street
C4	Alfred Street	A1	Mountjoy Road
A3	Back Spring Street	B2	New North Parade
B1	Bath Street	A2	New North Road
C2	Beast Market	B4	New Street
A1	Belmont Street	C2	Northumberland Street
A4	Bow Street	D2	Old Leeds Road
C2	Brook Street	C3	Old Gate
C2	Byram Street	A3	Old South Street
B1	Cambridge Road	B4	Outcote Bank
B1	Castlegate	C4	Page Street
A3	Cecil Street	A2	Park Avenue
C4	Chapel Street	C4	Peel Street
B1	Clare Hill	C2	Pine Street
B1	Claremont Street	A2	Portland Street
B3	Cloth Hall Street	C4	Princess Street
D4	Colne Street	A4	Prospect Street
C4	Corporation Street	D2	Quay Street
C3	Cross Church Street	C3	Queen Street
A4	Cross Grove Street	C4	Queensgate
D4	Day Street	B2	Railway Street
B3	Dundas Street	C3	Ramsden Street
A1	Elmwood Avenue	B1	Rook Street
A4	Fenton Square	D3	St Andrews Road
D4	Firth Street	B2	St George's Square
A2	Fitzwilliam Street	B1	St John's Road
B1	Fitzwilliam Street	C2	St Peter's Street
B3	Fox Street	D4	Sand Street
D4	Garforth Street	C2	Southgate
D1	Gas Works Street	A4	Springgrove Street
B3	George Street	A3	Spring Street
C1	Great Northern Street	A3	Springwood Avenue
A3	Greenhead Road	A3	Springwood Street
B3	Half Moon Street	B2	Station Street
B3	Henry Street	A2	Trinity Street
B3	High Street	B3	Westgate
A1	Highfields Road	A3	Upper George Street
B3	Imperial Arcade	B3	Upperhead Row
B2	John William Street	C3	Venn Street
C3	King Street	C3	Victoria Lane
D4	Kings Mill Lane	D3	Wakefield Road
C2	Kirkgate	A3	Water Street
C2	Lord Street	D2	Watergate
C1	Lower Fitzwilliam Street	A2	Waverley Road
A3	Lynton Avenue	A1	Wentworth Street
A4	Manchester Road	C1	William Street
C3	Market Place	C2	Wood Street
B3	Market Street	C3	Zetland Street

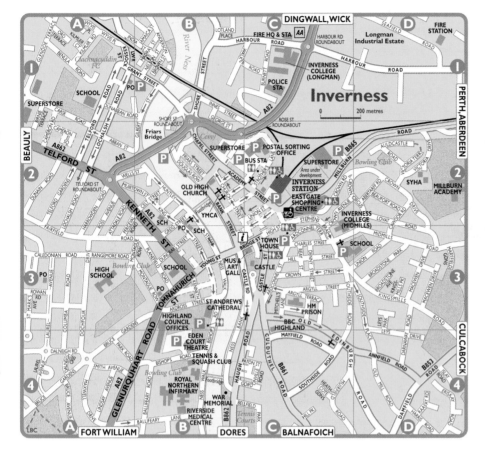

Inverness

D2	Abertarff Road	A4	Glenurquhart Road
B2	Academy Street	B1	Grant Street
B1	Anderson Street	B3	Greig Street
D4	Annfield Road	C1	Harbour Road
C3	Ardconnel Street	A2	Harrowden Road
C3	Ardconnel Terrace	B4	Haugh Road
B3	Ardross Street	C3	High Street
C3	Argyll Street	C3	Hill Street
C3	Argyll Terrace	B2	Huntley Street
A2	Attadale Road	A1	India Street
D2	Auldcastle Road	A2	Kenneth Street
B4	Ballifeary Lane	B2	King Street
B4	Ballifeary Road	D3	Kingsmills Road
B2	Bank Street	A3	Laurel Avenue
D2	Beaufort Road	D4	Leys Drive
A1	Benula Road	A2	Lochalsh Road
B4	Bishop's Road	D2	Lovat Road
C3	Bridge Street	A1	Lower Kessock Street
D3	Broadstone Park	D3	Macewen Drive
A4	Bruce Gardens	A4	Maxwell Drive
C1	Burnett Road	C4	Mayfield Road
A3	Caledonian Road	D3	Midmills Road
A2	Cameron Road	C2	Millburn Road
A1	Carse Road	B3	Montague Row
C3	Castle Road	C4	Muirfield Road
C3	Castle Street	A2	Muirtown Street
D2	Cawdor Road	B4	Ness Bank
B2	Celt Street	B4	Ness Walk
B2	Chapel Street	C3	Old Edinburgh Road
C3	Charles Street	D4	Old Mill Road
B2	Church Street	B3	Planefield Road
A3	Columba Road	A3	Rangemore Road
C2	Crown Avenue	D1	Seafield Road
C2	Crown Circus	B1	Shore Street
D2	Crown Drive	D3	Southside Place
C2	Crown Road	C4	Southside Road
C3	Crown Street	C2	Stephens Brae
C4	Culduthel Road	C2	Strother's Lane
A4	Dalneigh Road	A2	Telford Gardens
D4	Damfield Road	A2	Telford Road
D4	Darnaway Road	A2	Telford Street
A3	Dochfour Drive	B3	Tomnahurich Street
B2	Douglas Row	D3	Union Road
A2	Dunain Road	C2	Union Street
A3	Fairfield Road	D2	Victoria Drive
B2	Friars Street	B1	Walker Road
B2	Gilbert Street	A2	Wells Street
A1	Glendoe Terrace	B3	Young Street

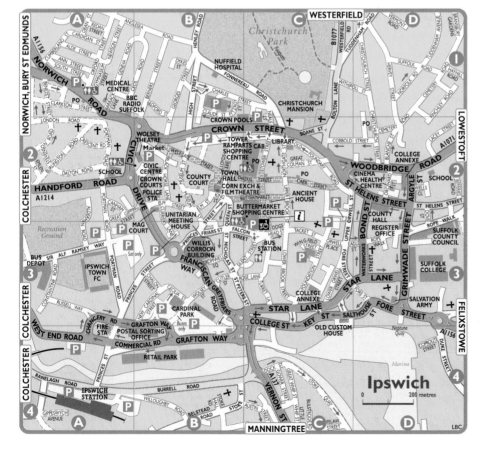

Ipswich

A1	Anglesea Road	B1	High Street
A1	Ann Street	C3	Key Street
D2	Argyle Street	B2	King Street
B4	Belstead Road	D2	Lacey Street
B1	Berners Street	B2	Lloyds Avenue
B2	Black Horse Lane	A2	London Road
C1	Bolton Lane	C3	Lower Brook Street
D3	Bond Street	B2	Museum Street
A2	Burlington Road	B3	New Cardinal Street
B4	Burrell Road	C2	Northgate Street
C2	Buttermarket	A1	Norwich Road
A1	Cardigan Street	C2	Old Foundary Road
C2	Carr Street	A1	Orford Street
B1	Cecil Road	A2	Orwell Place
B3	Cecilia Street	A2	Portman Road
D2	Cemetery Road	A4	Princes Street
A3	Chancery Road	B2	Queen Street
B1	Charles Street	A4	Ranelagh Road
D1	Christchurch Street	D3	Rope Walk
A2	Civic Drive	C3	Rose Lane
A1	Clarkson Street	A3	Russell Way
B1	Claude Street	B1	St Georges Street
C2	Cobbold Street	D2	St Helens Street
C3	College Street	B3	St Nicholas Street
A4	Commercial Road	B3	St Peters Street
A3	Constantine Road	C3	Salthouse Street
B2	Crown Street	C2	Silent Street
A1	Cumberland Street	A3	Sir Alf Ramsey Way
B3	Cutler Street	C2	Soane Street
A2	Dalton Road	C3	Star Lane
C4	Dock Street	C4	Stoke Quay
C3	Dogs Head Street	B4	Stoke Street
D4	Duke Street	D1	Suffolk Road
B2	Elm Street	C3	Tacket Street
B3	Falcon Street	C2	Tavern Street
B1	Fonnereau Road	C2	Tower Street
C3	Fore Street	C1	Tuddenham Road
C3	Foundation Street	C1	Turret Lane
B3	Franciscan Way	C2	Upper Brook Street
B3	Friars Street	C3	Upper Orwell Street
A1	Geneva Road	A3	Vernon Street
B3	Grafton Way	D3	Waterworks Street
C2	Great Colman Street	A4	West End Road
B3	Greyfriars Road	C1	Westerfield Road
D3	Grimwade Street	B2	Westgate Street
A2	Handford Road	B4	Willoughby Road
B1	Henley Road	B3	Wolsey Street
D1	Hervey Street	D2	Woodbridge Road

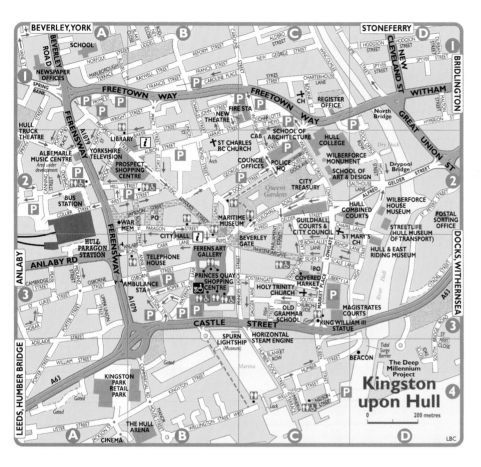

Kingston upon Hull

A4	Adelaide Street	C3	Market Place
B2	Albion Street	A1	Marlborough Terrace
C2	Alfred Gelder Street	A3	Midland Street
A3	Anlaby Road	A2	Mill Street
B3	Anne Street	B3	Myton Street
B2	Baker Street	D1	New Cleveland Street
A1	Beverley Road	C1	New George Street
C3	Bishop Lane	A1	Norfolk Street
C4	Blanket Row	A3	Osborne Street
B2	Bond Street	B2	Paragon Street
C1	Bourne Street	C3	Parliament Street
C3	Bowlalley Lane	A3	Pease Street
A2	Brook Street	B1	Percy Street
A2	Canning Street	A4	Porter Street
B1	Caroline Place	C3	Posterngate
B1	Caroline Street	C3	Princes Dock Street
B3	Carr Lane	A1	Prospect Street
B3	Castle Street	C4	Queen Street
C2	Chapel Lane	C2	Queens Dock Avenue
B1	Charles Street	B1	Raywell Street
C1	Charlotte Street Mews	B1	Reform Street
C1	Charterhouse Lane	B3	Roper Street
A2	Collier Street	A3	St Lukes Street
B4	Commercial Road	D2	St Peters Street
C3	Dagger Lane	B2	Savile Street
C2	Dock Street	C3	Scale Lane
A1	Ferensway	C3	Silver Street
C3	Fish Street	D4	South Bridge Road
A1	Freetown Way	C3	South Churchside
B2	George Street	B2	South Street
D2	Great Union Street	A1	Spring Bank
C2	Guildhall Road	A2	Spring Street
D2	High Street	D1	Spyvee Street
D1	Hodgson Street	B2	Story Street
C4	Humber Dock Street	C1	Sykes Street
C4	Humber Street	C3	Trinity House Lane
D1	Hyperion Street	A3	Upper Union Street
B2	Jameson Street	B3	Waterhouse Lane
B2	Jarratt Street	C4	Wellington Street
B1	John Street	B4	Wellington Street West
B2	King Edward Street	A2	West Street
B4	Kingston Street	C3	Whitefriargate
C3	Liberty Lane	C2	Wilberforce Drive
D1	Lime Street	A4	William Street
A4	Lister Street	C1	Wincolmlee
A2	Lombard Street	D1	Witham
C3	Lowgate	C1	Worship Street
B4	Manor House Street	A1	Wright Street

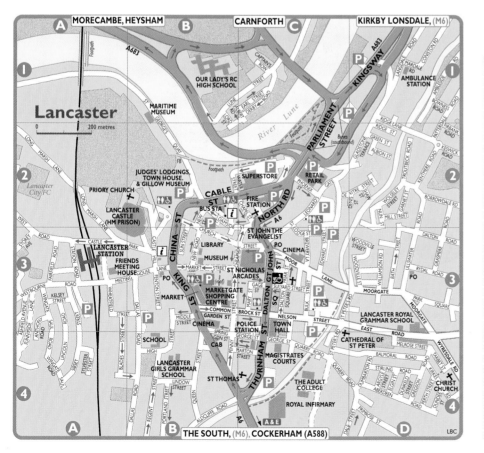

Lancaster

D4	Aberdeen Road	A2	Long Marsh Lane
B4	Aldcliffe Road	B1	Lord Street
D1	Ambleside Road	B1	Lune Street
D4	Balmoral Road	B3	Market Street
D3	Bath Street	C4	Marton Street
A4	Blades Street	C3	Mary Street
D2	Borrowdale Road	A3	Meeting House Lane
C3	Brewery Lane	D4	Melrose Street
C3	Brock Street	B3	Middle Street
C3	Bulk Street	C3	Moor Lane
B2	Cable Street	D3	Moorgate
C1	Captain's Row	C3	Nelson Street
B3	Castle Hill	B3	New Road
A3	Castle Park	B2	New Street
C2	Chapel Street	C2	North Road
B3	Cheapside	D3	Park Square
B3	China Street	C2	Parliament Street
B3	Church Street	D2	Patterdale Road
B3	Common Garden Street	B4	Penny Street
D4	Dale Street	C2	Phoenix Street
B3	Dallas Road	B4	Portland Street
C3	Dalton Square	C4	Quarry Road
B2	Damside Street	B4	Queen Street
D2	De Vitre Street	B4	Regent Street
C1	Derby Road	D1	Ridge Lane
D4	Dumbarton Road	D3	Rydal Road
C1	Earl Street	B1	St George's Quay
D3	East Road	C2	St Leonard's Gate
C3	Edward Street	C4	St Peter's Road
D4	Elgin Street	A4	Sibsey Street
A3	Fairfield Road	B4	Spring Garden Street
B3	Fenton Street	A3	Station Road
C3	Friar Street	D4	Stirling Road
C3	Gage Street	C3	Sulyard Street
C4	George Street	B3	Sun Street
D2	Gladstone Terrace	C4	Thurnham Street
D3	Grasmere Road	D2	Troutbeck Road
C3	Great John Street	D3	Ullswater Road
D2	Green Street	B2	Water Street
D4	Gregson Road	A2	West Road
B4	High Street	A3	Westbourne Road
D2	Kentmere Road	A3	Wheatfield Street
B3	King Street	D3	Williamson Road
D1	Kingsway	A4	Wingate Saul Road
D4	Kirkes Road	D2	Wolseley Street
D1	Langdale Road	D3	Woodville Street
A4	Lincoln Road	D4	Wyresdale Road
C3	Lodge Street		

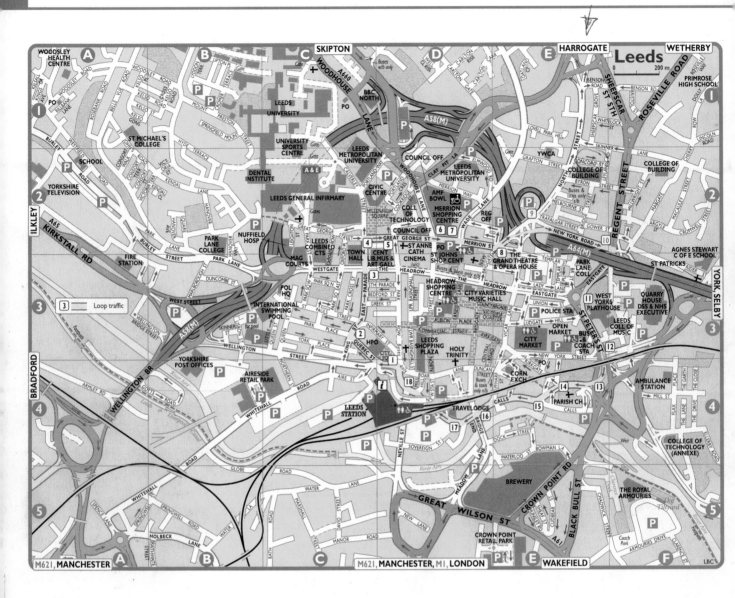

Leeds

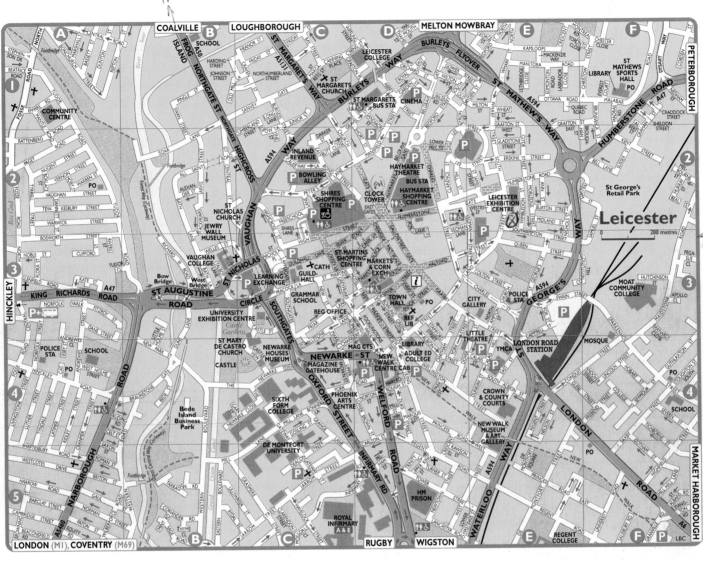

Leicester

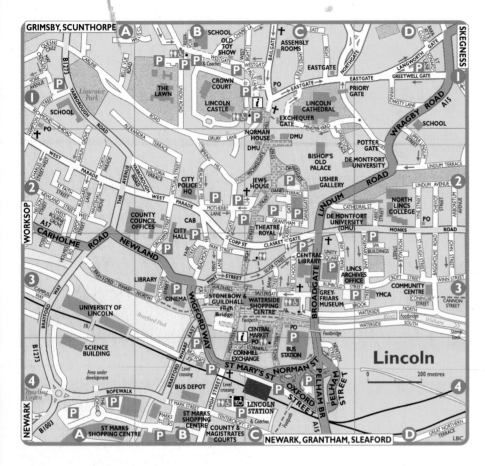

Lincoln

D2	Abbey Street	D2	Monks Road
B2	Alexandra Terrace	D3	Montague Street
A2	Ashlin Grove	B2	Motherby Lane
D3	Baggholme Road	A3	Newland
C1	Bailgate	A2	Newland Street West
C3	Bank Street	C4	Newton Street
B2	Beaumont Fee	C4	Norman Street
B4	Brayford Street	A2	North Parade
A3	Brayford Way	C1	Northgate
B4	Brayford Wharf East	B3	Orchard Street
A3	Brayford Wharf North	C4	Oxford Street
C3	Broadgate	B3	Park Street
D3	Brook Street	C4	Pelham Bridge
A3	Carholme Road	C4	Pelham Street
A1	Carline Road	A1	Queens Crescent
D2	Cathedral Street	B1	Reservoir Street
A2	Charles Street West	A1	Richmond Road
D2	Cheviot Street	A4	Ropewalk
C3	Clasket Gate	D3	Rosemary Lane
D3	Coningsby Street	A2	Rudgard Lane
C4	Cornhill	C3	Rumbold's Street
B3	Corporation Street	D3	St Hugh Street
D3	Croft Street	B4	St Mark Street
C2	Danes Terrace	B4	St Mary's Street
C2	Danesgate	C1	St Paul's Lane
A2	Depot Street	C3	Saltergate
B2	Drury Lane	C3	Silver Street
C1	East Bight	C4	Sincil Street
C1	Eastgate	B2	Spring Hill
C2	Flaxengate	C2	Steep Hill
C3	Free School Lane	C2	Strait
C3	Friars Lane	B4	Tentercroft Street
C2	Grantham Street	A2	The Avenue
D1	Greetwell Gate	B1	Union Road
B3	Guildhall Street	C3	Unity Square
A1	Hampton Street	D2	Upper Lindum Street
B4	High Street	B2	Victoria Street
B2	Hungate	B2	Victoria Terrace
C1	James Street	D2	Vine Street
D1	Langworth Gate	D3	Waterside North
D2	Lindum Avenue	D3	Waterside South
C2	Lindum Road	A2	West Parade
D2	Lindum Terrace	B1	Westgate
A1	May Crescent	A2	Whitehall Grove
C2	Michaelgate	B3	Wigford Way
C1	Minster Yard	D1	Winnowsty Lane
B3	Mint Lane	D1	Wragby Road
B3	Mint Street	A1	Yarborough Road

Llandudno

A1	Abbey Road	C4	Jacksons Court
C2	Adelphi Street	A2	James Street
B3	Albert Street	B3	Jubilee Street
C3	Argyll Road	A4	King's Avenue
A1	Arvon Avenue	A4	King's Place
B3	Augusta Street	A4	King's Road
B2	Back Madoc Street	A1	Llewelyn Avenue
B2	Bodafon Street	A3	Lloyd Street
A1	Bodhyfryd Road	B2	Madoc Street
B2	Brookes Street	A2	Maelgwyn Road
B4	Builder Street	C4	Maesdu Road
A4	Builder Street West	A2	Market Street
B4	Cae Bach	A1	Masonic Street
D4	Cae Clyd	C3	Mostyn Broadway
A4	Cae Mawr	C2	Mostyn Crescent
A2	Caroline Road	A1	Mostyn Street
A2	Chapel Street	C2	Nevill Crescent
C3	Charlotte Road	A2	New Street
B3	Charlton Street	B3	Norman Road
A1	Church Walks	B1	North Parade
A3	Claremont Road	A1	Old Road
D4	Clarence Crescent	B3	Oxford Road
D4	Clarence Drive	D3	Penrhyn Crescent
A2	Clement Avenue	A1	Plas Road
A2	Clifton Road	B1	Prince Edwards Square
B2	Clonmell Street	A3	St Andrews Avenue
C3	Conway Road	A3	St David's Place
B4	Council Street West	A3	St David's Road
A1	Court Street	B2	St George's Crescent
B4	Cwm Road	B2	St George's Place
A2	Deganwy Avenue	A2	St Mary's Road
A4	Dyffryn Road	A3	St Seiriol's Road
C4	Fforddd Dewi	B2	Somerset Street
B4	Fforddd Gwynedd	B1	South Parade
C4	Fforddd Las	A2	Taliesin Street
C4	Fforddd Morfa	B3	Thorpe Street
C4	Fforddd Penrhyn	A4	Trinity Avenue
C4	Fforddd Tudno	B3	Trinity Square
B3	Garage Street	A1	Tudno Street
A2	Garden Street	C3	Tudor Crescent
A2	George Street	C3	Tudor Road
B1	Glan Y Mor Parade	A1	Ty Gwyn Road
B2	Gloddaeth Crescent	B1	Ty Isa Road
A2	Gloddaeth Street	D3	Ty'n Y Ffrith Road
A1	Hill Terrace	A1	Vardre Lane
B4	Howard Place	C2	Vaughan Street
B4	Howard Road	B4	Wern Y Wylan
B4	Hywel Place	A2	York Road

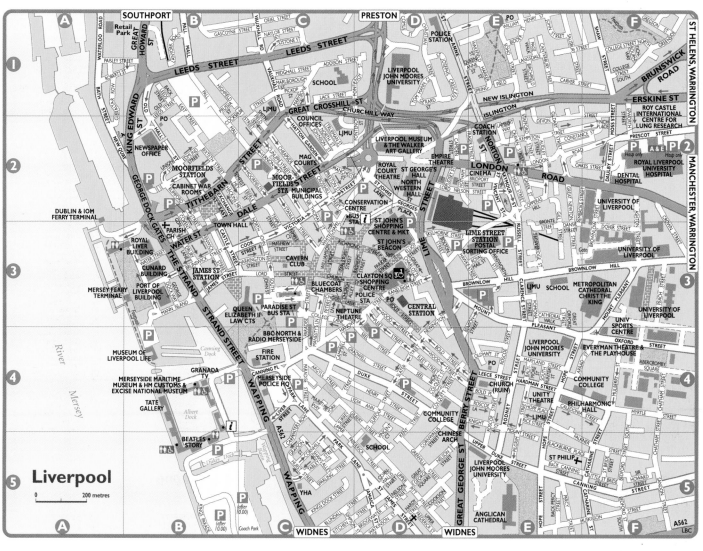

Liverpool

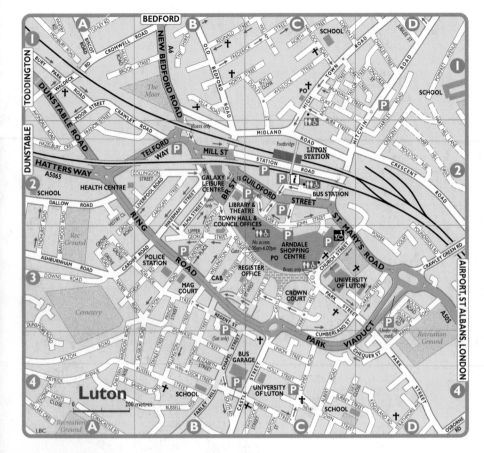

Luton

B3	Adelaide Street	A2	Hazelbury Crescent
C4	Albert Road	C4	Hibbert Street
B2	Alma Street	C1	High Town Road
A3	Ashburnham Road	D2	Hitchin Road
A1	Avondale Road	C4	Holly Street
C1	Back Street	B2	Inkerman Street
A1	Biscot Road	C2	John Street
A3	Brantwood Road	B3	King Street
B2	Bridge Street	C4	Latimer Road
A1	Brook Street	B2	Liverpool Road
C1	Brunswick Street	D4	Manor Road
C2	Burr Street	A4	Meyrick Avenue
A1	Bury Park Road	C2	Midland Road
B3	Buxton Road	B2	Mill Street
A3	Cardiff Grove	A4	Milton Road
A3	Cardiff Road	A1	Moor Street
B2	Cardigan Street	A3	Napier Road
B4	Castle Street	B1	New Bedford Road
B4	Chapel Street	C4	New Town Street
D1	Charles Street	B1	Old Bedford Road
D4	Chequer Street	C3	Park Street
C3	Church Street	C3	Park Street West
D1	Concorde Street	C4	Park Viaduct
D3	Crawley Green Road	D3	Power Court
A1	Crawley Road	B3	Princess Street
D2	Crescent Rise	B3	Regent Street
D2	Crescent Road	B1	Reginald Street
A1	Cromwell Road	B2	Ring Road
C4	Cumberland Street	A3	Rothesay Road
A2	Dallow Road	B4	Russell Rise
A3	Downs Road	B4	Russell Street
C1	Dudley Street	C2	St Mary's Road
C1	Duke Street	B4	Salisbury Road
B4	Dumfries Street	C2	Silver Street
B3	Dunstable Place	B4	Stanley Street
A1	Dunstable Road	C2	Station Road
B4	Farley Hill	C4	Surrey Street
B1	Frederick Street	B2	Telford Way
B3	George Street	A4	Tenzing Grove
B3	George Street West	C4	Union Street
B3	Gordon Street	B3	Upper George Street
A3	Grove Road	D3	Vicarage Street
C2	Guildford Street	A1	Waldeck Road
D2	Hart Hill Drive	B4	Wellington Street
D2	Hartley Road	C1	Wenlock Street
B4	Hastings Street	B4	Windsor Street
A2	Hatters Way	A4	Winsdon Road
C1	Havelock Road	C1	York Street

Maidstone

D1	Albany Street	C3	Lower Stone Street
D2	Albion Place	C1	Lucerne Street
D1	Allen Street	B2	Market Buildings
D3	Ashford Road	B2	Market Street
D2	Astley Street	C2	Marsham Street
B3	Bank Street	D4	Meadow Walk
B4	Barker Road	B3	Medway Street
D4	Birch Tree Way	C4	Melville Road
B3	Bishops Way	B3	Mill Street
D3	Blythe Road	D4	Mote Avenue
C1	Brewer Street	C4	Mote Road
A3	Broadway	B2	Museum Street
C4	Brunswick Street	C4	Orchard Street
C4	Brunswick Street East	C3	Palace Avenue
A1	Buckland Hill	D1	Princes Street
A2	Buckland Road	C4	Priory Road
C1	Camden Street	C4	Pudding Lane
D3	Chancery Lane	D2	Queen Anne Road
A4	Charles Street	A4	Reginald Road
C2	Church Street	C3	Romney Place
B4	College Avenue	B2	Rose Yard
C4	College Road	A4	Rowland Close
C1	County Road	A2	St Annes Court
D2	Cromwell Road	B2	St Faiths Street
A4	Douglas Road	D1	St Luke's Avenue
B2	Earl Street	D1	St Lukes Road
D4	Elm Grove	A2	St Peter Street
B1	Fairmeadow	B1	Sandling Road
A4	Florence Road	D2	Sittingbourne Road
D1	Foley Street	D3	Square Hill Road
C4	Foster Street	B1	Staceys Street
C3	Gabriel's Hill	B1	Station Road
C4	George Street	A3	Terrace Road
D4	Greenside	A4	Tonbridge Road
A4	Hart Street	D2	Tufton Street
D4	Hastings Road	C2	Union Street
D1	Heathorn Street	C4	Upper Stone Street
C1	Hedley Street	D2	Vinters Road
B3	High Street	D3	Wat Tyler Way
D1	Holland Road	B2	Waterside
C1	James Street	B1	Week Street
C1	Jeffrey Street	C1	Well Road
C3	King Street	A4	Westree Road
D4	Kingsley Road	C1	Wheeler Street
C4	Knightrider Street	C1	Wollett Street
A1	Lesley Place	C2	Wyatt Street
A3	London Road	C2	Wyke Manor Road
B1	Lower Boxley Road		

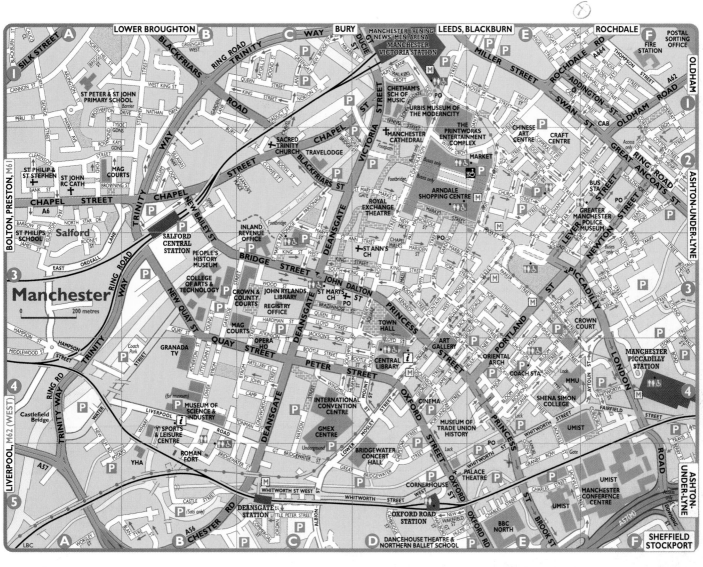

Manchester

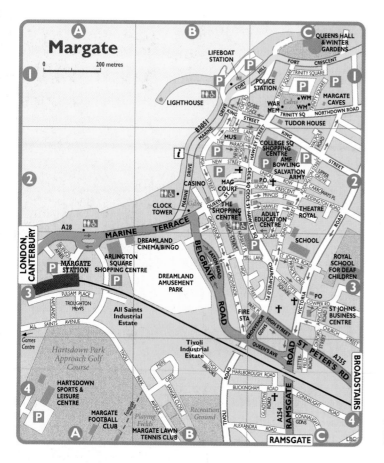

Margate

C2	Addington Road	C3	St John's Road
C2	Addington Street	C3	St John's Street
B4	Alexandra Road	C4	St Peter's Road
A3	All Saints Avenue	B4	Sanger Close
C3	Arnold Road	C4	Setterfield Road
B3	Belgrave Road	B2	The Parade
B4	Buckingham Road	B4	Tivoli Brooks
A3	Buenos Ayres	A4	Tivoli Park Avenue
C2	Carroways Place	B4	Tivoli Road
C2	Cecil Square	C1	Trinity Square
C2	Cecil Street	A3	Troughton Mews
C3	Charlotte Square	C2	Union Crescent
C3	Church Street	C2	Union Row
C3	Churchfield Place	C2	Upper Grove
C1	Cobbs Place	C3	Victoria Road
C4	Connaught Gardens	C2	Walpole Road
C4	Connaught Road		
C3	Cowper Road		
B3	Eaton Road		
C1	Fort Crescent		
B1	Fort Hill		
B1	Fort Road		
A3	Fulsam Place		
C4	Gladstone Road		
C3	Grosvenor Gardens		
B2	Grosvenor Place		
C2	Hawley Square		
C2	Hawley Street		
B3	Herbert Place		
B2	High Street		
B1	King Street		
B2	Love Lane		
B2	Marine Drive		
A3	Marine Terrace		
B4	Marlborough Road		
B4	Mere Gate		
C3	Mill Lane		
A3	Naylands		
B2	New Cross Street		
B2	New Street		
C1	Northdown Road		
C4	Oxford Street		
C3	Park Place		
C3	Prince's Crescent		
C2	Princes Street		
B2	Queen Street		
C4	Queens Avenue		
C4	Ramsgate Road		

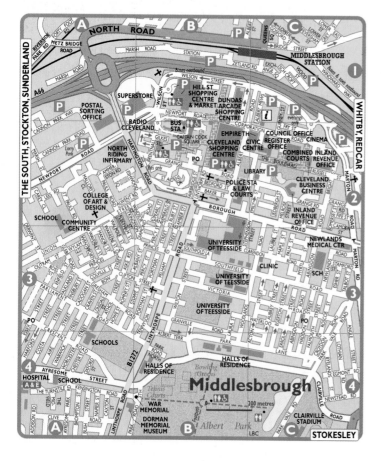

Middlesbrough

C4	Abingdon Road	A3	Enfield Street	A3	Outram Street
C4	Acton Street	C4	Errol Street	A4	Oxford Street
A4	Aire Street	C3	Esher Street	C3	Palm Street
C1	Albert Mews	A2	Eshwood Square	B4	Park Lane
B2	Albert Road	A3	Essex Street	B4	Park Road North
B1	Albert Street	C1	Exchange Square	B4	Park Road South
B4	Albert Terrace	B2	Fairbridge Street	C4	Park Vale Road
A2	Alwent Road	A3	Falkland Street	A3	Parliament Road
B2	Amber Street	C4	Falmouth Street	B2	Pearl Street
A2	Ammerston Road	C2	Fife Street	B3	Pelham Street
C3	Angle Street	A3	Finsbury Street	B3	Percy Street
A3	Aske Road	A2	Fleetham Street	B3	Portman Street
A3	Athol Street	C2	Fry Street	A3	Princes Road
C3	Aubrey Street	B2	Garnet Street	C1	Queens Square
A4	Ayresome Park Road	B2	Gilkes Street	A3	Romney Street
A4	Ayresome Street	A3	Glebe Road	C3	Roscoe Street
B2	Baker Street	B2	Grange Road	B2	Ruby Street
B2	Bedford Street	B3	Granville Road	C2	Russell Street
B2	Borough Road	B3	Gresham Road	B2	St Aidens Drive
A3	Bow Street	C2	Gurney Street	A2	St Pauls Road
B2	Brentnall Street	C4	Haddon Street	C2	Somerset Street
C1	Bridge Street	A4	Harford Street	B3	Southfield Road
C2	Bright Street	A2	Hartington Road	B3	Southfold Lane
A4	Brompton Street	A3	Howe Street	C3	Stamford Street
C4	Byelands Street	C2	Jedbergh Street	B1	Station Street
A3	Cadogan Street	A4	Kensington Road	B3	Stephenson Street
A2	Cannon Park Road	A2	Kingston Street	B3	Stowe Street
A2	Cannon Park Way	B3	Laura Street	C3	Talbot Street
B2	Captain Cook Square	C3	Laurel Street	B3	Tennyson Street
A2	Carey Close	A2	Lees Road	C2	The Boulevard
A4	Caxton Street	A4	Linthorpe Road	A4	The Turnstile
A4	Chester Street	A3	Lonsdale Road	A3	Union Street
C4	Clairville Road	C4	Lothian Road	B3	Victoria Road
C3	Clarendon Road	C1	Lower Feversham Street	A3	Walpole Street
A3	Clifton Street	C1	Lower Gosford Street	A3	Warren Street
A4	Clive Road	A3	Manor Street	A4	Warwick Street
A3	Colville Street	C3	Maple Street	C3	Waterloo Road
B2	Corporation Road	A2	Marsh Road	A3	Waverley Street
A4	Costa Street	A2	Marsh Street	A3	Wentworth Street
A3	Craven Street	C2	Marton Road	B1	Wilson Street
A4	Crescent Road	C2	Melrose Street	B3	Wilton Street
C4	Croydon Road	A1	Metz Bridge Road	B2	Windsor Street
A3	Derwent Street	C3	Myrtle Street	C1	Windward Way
B3	Diamond Road	A4	Napier Street	C1	Wood Street
C3	Egerton Street	C3	Newlands Road	B3	Woodlands Road
C4	Egmont Road	A2	Newport Road	A4	Worcester Street
B2	Emerald Street	C4	Newstead Road	A3	Wylam Street
C2	Emily Street	A1	North Road	B1	Zetland Road

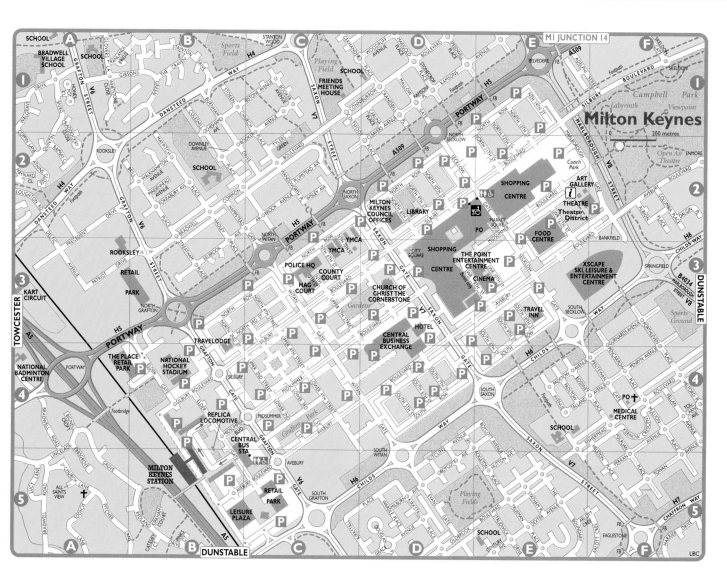

Milton Keynes

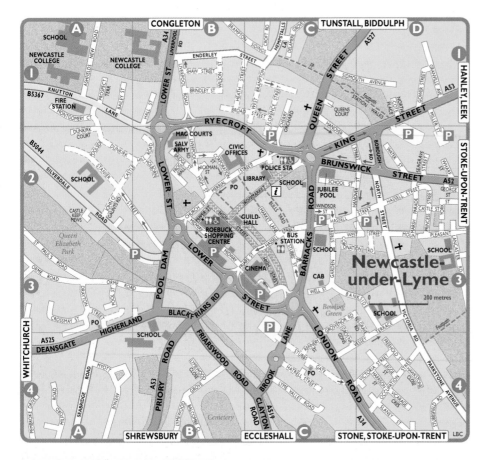

Newcastle-under-Lyme

A1	Ashfields New Road	D4	Legge Street
C3	Bankside	B1	Liverpool Road
C3	Barracks Road	C4	London Road
D3	Belgrave Road	B2	Lower Street
B3	Blackfriars Road	C4	Lyme Valley Road
D2	Borough Road	B4	Lymewood Grove
B1	Brampton Sidings	C2	Market Lane
B2	Bridge Street	D2	Marsh Parade
B1	Brindley Street	B2	Merrial Street
B1	Broad Street	B2	Midway
C4	Brook Lane	D1	Miller Street
C2	Brunswick Street	A1	Montgomery Court
C2	Bulls Yard	D3	Mount Pleasant
A2	Castle Hill Road	A4	Myott Avenue
D2	Castle Street	D2	North Street
C1	Cherry Orchard	D1	Northcote Place
B2	Church Street	D4	Occupation Street
C4	Clayton Road	A3	Orme Road
C3	Coronation Road	D4	Parkstone Avenue
B2	Corporation Street	B2	Pepper Street
A3	Crossmay Street	B3	Pool Dam
A4	Deansgate	A2	Poolside
A3	Drayton Street	D2	Princess Street
A2	Dunkirk	B4	Priory Road
B1	Enderley Street	C1	Queen Street
C1	Florence Street	C4	Refinery Street
D4	Freehold Street	B1	Ryecroft
B3	Friars Street	A3	St Paul's Road
B4	Friarswood Road	C2	School Street
B2	Frog Hall	A4	Seabridge Road
C3	Garden Street	D2	Seagrave Street
D1	Gower Street	B1	Shaw Street
D1	Granville Avenue	C1	Sidmouth Avenue
C4	Grosvenor Gardens	A2	Silverdale Road
C3	Grosvenor Road	D4	Slaney Street
B1	Hall Street	A2	Stanier Street
C2	Hanover Street	D1	Station Walks
D4	Harrison Street	C4	Stubbs Gate
C2	Hassell Street	C3	Stubbs' Street
C4	Hatrell Street	D4	Vessey Terrace
B1	Heath Street	D3	Victoria Road
C1	Hempstalls Lane	D4	Victoria Street
B2	High Street	D2	Water Street
A3	Higherland	C3	Well Street
C2	Ironmarket	C1	West Brampton
A2	John O'Gaunts Road	C3	West Street
C2	King Street	B1	Wilson Street
A1	Knutton Lane	C2	Windsor Street

Newport

B3	Albert Terrace	B3	Jones Street
A1	Allt Yr Yn Avenue	C4	Keynsham Avenue
A1	Allt Yr Yn Road	C4	King Street
B3	Bailey Street	C2	Kingsway
B3	Baneswell Road	A3	Llanthewy Road
D2	Bedford Road	D1	Llanvair Road
B3	Blewitt Street	B1	Locke Street
C1	Bond Street	C4	Lower Dock Street
B2	Bridge Street	B1	Lucas Street
A3	Bryngwyn Road	C4	Mellon Street
A4	Brynhyfryd Avenue	B2	Mill Street
A4	Brynhyfryd Road	B3	North Street
A3	Caerau Crescent	A2	Oakfield Road
A3	Caerau Road	C4	Park Square
D1	Caerleon Road	C1	Pugsley Street
C4	Cardiff Road	C4	Queen Street
C4	Caroline Street	B1	Queen's Hill
D2	Cedar Road	B1	Queen's Hill Crescent
C3	Charles Street	B2	Queensway
D2	Chepstow Road	D1	Riverside
C2	Clarence Place	C2	Rodney Parade
B3	Clifton Place	C2	Rodney Road
B4	Clifton Road	B1	Rose Street
A3	Clyffard Crescent	D1	Rudry Street
A2	Clytha Park Road	A3	St Edward Street
D2	Colne Street	A1	St Marks Crescent
A1	Coltsfoot Close	B3	St Mary Street
A1	Comfrey Close	C2	St Vincent Road
C3	Commercial Street	C3	School Lane
D1	Corelli Street	B4	St Woolos Place
D2	Corporation Road	B3	St Woolos Road
C3	Cross Lane	A2	Serpentine Road
B2	Devon Place	C2	Skinner Street
B4	Dewsland Park Road	A1	Sorrel Drive
B3	East Street	A3	Spencer Road
D1	East Usk Road	B2	Stanley Road
B1	Factory Road	A4	Stow Hill
A2	Fields Park Road	A4	Stow Park Avenue
A2	Fields Road	D1	Tregare Street
B4	Friars Road	A3	Tunnel Terrace
C4	George Street	C3	Usk Way
A2	Godfrey Road	B4	Vicarage Hill
A2	Gold Tops	B3	Victoria Place
D2	Grafton Road	C4	Victoria Road
B3	Graham Street	B3	Victoria Street
D4	Granville Street	B3	West Street
B2	High Street	A3	Windsor Terrace
C3	Hill Street	A4	York Place

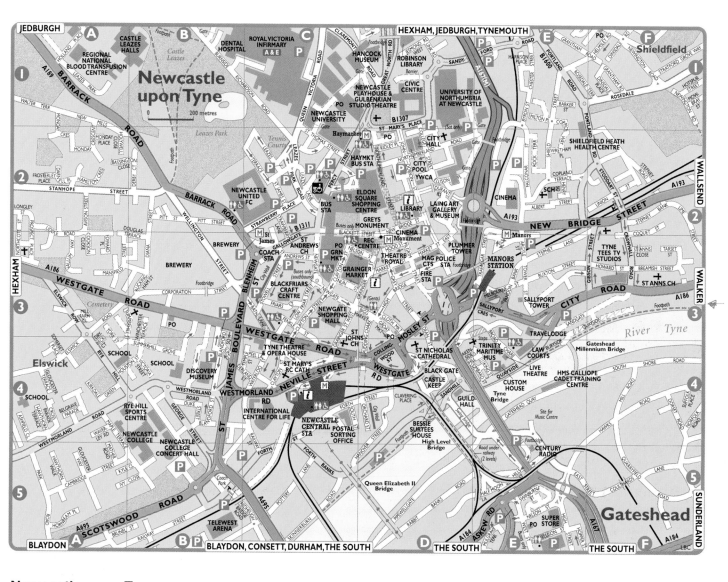

Newcastle upon Tyne

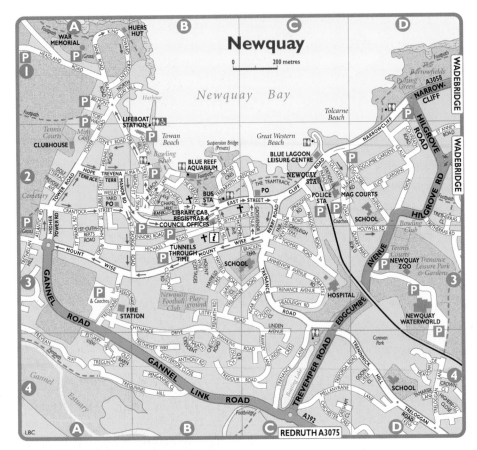

Newquay

C3	Agar Road	B2	Marcus Hill
C2	Albany Road	B3	Mayfield Road
B2	Alma Place	D4	Meadowside
B4	Anthony Road	C4	Mellanvrane Lane
A3	Atlantic Road	B2	Mitchell Avenue
B2	Bank Street	A3	Mount Wise
B2	Beach Road	D2	Narrowcliff
B2	Beachfield Avenue	A1	North Quay Hill
A1	Beacon Road	C2	Pargolla Road
C2	Berry Road	B4	Pengannel Close
C3	Bracken Terrace	D3	Quarry Park Road
B2	Broad Street	C4	Rawley Lane
B2	Chapel Hill	C3	Robartes Road
C4	Chichester Crescent	A3	St Cuthberts Road
B3	Chynance Drive	B3	St George's Road
B4	Chyverton Close	A3	St John's Road
C2	Cliff Road	A3	St Michael's Road
D2	Colvreath Road	A3	St Piran's Road
A2	Crantock Street	C3	St Thomas Road
A1	Dane Road	B2	Seymour Avenue
B2	East Street	C2	Springfield Road
C3	Edgcumbe Avenue	C2	Station Parade
D2	Edgcumbe Gardens	A2	Sydney Road
D2	Eliot Gardens	B2	The Crescent
B3	Ennors Road	C2	Tolcarne Road
A2	Fernhill Road	C2	Tor Road
B2	Fore Street	A2	Tower Road
B4	Gannel Link Road	B2	Trebarwith Crescent
A3	Gannel Road	B4	Tredour Road
B2	Gover Lane	C4	Treforda Road
C2	Grosvenor Avenue	A3	Tregunnel Hill
B2	Harbour Hill	B3	Trelawney Road
B4	Hawkins Road	D4	Treloggan Lane
A1	Headland Road	D4	Treloggan Road
C3	Headleigh Road	B4	Trembath Crescent
A2	Higher Tower Road	C3	Trenance Avenue
D2	Hilgrove Road	C4	Trenance Lane
D3	Holywell Road	C3	Trenance Road
A2	Hope Terrace	B3	Trenarth Road
B2	Island Crescent	D4	Treninnick Hill
A2	Jubilee Street	D3	Tretherras Road
A1	King Edward Crescent	B4	Trethewey Way
B2	King Street	A4	Trevean Way
C3	Lanhenvor Avenue	C4	Trevemper Road
C3	Linden Avenue	A2	Trevena Terrace
C4	Linden Crescent	D2	Ulalia Road
B3	Listry Road	B3	Vivian Close
A2	Manor Road	A2	Wesley Yard

Northampton

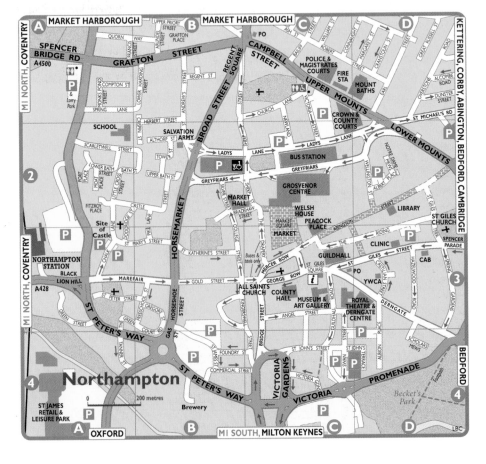

C3	Abington Street	B1	Lower Harding Street
D2	Albert Place	D2	Lower Mounts
D4	Albion Place	A3	Marefair
B2	Althorp Street	D1	Margaret Street
C3	Angel Street	C2	Market Square
B1	Arundel Street	C3	Mercer Row
C1	Ash Street	A2	Moat Place
C1	Bailiff Street	A1	Monks Pond Street
A2	Bath Street	C2	Newland
A3	Black Lion Hill	D1	Overstone Road
B2	Bradshaw Street	B3	Pike Lane
C4	Bridge Street	A1	Quorn Way
B2	Broad Street	B1	Regent Square
C1	Campbell Street	B1	Regent Street
D3	Castilian Street	C1	Robert Street
B2	Castle Street	B1	St Andrews Street
A3	Chalk Lane	C3	St Giles Square
C1	Church Lane	D3	St Giles Street
B3	College Street	D2	St Giles Terrace
B4	Commercial Street	B4	St James Street
A1	Compton Street	C4	St John's Street
C1	Connaught Street	D4	St John's Terrace
B3	Court Road	B3	St Katherine's Street
D1	Cranstoun Street	A3	St Mary's Street
B2	Crispin Street	D1	St Michael's Road
D3	Derngate	A3	St Peter Street
A3	Doddridge Street	A3	St Peter's Way
D1	Dunster Street	B4	St Peter's Way
D1	Earl Street	A2	Scarletwell Street
B4	Foundry Street	C2	Sheep Street
A1	Francis Street	B2	Silver Street
B3	Freeschool Street	A1	Spencer Bridge Road
B4	Gas Street	D3	Spencer Parade
C3	George Row	D3	Spring Gardens
B3	Gold Street	A1	Spring Lane
A1	Grafton Street	C4	Swan Street
A3	Green Street	A4	Tanner Street
B3	Gregory Street	C2	The Drapery
B2	Greyfriars	A3	The Green
C3	Guildhall Road	C3	The Riding
D3	Hazelwood Road	B2	Tower Street
B1	Herbert Street	B2	Upper Bath Street
B3	Horsemarket	C1	Upper Mounts
B3	Horseshoe Street	B1	Upper Priory Street
B3	Kingerswell Street	C4	Victoria Gardens
B2	Lady's Lane	C4	Victoria Promenade
A2	Little Cross Street	C1	Victoria Street
A2	Lower Bath Street	D2	Wellington Street
		C1	William Street

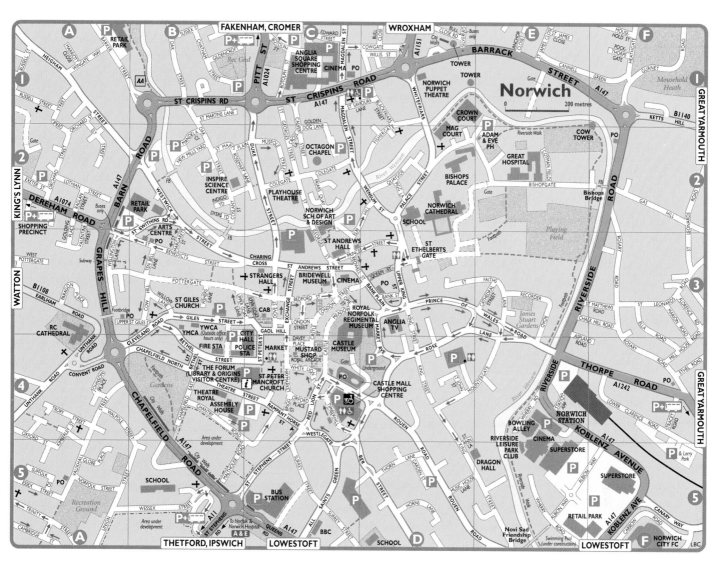

Norwich

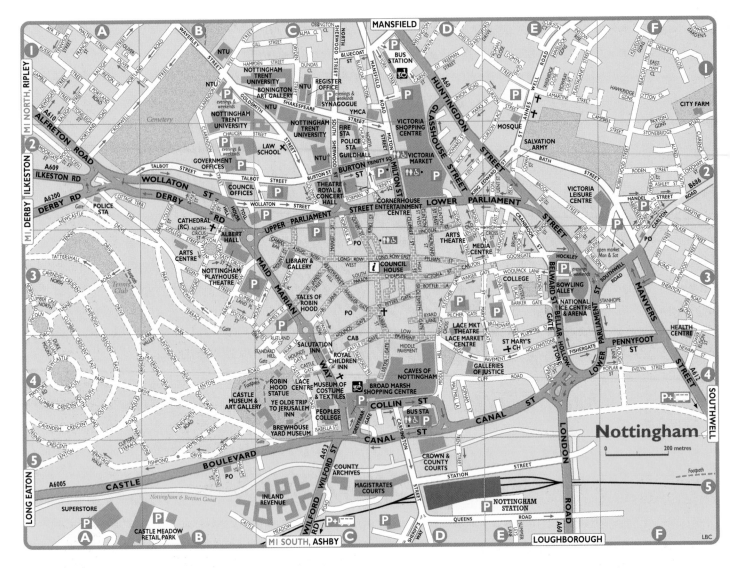

Nottingham

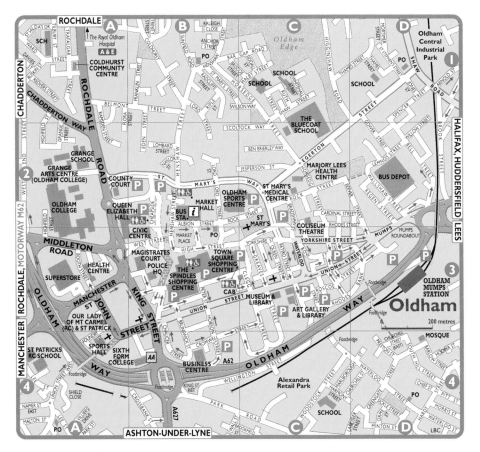

Oldham

B2	Albion Street	B3	Market Place
B1	Bar Gap Road	C4	Marlborough Street
D4	Barlow Street	A3	Middleton Road
D2	Beever Street	D4	Morris Street
D2	Bell Street	D3	Mumps
A1	Belmont Street	A3	Oldham Way
C2	Ben Brierley Way	B4	Park Road
A3	Booth Street	B3	Peter Street
C3	Bow Street	D4	Preston Street
C2	Bradshaw Street	C3	Queen Street
D2	Brook Street	B1	Radcliffe Street
B4	Brunswick Street	A1	Ramsden Street
C2	Cardinal Street	A1	Redvers Street
A1	Chadderton Way	D2	Regent Street
B4	Chaucer Street	C3	Retiro Street
B2	Cheapside	C3	Rhodes Bank
C4	Churchill Street	C2	Rhodes Street
C3	Clegg Street	B1	Rifle Street
B1	Coldhurst Street	A1	Rochdale Road
B4	Cromwell Street	B2	Rock Street
B4	Crossbank Street	C3	Roscoe Street
B2	Eden Street	A1	Ruskin Street
C2	Egerton Street	C1	Ruth Street
A4	Foundry Street	B1	St Mary's Street
B1	Franklin Street	B2	St Mary's Way
D2	Gower Street	D1	St Stephen's Street
A2	Grange Street	B2	Scoltock Way
C3	Greaves Street	D1	Shaw Road
D4	Greengate Street	C1	Shaw Street
D4	Hardy Street	D4	Sickle Street
C4	Harmony Street	D4	South Hill Street
B2	Henshaw Street	D1	Spencer Street
C1	Higginshaw Road	B1	Sunfield Road
B3	High Street	C1	Thames Street
A2	Highfield Street	A1	Tilbury Street
B3	Hobson Street	A1	Trafalgar Street
D4	Hooper Street	B3	Union Street
C1	Horsedge Street	A4	Union Street West
C2	Jesperson Street	B4	Wall Street
A3	John Street	D2	Wallshaw Street
D1	Jones Street	A1	Ward Street
B3	King Street	C3	Waterloo Street
A4	Lee Street	B4	Wellington Street
D2	Lemnos Street	A2	West End Street
B2	Lombard Street	B3	West Street
B1	Lord Street	D2	Willow Street
C1	Malby Street	C4	Woodstock Street
A3	Manchester Street	C3	Yorkshire Street

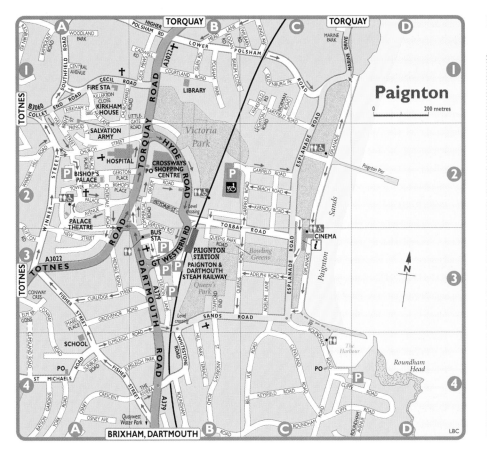

Paignton

C3	Adelphi Lane	C1	Leighton Road
C3	Adelphi Road	B1	Littlegate Road
B1	Barum Close	B1	Logan Road
A4	Batson Gardens	B1	Lower Polsham Road
A1	Baymount Road	A3	Mabel Place
C2	Beach Road	C1	Marine Drive
C4	Bell Vue Road	C1	Marine Park
A2	Bishop's Place	B1	Mead Lane
A1	Brent Street	A3	Midvale Road
B1	Cadwell Road	A1	Mill Lane
B1	Cecil Mews	A3	New Street
A1	Cecil Road	C1	Norman Road
A1	Central Avenue	C1	Oldenburg Park
A2	Church Street	A4	Osney Avenue
A1	Churchward Road	A4	Osney Crescent
C4	Cleveland Road	A2	Palace Avenue
C4	Cliffe Road	A2	Palace Place
A3	Clifton Road	B1	Polsham Park
A4	Climsland Road	A2	Princes Street
A1	Colley End Road	B3	Queens Park Road
B2	Commercial Road	B3	Queens Road
A3	Conway Crescent	A1	Redburn Road
A4	Conway Road	D4	Roundham Avenue
B1	Courtland Road	B4	Roundham Road
A2	Coverdale Road	B4	St Andrews Road
A3	Curledge Street	A4	St Michaels Road
B3	Dartmouth Road	B3	Sands Road
B2	Dendy Road	A1	Southfield Road
A3	Elm Bank Gardens	B3	Stafford End
B4	Elmsleigh Park	B3	Station Lane
A4	Elmsleigh Road	C1	Steartfield Road
C3	Esplanade	A4	Sunbury Road
C3	Esplanade Road	B4	The Riviera
A3	Fisher Street	B2	Torbay Road
C2	Garfield Road	B2	Torquay Road
A2	Gerston Place	A3	Totnes Road
B2	Gerston Road	A2	Tower Road
B1	Glen Road	B2	Victoria Street
B3	Great Western Road	C1	Warefield Road
A3	Grosvenor Road	A1	Well Street
B1	Higher Polsham Road	B4	Whitestone Road
B4	Hill Park Terrace	C1	Wilbarn Road
B2	Hyde Road	A2	Winner Hill Road
C2	Kernou Road	A2	Winner Street
C4	Keysfield Road	A1	Woodland Park
A1	Killerton Close	A4	York Road
C1	Kings Avenue		
A1	Kirkham Street		

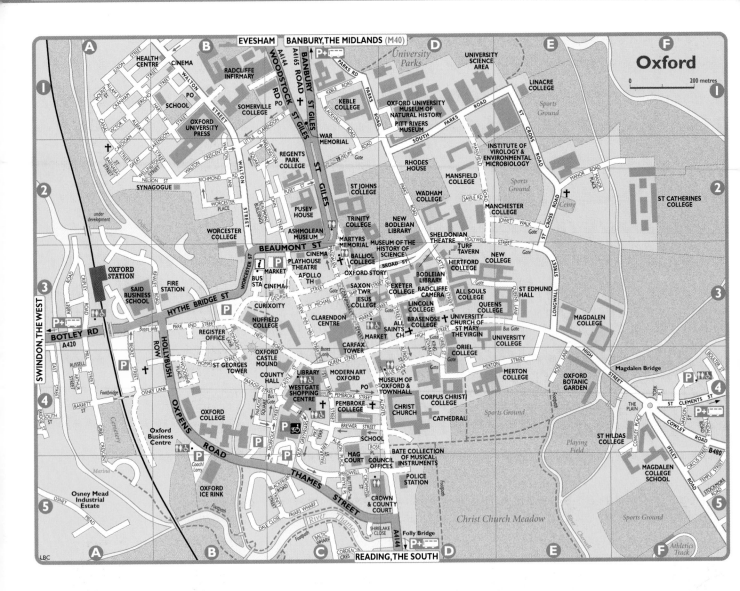

Oxford

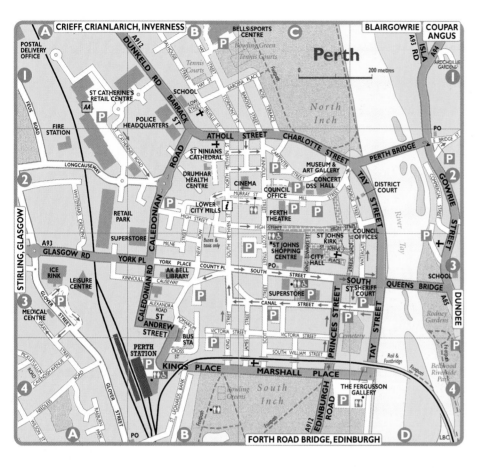

Perth

B3	Alexandra Road		A4	Raeburn Park
D1	Ardchoillie Gardens		C1	Rose Terrace
B2	Atholl Street		B3	St Andrew Street
B1	Balhousie Street		A2	St Catherines Road
B1	Barossa Place		D3	St John Street
C1	Barossa Street		C3	St Johns Place
B1	Barrack Street		B4	St Leonards Bank
B3	Caledonian Road		C3	Scott Street
C3	Canal Street		B3	South Methven Street
C2	Carpenter Street		C3	South Street
A4	Cavendish Avenue		C4	South William Street
C2	Charlotte Street		B1	Stormont Street
D2	Commercial Street		D2	Tay Street
B3	County Place		B3	Victoria Street
B4	Cross Street		D3	Watergate
B1	Dunkeld Road		A2	Whitefriars Crescent
D2	East Bridge Street		A4	Wilson Street
C4	Edinburgh Road		B3	York Place
A1	Feus Road			
D2	George Street			
A3	Glasgow Road			
A3	Glover Street			
D2	Gowrie Street			
A3	Gray Street			
B2	Hay Street			
B2	High Street			
D1	Isla Road			
C4	James Street			
C3	King Edward Street			
B4	King Street			
B4	Kings Place			
B3	Kinnoull Causeway			
C2	Kinnoull Street			
A2	Longcauseway			
B1	Low Street			
C4	Marshall Place			
B1	Melville Street			
C2	Mill Street			
B3	Milne Street			
C2	Murray Street			
A4	Needless Road			
B3	New Row			
B2	North Methven Street			
D2	Perth Bridge			
A4	Pickletullum Road			
B3	Pomarium Street			
C4	Princes Street			
D3	Queens Bridge			

Peterborough

C3	Bishops Road		D2	South Street
D1	Boongate		D2	Star Road
A1	Bourges Boulevard		A2	Station Road
B3	Bridge Street		B3	Trinity Street
A1	Bright Street		B3	Versen Platz
B1	Broadway		C2	Vineyard Road
B2	Cathedral Square		D2	Wake Road
B2	Church Street		D1	Wellington Street
C2	City Road		B3	Wentworth Street
A2	Cowgate		A1	Westgate
A1	Cromwell Road		B2	Wheel Yard
B2	Cross Street			
A1	Deacon Street			
D1	Dickens Street			
B4	East Station Road			
D2	Eastgate			
B2	Exchange Street			
D2	Fengate Close			
B1	Fitzwilliam Street			
D4	Frank Perkins Parkway			
B1	Geneva Street			
A4	George Street			
A1	Gladstone Street			
C2	Granby Street			
C3	Gravel Walk			
D2	Hereward Street			
A4	Jubilee Street			
A3	Lea Gardens			
B1	Lincoln Road			
B2	Long Causeway			
B1	Manor House Street			
A1	Mayors Walk			
B2	Midgate			
D1	Morris Street			
D2	Nene Street			
C1	New Road			
B1	North Street			
B1	Northminster Road			
B4	Oundle Road			
B1	Park Road			
D4	Potters Way			
B2	Priestgate			
B2	Queen Street			
A2	River Lane			
B3	Rivergate			
A1	Russell Street			
C2	St Johns Street			
B3	St Peters Road			

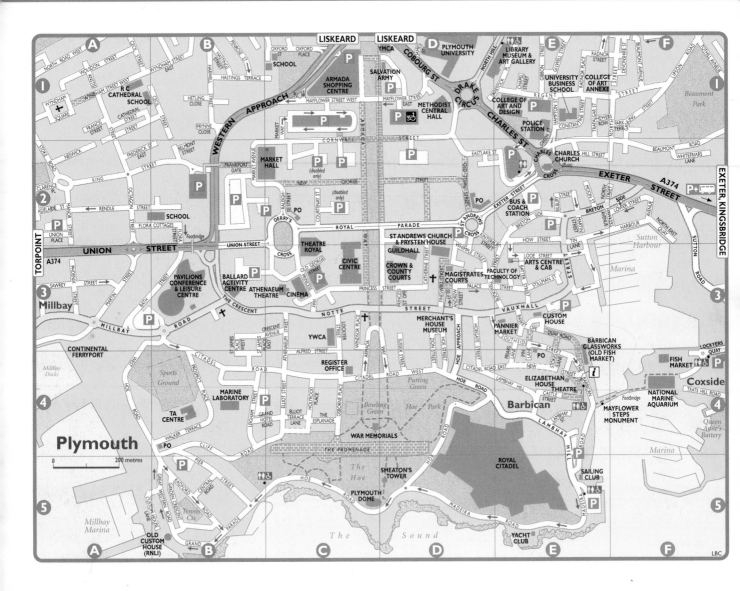

Plymouth

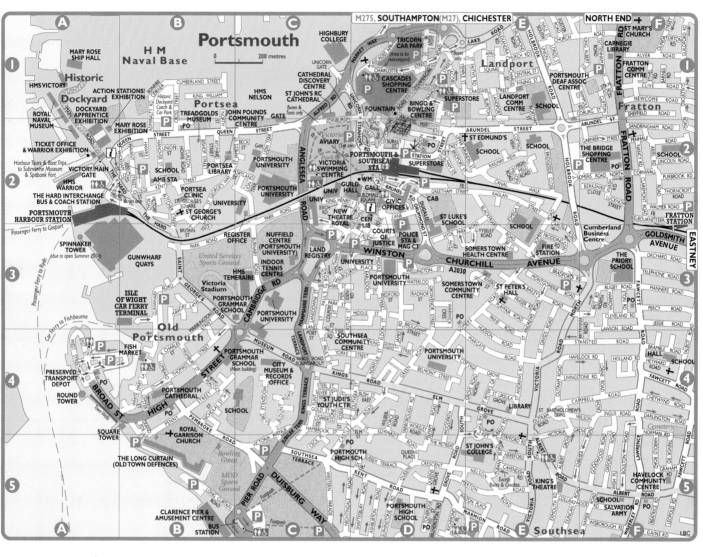

Portsmouth

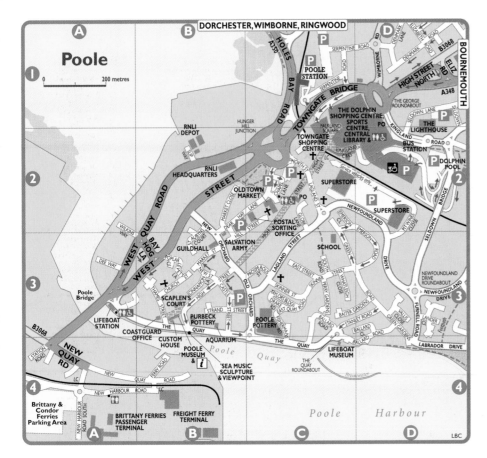

Poole

C3	Baiter Gardens	C3	Prosperous Street
D3	Ballard Close	B3	St Aubyns Court
C3	Ballard Road	D1	Seldown
B3	Bay Hog Lane	D2	Seldown Bridge
B3	Castle Street	D1	Seldown Lane
C2	Chapel Lane	C1	Serpentine Road
B3	Church Street	C3	Skinner Street
B3	Cinnamon Lane	B2	Slip Way
B2	Dear Hay Lane	C3	South Road
A3	Dee Way	C3	Stanley Road
D1	Denmark Lane	A4	Station Road
D1	Denmark Road	B3	Strand Street
C3	Drake Road	C3	Taylors Buildings
C3	East Quay Road	B3	Thames Street
C3	East Street	B3	The Quay
D1	Elizabeth Road	C1	Towngate Bridge
C2	Emerson Close	D3	Vallis Close
D3	Emerson Road	B3	West Street
C2	Falkland Square	A3	West Quay Road
B4	Ferry Road	C3	Whatleigh Close
C3	Fishermans Road	A2	Wilkins Way
D3	Furnell Road	D1	Wimborne Road
C2	Globe Lane		
D3	Green Gardens		
C3	Green Road		
B3	High Street		
D1	High Street North		
B3	Hill Street		
C1	Holes Bay Road		
C2	Kingland Crescent		
D2	Kingland Road		
D4	Labrador Drive		
C2	Lagland Street		
D3	Lander Close		
B3	Levet's Lane		
B2	Market Close		
B3	Market Street		
A4	New Harbour Road		
A4	New Harbour Road South		
B2	New Orchard		
A4	New Quay Road		
B3	New Street		
D2	Newfoundland Drive		
C2	North Street		
C3	Old Orchard		
C3	Perry Gardens		
D2	Pitwines Close		
B3	Poplar Close		

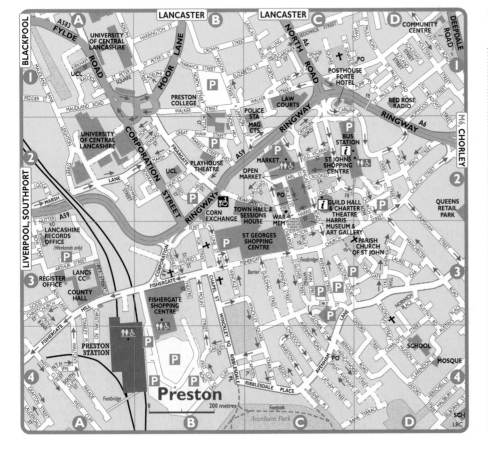

Preston

A1	Adelphi Street	A2	Ladywell Street
A3	Arthur Street	C2	Lancaster Road
C4	Avenham Lane	C1	Lancaster Road North
C4	Avenham Road	D3	Laurel Street
C3	Avenham Street	B1	Lawson Street
C4	Bairstow Street	A2	Leighton Street
C4	Berwick Road	C2	Lord Street
C2	Birley Street	C1	Lund Street
A3	Bow Lane	B3	Lune Street
B2	Bowran Street	D3	Manchester Road
C3	Cannon Street	B2	Market Street West
C1	Carlisle Street	A2	Marsh Lane
C4	Chaddock Street	A1	Maudland Bank
B3	Chapel Street	A1	Maudland Road
D4	Charlotte Street	C1	Melling Street
C3	Cheapside	B1	Moor Lane
D2	Church Row	B3	Mount Street
C3	Church Street	C1	North Road
D4	Clarendon Street	B1	North Street
C3	Corporation Street	D3	Oak Street
B2	Crooked Lane	C2	Old Vicarage Street
C2	Crooked Lane	C2	Orchard Street
B1	Crown Street	C2	Ormskirk Road
D2	Derby Street	D4	Oxford Street
C2	Earl Street	D2	Percy Street
B4	East Cliff	A3	Pitt Street
B4	East Cliff Road	D2	Pole Street
D1	Egan Street	D1	Pump Street
B1	Elizabeth Street	C4	Ribblesdale Place
B3	Fishergate	B2	Ringway
A4	Fishergate Hill	D4	St Austin's Place
B3	Fleet Street	D3	St Austin's Road
B3	Fox Street	C1	St Ignatius Square
C4	Frenchwood Street	D1	St Pauls Road
B2	Friargate	D1	St Pauls Square
A1	Fylde Road	A1	St Peter's Square
C3	Glover Street	B1	St Peter's Street
C4	Great Avenham Street	B2	Seed Street
B2	Great Shaw Street	D3	Shepherd Street
D3	Grimshaw Street	D1	South Meadow Street
C3	Guildhall Street	C4	Starkie Street
B1	Harrington Street	C3	Syke Street
C2	Harris Street	B1	Walker Street
B2	Heatley Street	A4	Walton's Parade
B2	Hill Street	B1	Warwick Street
D1	Holsteins Street	A4	West Cliff
D1	Hopwood Street	B3	Winckley Square
C3	Jacson Street	B3	Winckley Street
D3	Knowsley Street		

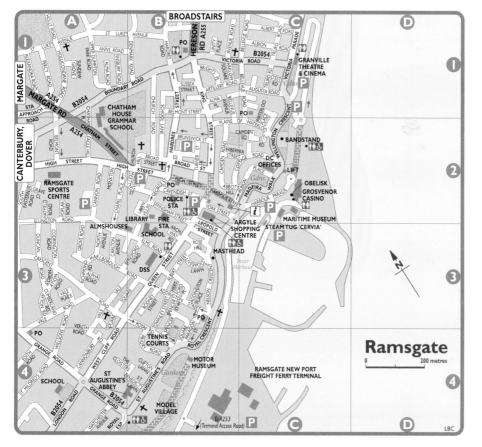

Ramsgate

B2	Abbots Hill	B2	Harbour Street
B3	Addington Street	B1	Hardres Road
C1	Albert Road	B2	Hardres Street
B3	Albert Street	B1	Hereson Road
C2	Albion Place	B2	Hibernia Street
C1	Albion Road	A2	High Street
A1	Alma Road	A1	Hollicondane Road
A1	Anns Road	B1	King Street
B1	Arklow Square	B2	Lawn Villas
B1	Artillery Road	B3	Leopold Street
C1	Augusta Road	B3	Liverpool Lawn
B1	Avenue Road	A4	London Road
A3	Ayton Road	C2	Madeira Walk
A2	Belgrave Close	A1	Margate Road
B1	Bellevue Avenue	A3	Marlborough Road
C1	Bellevue Road	B2	Meeting Street
A2	Belmont Road	A2	Monkton
B1	Belmont Street	B3	Nelson Crescent
B3	Beresford Road	A3	North Avenue
A1	Boundary Road	B4	Paragon Street
B1	Brights Place	A1	Percy Road
B2	Broad Street	B2	Plains of Waterloo
B2	Brunswick Street	B4	Priory Road
B2	Camden Road	B3	Queen Street
A2	Cannon Road	A3	Richmond Road
A4	Cannonbury Road	B3	Rose Hill
A3	Carlton Avenue	B4	Royal Crescent
B2	Cavendish Street	A4	Royal Esplanade
A2	Chapel Place	B3	Royal Road
A1	Chatham Place	B4	St Augustine's Road
A2	Chatham Street	B4	St Benedict's Lawn
B1	Church Road	A1	St Luke's Avenue
A3	Codrington Road	B1	School Lane
A3	Coronation Road	B3	Spencer Square
C2	Cottage Road	A1	Station Approach Road
A3	Crescent Road	B1	Sussex Street
B1	Denmark Road	B3	Townley Street
A3	Duncan Road	C1	Truro Road
A2	Eagle Hill	B2	Turner Street
B2	Effingham Street	A1	Upper Dumpton Park Road
C2	Elizabeth Road	A3	Vale Road
A2	Ellington Road	A3	Vale Square
B3	Elms Road	C1	Victoria Parade
A1	Finsbury Road	B1	Victoria Road
B2	George Street	C2	Wellington Crescent
A4	Grange Road	A4	West Cliff Road
A3	Grove Road	A4	Willsons Road
C2	Harbour Parade	B2	York Street

Reading

A1	Abattoirs Road	C3	Kennet Side
C2	Abbey Square	D3	Kennet Street
C2	Abbey Street	C1	Kings Meadow Road
C2	Abbots Walk	D3	Kings Road
A1	Addison Road	C4	London Road
A3	Anstey Road	C3	London Street
A1	Barry Place	A1	Meadow Road
D3	Betam Road	B3	Minster Street
B2	Blagrave Street	C4	Mount Pleasant
B3	Bridge Street	C1	Napier Road
B3	Broad Street	A1	Northfield Road
A4	Brook Street West	D3	Orts Road
A1	Cardiff Road	A3	Oxford Road
A3	Carey Street	B4	Pell Street
A4	Castle Hill	B2	Queen Victoria Street
A3	Castle Street	C3	Queens Road
B3	Chain Street	D4	Redlands Road
A2	Cheapside	B3	Rose Walk
A4	Coley Hill	A1	Ross Road
A4	Coley Place	A2	Sackville Street
D4	Craven Road	C4	St Giles Close
B2	Cross Street	D3	St Johns Road
B4	Crossland Road	B3	St Mary's Butts
C4	Crown Road	B4	Sherman Road
B4	Deansgate Road	C3	Sidmouth Street
C3	Duke Street	C4	Silver Street
C3	East Street	B3	Simmonds Street
A2	Eaton Place	C3	South Street
D3	Eldon Road	B4	Southampton Street
D3	Eldon Terrace	A2	Stanshawe Road
A4	Field Road	B2	Station Hill
B4	Fobney Street	B2	Station Road
B2	Forbury Road	B3	Swan Place
B2	Friar Street	A1	Swansea Road
A4	Garnet Hill	D3	The Grove
A4	Garnet Street	A2	Tudor Road
B2	Garrard Street	B2	Union Street
D2	Gas Works Road	B4	Upper Brook Street
C1	George Street	A2	Vachel Road
A2	Great Knollys Street	B2	Valpy Street
A2	Greyfriars Road	B1	Vastern Road
B3	Gun Street	D3	Watlington Street
B4	Henry Street	A3	Waylen Street
A3	Howard Street	A2	Weldale Street
A3	Jesse Terrace	A2	West Street
B4	Katesgrove Lane	A4	Wolseley Street
D2	Kenavon Drive	A1	York Road
C4	Kendrick Road	A3	Zinzan Street

St Andrews

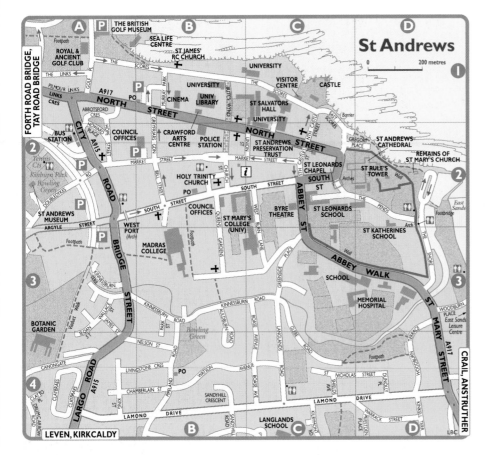

Scarborough

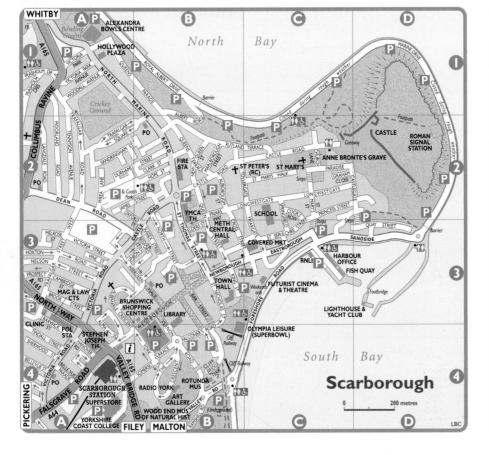

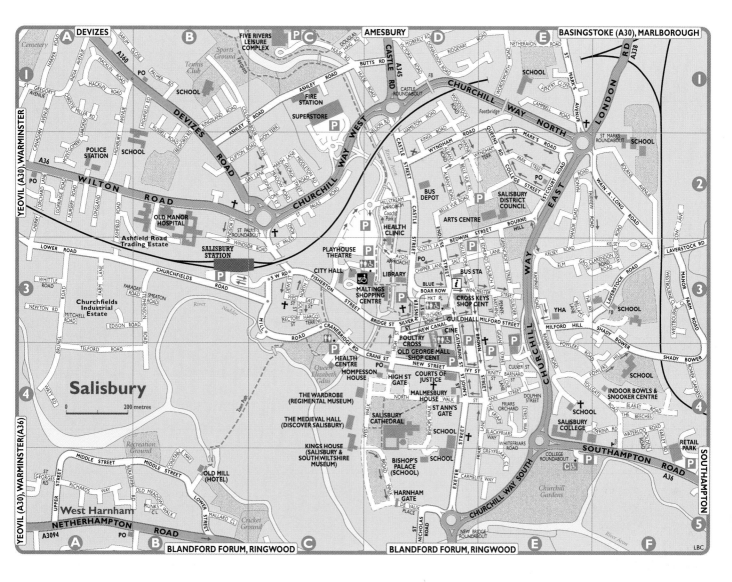

Salisbury

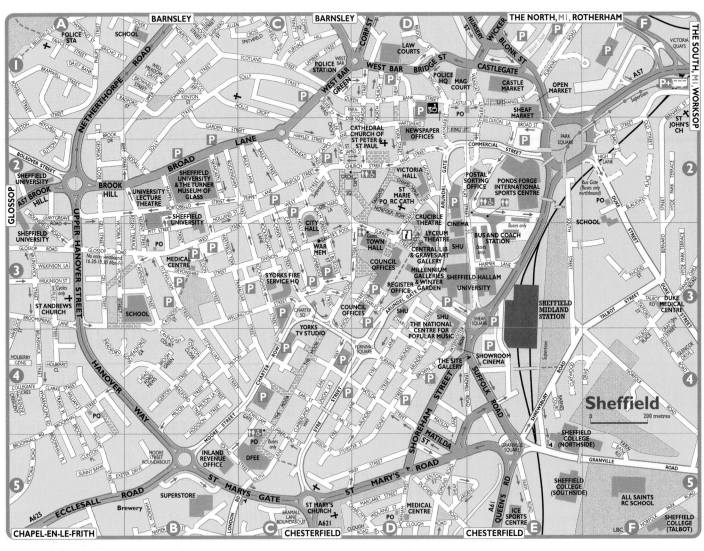

Sheffield

Shrewsbury

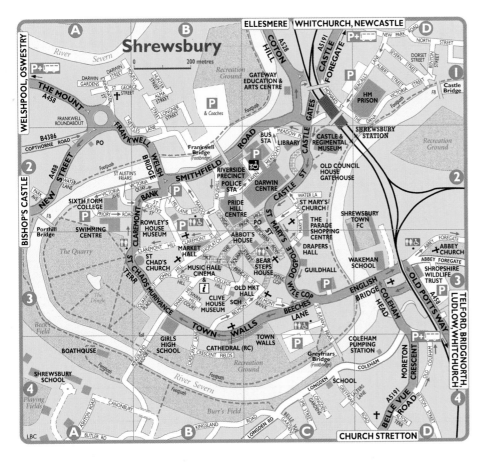

Southend-on-Sea

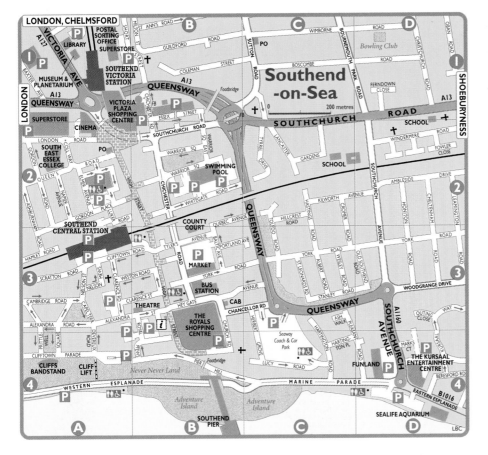

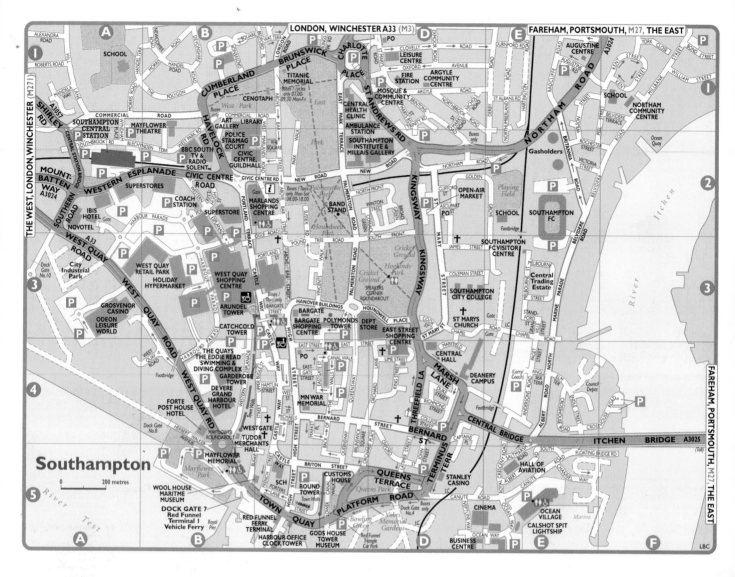

Southampton

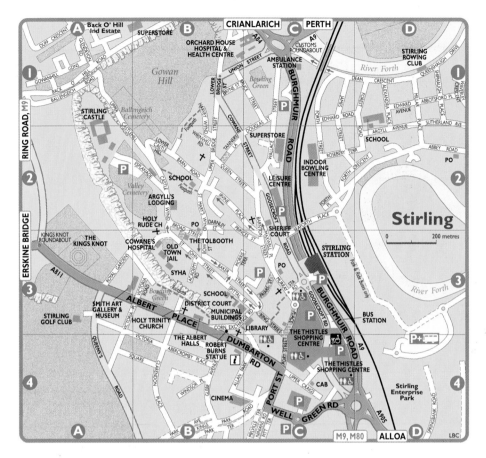

Stirling

D2	Abbey Road	D1	Millar Place
D1	Abbotsford Place	B3	Morris Terrace
B4	Abercromby Place	C3	Murray Place
B3	Academy Road	C4	Ninians Road
B3	Albert Place	B4	Park Avenue
D1	Alexandra Place	B4	Park Terrace
B4	Allan Park	C4	Pitt Terrace
D2	Argyll Avenue	C4	Port Street
A1	Back O' Hill Road	B3	Princes Street
B3	Baker Street	B2	Queen Street
A1	Ballengeich Road	D1	Queenshaugh Drive
B2	Barn Road	A4	Queen's Road
C2	Barnton Street	C2	Rosebery Terrace
B1	Bayne Street	A3	Royal Gardens
B3	Bow Street	B3	St John Street
B2	Broad Street	B2	St Mary's Wynd
C1	Bruce Street	C2	Seaforth Place
C1	Burghmuir Road	D1	Shiphaugh Place
B2	Castle Wynd	B3	Spittal Street
B4	Clarendon Place	D4	Springbank Road
B3	Corn Exchange Road	C3	Station Road
B1	Cowane Street	D1	Sutherland Avenue
B2	Darnley Street	B2	Tannery Lane
D1	Dean Crescent	B1	Union Street
C2	Douglas Street	B2	Upper Bridge Street
A1	Duff Crescent	A1	Upper Castlehill
C4	Dumbarton Road	C4	Upper Craigs
D1	Edward Avenue	A3	Victoria Place
C1	Edward Road	B3	Victoria Road
B2	Esplanade	B4	Victoria Square
D1	Forest Road	C2	Wallace Street
C2	Forth Crescent	D1	Waverley Crescent
C2	Forth Place	C4	Well Green Road
C1	Forth Street	B2	Whinwell Road
C3	Friars Street	B4	Windsor Place
B4	Glebe Avenue		
A1	Glendevon Road		
C2	Goosecroft Road		
A1	Gowanhill Gardens		
B1	Harvey Wynd		
B2	Irvine Place		
C1	James Street		
C3	King Street		
B4	Kings Park Road		
B1	Lower Bridge Street		
B2	Lower Castle Hill		
C3	Maxwell Place		
C4	Melville Terrace		

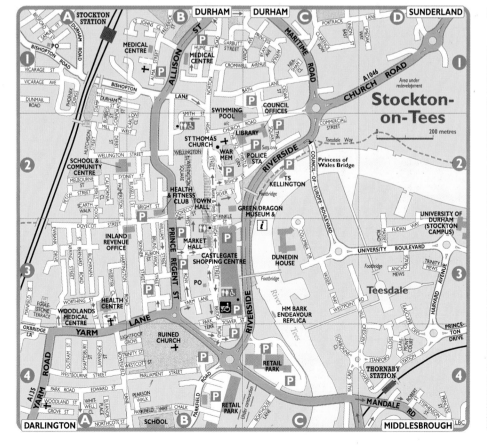

Stockton-on-Tees

B1	Allison Street	A2	Palmerston Street
B1	Alma Street	A4	Park Road
C1	Bath Lane	B3	Park Terrace
A1	Bedford Street	B4	Parkfield Road
B2	Bishop Street	B4	Parkfield Way
A1	Bishopton Lane	B4	Parliament Street
A1	Bishopton Road	A2	Petch Street
C4	Boathouse Lane	A1	Phoenix Sidings
A4	Bowesfield Lane	C1	Portrack Lane
B3	Bridge Road	B3	Prince Regent Street
B2	Bright Street	C1	Princess Avenue
B3	Brunswick Street	D4	Princeton Drive
A3	Buchanan Street	D3	Radcliffe Crescent
B4	Chalk Close	C3	Riverside
D4	Chapel Street	B2	Russell Street
B2	Church Road	C1	Ryan Avenue
D4	Claremont Court	A3	St Bernard Road
C1	Clarence Row	B1	St Johns Close
C3	Columbia Drive	A4	Shaftesbury Street
C2	Commercial Street	B2	Silver Street
A2	Corporation Street	B3	Skinner Street
C2	Council of Europe Boulevard	B2	Smith Street
B1	Cromwell Avenue	A1	Stamp Street
A2	Derby Street	D4	Stanford Close
A2	Dixon Street	D4	Station Street
A3	Dovecot Street	A2	Sydney Street
A1	Durham Road	A3	Tarring Street
A1	Durham Street	B2	The Square
A4	Edward Street	C2	Thistle Green
A3	Ewbank Drive	B3	Tower Street
B3	Finkle Street	C1	Union Street East
B1	Frederick Street	D3	University Boulevard
D3	Fudan Way	C3	Vasser Way
B1	Garbutt Street	A1	Vicarage Avenue
A3	Hartington Road	A1	Vicarage Street
D3	Harvard Avenue	C1	Wade Avenue
B2	High Street	A3	Webster Close
B1	Hume Street	B2	Wellington Square
A2	Hutchison Street	A2	Wellington Street
A4	Lawrence Street	B3	West Row
D4	Mandale Road	A4	Westbourne Street
C1	Maritime Road	C3	Westpoint Road
D3	Massey Road	B3	William Street
A2	Melbourne Street	A4	Woodland Street
A2	Mill Street West	A3	Worthing Street
B1	Norton Road	D3	Yale Crescent
A4	Outram Street	A4	Yarm Lane
A4	Oxbridge Lane	A4	Yarm Road

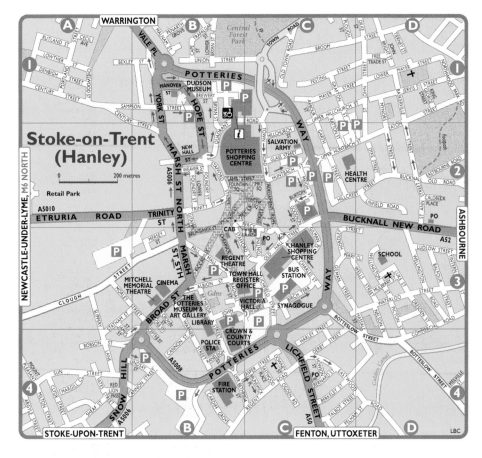

Stoke-on-Trent (Hanley)

B3	Albion Street	B2	Lower Foundry Street
B3	Bagnall Street	D1	Lower Mayer Street
D3	Balfour Street	C2	Market Lane
D1	Baskerville Street	C2	Market Square
C4	Berkeley Street	B2	Marsh Street North
B3	Bethesda Street	B3	Marsh Street South
C3	Birch Terrace	C1	Mayer Street
C3	Botteslow Street	C2	Meigh Street
B1	Brewery Street	A3	Morley Street
B3	Broad Street	D1	Mynors Street
C1	Broom Street	B2	New Hall Street
B3	Brunswick Street	C3	Old Hall Street
B1	Bryan Street	C1	Old Town Road
D2	Bucknall New Road	B3	Pall Mall
D2	Bucknall Old Road	C2	Parliament Row
C2	Burton Place	C2	Percy Street
B4	Cannon Street	B3	Piccadilly
A1	Century Street	D3	Picton Street
C3	Charles Street	A1	Portland Street
B3	Cheapside	B1	Potteries Way
A3	Clough Street	B2	Quadrant Road
A4	Clyde Street	B4	Raneleigh Street
D4	Commercial Road	C4	Regent Road
C4	Derby Street	A4	Robson Street
D3	Dresden Street	D2	St Ann Street
C4	Eastwood Road	D1	St John Street
D2	Eaton Street	A1	Sampson Street
A2	Etruria Road	A3	Slippery Lane
C1	Festing Street	A4	Snow Hill
B2	Foundry Street	B3	Stafford Street
B2	Fountain Square	A3	Statham Street
C2	Garth Street	A4	Sun Street
C3	Gilman Street	C4	Talbot Street
B2	Gitana Street	C2	Tontine Square
C2	Glass Street	C3	Tontine Street
C2	Goodson Street	C2	Town Road
C1	Grafton Street	B2	Trinity Street
B1	Hanover Street	B1	Union Street
C2	Hillchurch Street	C1	Upper Hillchurch Street
C2	Hillcrest Street	C2	Upper Huntbach Street
B1	Hope Street	B1	Vale Place
C2	Huntbach Street	B3	Warner Street
D1	Jervis Street	D3	Waterloo Street
D1	John Bright Street	B2	Weaver Street
B3	John Street	D3	Wellington Road
B2	Lamb Street	D3	Wells Street
C3	Lichfield Street	A4	Yates Street
B4	Lower Bethesda Street	B1	York Street

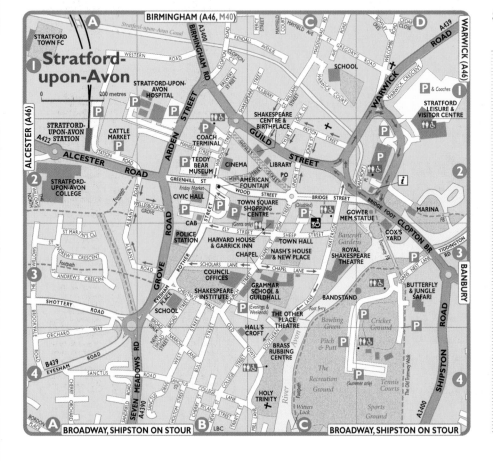

Stratford-upon-Avon

A3	Albany Road	B4	New Street
A2	Alcester Road	B3	Old Town
B2	Arden Street	A4	Orchard Way
C1	Avenue Road	C2	Payton Street
D2	Bancroft Place	C1	Percy Street
B1	Birmingham Road	B3	Rother Street
A4	Bordon Place	D1	Rowley Crescent
B1	Brewery Street	B4	Ryland Street
D2	Bridge Foot	A3	St Andrew's Crescent
C2	Bridge Street	C1	St Gregory's Road
B3	Broad Street	A3	St Martin's Close
B3	Broad Walk	B4	Sanctus Drive
A3	Brookvale Road	A4	Sanctus Road
B4	Bull Street	B4	Sanctus Street
D1	Cedar Close	A4	Sandfield Road
C3	Chapel Lane	B3	Scholars Lane
C3	Chapel Street	A4	Seven Meadows Road
A4	Cherry Orchard	B1	Shakespeare Street
B4	Cherry Street	C3	Sheep Street
B3	Chestnut Walk	D4	Shipston Road
B3	Church Street	A3	Shottery Road
D3	Clopton Bridge	C4	Southern Lane
B1	Clopton Court	A2	Station Road
B1	Clopton Road	D3	Swans Nest Lane
B4	College Lane	A3	The Willows
C4	College Street	A2	The Willows North
B3	Ely Street	D3	Tiddington Road
B3	Evesham Place	B4	Trinity Street
A4	Evesham Road	C2	Tyler Street
C1	Great Williams Street	C2	Union Street
B2	Greenhill Street	C1	Warwick Court
B3	Grove Road	D1	Warwick Crescent
C2	Guild Street	D1	Warwick Road
B2	Henley Street	C3	Waterside
C2	High Street	D1	Welcombe Road
B4	Holtom Street	B2	Wellesbourne Grove
C2	John Street	B4	West Street
B1	Kendall Avenue	A1	Western Road
C1	Lock Close	B2	Windsor Street
C1	Maidenhead Road	B2	Wood Street
B2	Mansell Street		
C1	Mayfield Avenue		
C1	Mayfield Court		
B2	Meer Street		
C4	Mill Lane		
C1	Mulberry Street		
B4	Narrow Lane		
B4	New Broad Street		

Sunderland

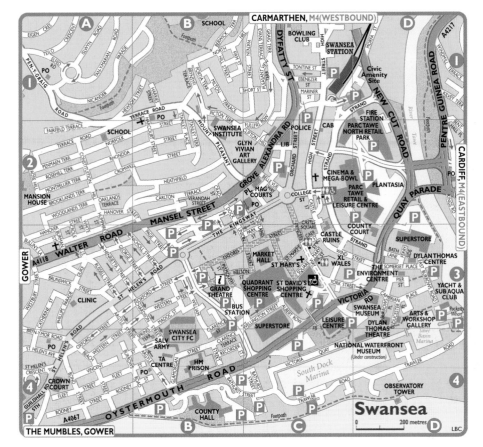

Swansea

C3	Albert Row	B3	Nelson Street
C2	Alexandra Road	D1	New Cut Road
A3	Argyle Street	A1	Nicander Parade
D3	Bath Lane	B3	Nicholl Street
B4	Bathurst Street	A2	Norfolk Street
A4	Beach Street	B1	North Hill
C2	Belle Vue Way	C2	Orchard Street
A4	Bond Street	A4	Oxford Street
A2	Brooklands Terrace	A4	Oystermouth Road
A3	Brunswick Street	B3	Page Street
B1	Brynsyfi Terrace	A1	Pen y Graig Road
A4	Burrows Road	A2	Penmaen Terrace
C3	Caer Street	D2	Pentre Guinea Road
D3	Cambrian Place	A3	Phillips Parade
B2	Carlton Terrace	B1	Picton Terrace
C3	Castle Square	D3	Pier Street
C2	Castle Street	B3	Plymouth Street
A3	Catherine Street	C2	Portland Street
C2	Clifton Hill	B1	Portia Terrace
C2	College Street	C3	Princess Way
A2	Constitution Hill	D2	Quay Parade
A2	Cromwell Street	A2	Rhondda Street
B2	Dock Union Street	B3	Richardson Street
A3	Duke Street	A4	Rodney Street
C1	Dyfatty Street	A2	Rosehill Terrace
D3	East Burrows Road	A3	Russell Street
A2	Fairfield Terrace	A3	St Helen's Road
B1	Firm Street	C3	St Mary Street
A4	Fleet Street	C3	St Mary's Square
C2	Fullers Row	D3	Somerset Place
A3	George Street	B2	Stanley Place
B4	Glamorgan Street	C2	Strand
D3	Gloucester Place	A1	Tan-y-Marian Road
C1	Graig Terrace	A2	Terrace Road
C2	Grove Place	B3	The Kingsway
A3	Hanover Street	C1	Tontine Street
B2	Harcourt Street	C4	Trawler Road
B2	Heathfield	C4	Victoria Quay
A3	Henrietta Street	C3	Victoria Road
A1	Hewson Street	A4	Vincent Street
C1	High Street	A3	Walter Road
B1	Hill Street	C1	Watkin Street
A1	Islwyn Road	C3	Wellington Street
B3	Madoc Street	A4	Western Street
B2	Mansel Street	B3	William Street
B1	Milton Terrace	C3	Wind Street
A2	Montpellier Terrace	A2	Woodlands Terrace
B2	Mount Pleasant	C3	York Street

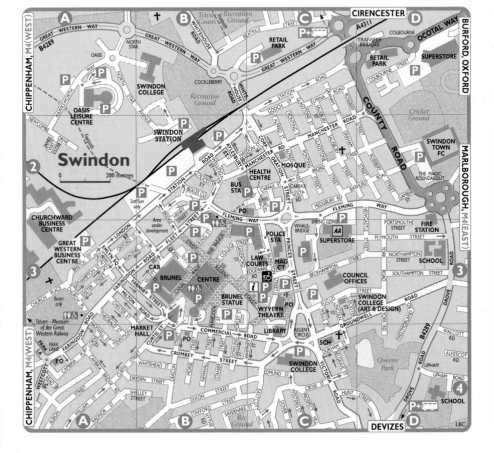

Swindon

C2	Alfred Street	B3	Havelock Street
B2	Aylesbury Street	A1	Hawksworth Way
A3	Bathampton Street	C2	Haydon Street
C2	Bathurst Road	B2	Henry Street
B2	Beales Close	C4	Hunt Street
C1	Beatrice Street	C3	Islington Street
C3	Beckhampton Street	A2	James Watt Close
C4	Belgrave Street	B3	King Street
B2	Bridge Street	C3	Leicester Street
A3	Bristol Street	C3	Lincoln Street
C2	Broad Street	A3	London Street
A4	Cambria Bridge Road	C2	Manchester Road
A4	Cambria Place	A4	Maxwell Street
B3	Canal Walk	A3	Milton Road
C2	Carfax Street	B3	Morley Street
A3	Chester Street	B4	Morse Street
A3	Church Place	D3	Newcastle Street
D1	Colbourne Street	A2	Newcombe Drive
B3	College Street	B4	Newhall Street
B4	Commercial Road	A1	North Star Avenue
C2	Corporation Street	D1	Ocotal Way
D1	County Road	A3	Oxford Street
B4	Crombey Street	A4	Park Lane
C4	Cross Street	D3	Plymouth Street
A4	Curtis Street	C2	Ponting Street
B4	Deacon Street	C3	Princes Street
B4	Dixon Street	B3	Queen Street
B4	Dowling Street	A3	Reading Street
D4	Drove Road	B3	Regent Street
B4	Dryden Street	C1	Rosebery Street
C4	Durham Street	C1	Salisbury Street
C4	Eastcott Hill	B3	Sandford Street
C3	Edgeware Road	D3	Southampton Street
C4	Edmund Street	B4	Stafford Street
C1	Elmina Road	B4	Stanier Street
A3	Emlyn Square	B2	Station Road
C3	Euclid Street	A4	Tennyson Street
A3	Exeter Street	B3	The Parade
A4	Faringdon Road	A3	Theobald Street
A3	Farnsby Street	C4	Victoria Road
B3	Fleet Street	B3	Villett Street
B2	Fleming Way	B2	Wellington Street
C1	Gladstone Street	C3	Wells Street
B2	Gloucester Street	A4	Westcott Place
C1	Gooch Street	B4	Whitehead Street
C1	Graham Street	B1	Whitehouse Road
A1	Great Western Way	C4	Whitney Street
C3	Groundwell Road	D3	York Road

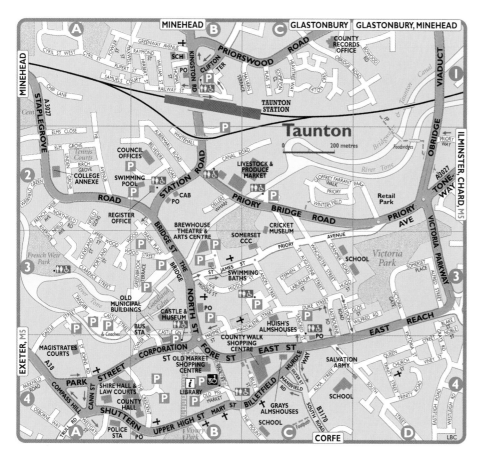

Taunton

B2	Albermarle Road		A1	Maxwell Street
D3	Alfred Street		B3	Middle Street
C4	Alma Street		B3	North Street
B2	Belvedere Road		A2	Northfield Road
C4	Billetfield		C1	Obridge Road
A2	Birch Grove		D2	Obridge Viaduct
B3	Bridge Street		B4	Old Pig Market
B2	Canal Road		A4	Park Street
A4	Cann Street		B4	Paul Street
C3	Canon Street		A3	Portland Street
B3	Castle Green		B1	Priorswood Road
A3	Castle Street		C3	Priory Avenue
D4	Church Street		C2	Priory Bridge Road
A3	Clarence Street		C2	Priory Park
A3	Cleveland Street		D4	Queen Street
B1	Clifton Terrace		B1	Railway Street
A4	Compass Hill		B1	Raymond Street
B4	Corporation Street		A1	Rupert Street
C3	Cranmer Road		C3	St Augustine Street
A1	Cyril Street		B3	St James Street
A1	Cyril Street West		A4	St Johns Road
B2	Dellers Wharf		A4	Shuttern
C3	Duke Street		C4	Silver Street
D3	East Reach		C4	South Road
C4	East Street		D4	South Street
C3	Eastbourne Road		A1	Staplegrove Road
D4	Eastleigh Road		B2	Station Road
C1	Eaton Crescent		C3	Stephen Street
A2	Elm Grove		C3	Tancred Street
B4	Fore Street		A2	The Avenue
A1	Fowler Street		B3	The Bridge
A2	French Weir Avenue		B4	The Crescent
D4	Grays Road		B1	Thomas Street
B3	Greenbrook Terrace		D2	Toneway
B1	Greenway Avenue		B4	Tower Street
B3	Hammet Street		D4	Trinity Road
C3	Haydon Road		D4	Trinity Street
C1	Heavitree Way		B4	Upper High Street
B1	Herbert Street		A3	Upper Wood Street
C4	Hurdle Way		D3	Victoria Gate
B1	Kingston Road		D2	Victoria Parkway
C3	Laburnum Street		D4	Victoria Street
A2	Linden Grove		D4	Viney Street
B3	Lower Middle Street		B1	William Street
C3	Magdalene Street		C3	Winchester Street
C1	Malvern Terrace		C2	Winters Field
C4	Mansfield Road		B3	Wood Street
B4	Mary Street		B3	Yarde Place

Torquay

B2	Abbey Road		D3	Meadfoot Road
D1	Alexandra Road		C2	Melville Street
D2	Alpine Road		D1	Middle Warberry Road
C1	Ash Hill Road		A1	Mill Lane
A1	Avenue Road		D3	Montpelier Terrace
A2	Bampfylde Road		B1	Morgan Avenue
A2	Bath Lane		C3	Palk Street
D4	Beacon Hill		D4	Park Hill Road
A1	Belgrave Road		D1	Pennsylvania Road
D3	Braddons Hill Road		C2	Pimlico
D3	Braddons Hill Road East		C1	Potters Hill
D3	Braddons Hill Road West		C1	Princes Road
D2	Braddons Street		D1	Princes Road West
A1	Bridge Road		C2	Queen Street
D1	Camden Road		A3	Rathmore Road
C3	Cary Parade		C3	Rock Road
C2	Cary Road		D1	Rosehill Road
B1	Castle Circus		B1	St Efride's Road
C1	Castle Lane		B2	St Lukes Road
C1	Castle Road		C2	St Lukes Road North
D1	Cavern Road		C2	St Lukes Road South
C1	Chatsworth Road		C1	St Marychurch Road
A2	Chestnut Avenue		B2	Scarborough Road
A1	Church Lane		A4	Seaway Lane
A1	Church Street		B2	Sheddon Hill
A1	Cleveland Road		A1	South Street
D2	Clifton Terrace		C2	Stentiford Hill Road
B2	Croft Hill		D3	Strand
B2	Croft Road		C2	Temperance Street
A1	East Street		A3	The Kings Drive
C1	Ellacombe Road		D3	The Terrace
A3	Falkland Road		B1	Thurlow Road
C3	Fleet Street		A1	Tor Church Road
D2	Grafton Road		B1	Tor Hill Road
A4	Hennapyn Road		A4	Torbay Road
B1	Higher Union Lane		D3	Torwood Street
D2	Hillesdon Road		B1	Trematon Avenue
D1	Hoxton Road		B1	Union Street
A1	Laburnum Street		D3	Upper Braddons Hill Road
D1	Lower Ellacombe Church Road		A1	Vansittart Road
			D3	Vaughan Parade
D2	Lower Warberry Road		D4	Victoria Parade
A1	Lucius Street		C1	Victoria Road
B1	Lymington Road		A2	Walnut Road
C2	Madrepore Road		C1	Warberry Road West
B1	Magdalene Road		C2	Warren Hill
C1	Market Street		C2	Warren Road
D4	Meadfoot Lane		C1	Wellington Road

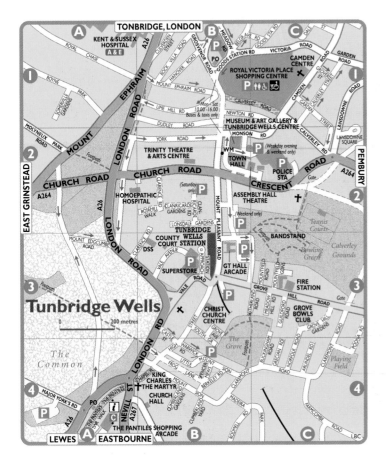

Tunbridge Wells

C4	Arundel Road
B1	Belgrave Road
B4	Berkeley Road
A1	Boyne Park
C4	Buckingham Road
B1	Calverley Road
C1	Calverley Street
C1	Camden Road
B3	Castle Street
B4	Chapel Place
A2	Church Road
B2	Clanricarde Gardens
B2	Clanricarde Road
B4	Claremont Road
B2	Clarence Road
C2	Crescent Road
B1	Culverden Street
B4	Cumberland Gardens
B4	Cumberland Yard
C1	Dale Street
B1	Dudley Road
C4	Farmcombe Road
B4	Frog Lane
C1	Garden Road
C1	Garden Street
B1	Goods Station Road
C4	Grecian Road
B1	Grosvenor Road
B3	Grove Avenue
C3	Grove Hill Gardens
C3	Grove Hill Road
C1	Grover Street
C3	Guildford Road
B1	Hanover Road
B4	High Street
C1	Lansdowne Road
C2	Lansdowne Square
B1	Lime Hill Road
B4	Little Mount Sion
A2	London Road
B2	Lonsdale Gardens
B4	Madeira Park
A4	Major York's Road
C3	Meadow Hill Road
B1	Meadow Road
A2	Molyneux Park Road
B2	Monson Road
A3	Mount Edgcumbe Road

A2	Mount Ephraim
B1	Mount Ephraim Road
B2	Mount Pleasant Road
B4	Mount Sion
C3	Mountfield Gardens
C3	Mountfield Road
A4	Nevill Street
B1	Newton Road
C4	Norfolk Road
C4	Poona Road
B1	Rock Villa Road
B4	Rodmell Road
B2	Rosehill Walk
A1	Royal Chase
A1	Somerville Gardens
B3	South Grove
B4	Spencer Mews
B3	Station Approach
C3	Sutherland Road
A4	The Pantiles
A4	The Pantiles Lower Walk
B3	Vale Avenue
B3	Vale Road
C1	Victoria Road
B4	Warwick Road
B2	York Road

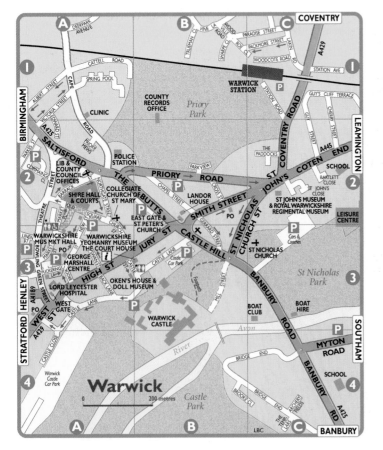

Warwick

A1	Albert Street
C4	Archery Fields
A3	Back Lane
C4	Banbury Road
A2	Barrack Street
C2	Bartlett Close
A3	Bowling Green Street
C4	Bridge End
A3	Brook Street
B4	Brooke Close
A1	Cape Road
A4	Castle Close
B3	Castle Hill
A3	Castle Lane
A3	Castle Street
A1	Cattell Road
B2	Chapel Street
C1	Cherry Street
A3	Church Street
A2	Commainge Close
C2	Coten End
C2	Coventry Road
B2	Cross Street
A1	Deerpark Avenue
A2	Edward Street
B3	Gerrard Street
C1	Guy Street
C1	Guy's Cliff Terrace
A3	High Street
B3	Jury Street
C1	Lakin Road
A3	Linen Street
A2	Market Place
A3	Market Street
C4	Myton Road
A3	New Street
A2	Northgate Street
A2	Old Square
C1	Packmore Street
C1	Paradise Street
A2	Parkes Street
B2	Parkview
A2	Priory Mews
B2	Priory Road
A3	Puckerings Lane
B1	Roe Close
C2	St John's
C2	St John's Close

B3	St Nicholas Church Street
A2	Saltisford
B1	Sharpe Close
B2	Smith Street
A1	Spring Pool
C1	Station Avenue
C1	Station Road
A3	Swan Street
B2	The Butts
C2	The Paddocks
C4	The Templars
A2	Theatre Street
B1	Trueman Close
A1	Victoria Street
B1	Vine Lane
A3	West Street
C1	Woodcote Road
B1	Woodville Road

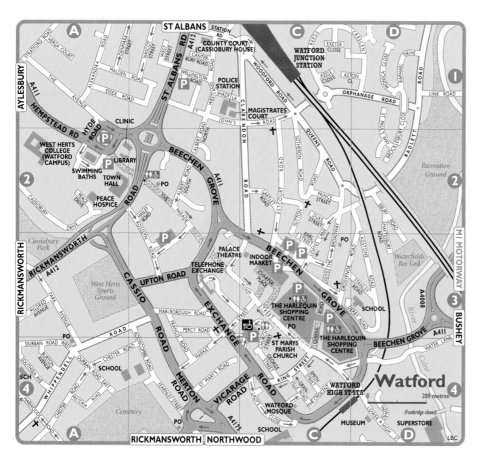

Watford

B4	Addiscombe Road	B4	Merton Road
B2	Albert Road North	A3	Mildred Avenue
B2	Albert Road South	D1	Monica Close
A1	Alexandra Road	B1	Nascot Street
D1	Aston Close	D4	New Road
C3	Beechen Grove	C1	Orphanage Road
D2	Brocklesbury Close	A3	Park Avenue
A4	Burton Avenue	A2	Peace Drive
B1	Canterbury Road	B3	Percy Road
B3	Cassio Road	A4	Pretoria Road
A2	Cassiobury Drive	C2	Prince Street
C3	Charter Place	C3	Queens Road
A4	Chester Road	C2	Queens Road
C4	Church Street	D2	Radlett Road
C1	Clarendon Road	D1	Raphael Drive
A1	Denmark Street	C1	Reeds Crescent
D3	Derby Road	A3	Rickmansworth Road
C2	Duke Street	B2	Rosslyn Road
A4	Durban Road East	B1	St Albans Road
A4	Durban Road West	B1	St John's Road
C3	Earl Street	B4	St Mary's Road
D2	Ebury Road	D1	St Paul's Way
A1	Essex Road	B1	Shady Lane
C2	Estcourt Road	D2	Shaftesbury Road
B3	Exchange Road	C4	Smith Street
C1	Exeter Close	C2	Sotheron Road
B4	Fearnley Street	A4	Southsea Avenue
B3	Francis Road	D3	Stanley Road
C2	Gartlet Road	B1	Station Road
C4	George Street	A1	Stratford Road
D3	Gladstone Road	C2	Sutton Road
C4	Granville Road	A1	The Avenue
C3	Grosvenor Road	C3	The Broadway
A4	Harwoods Road	C4	The Crescent
B2	Hasley Road	B2	The Parade
A1	Hempstead Road	B3	Upton Road
A1	Herga Court	B4	Vicarage Road
C3	High Street	D4	Water Lane
A2	Hyde Road	B1	Wellington Road
C1	Keele Close	B1	West Street
C4	King Street	B1	Westland Road
C4	Lady's Close	A4	Whippendell Road
D1	Link Road	C1	Woodford Road
C3	Loates Lane		
D4	Lower High Street		
A1	Malden Road		
B4	Market Street		
B3	Marlborough Road		

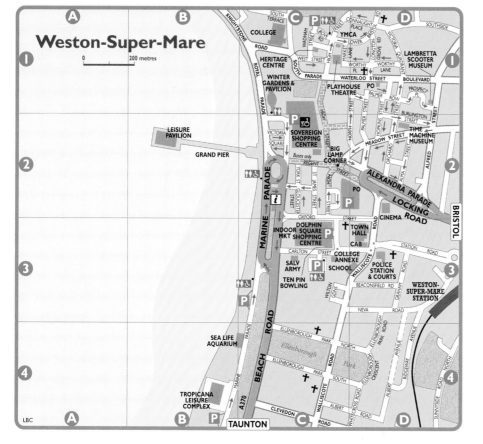

Weston-Super-Mare

D4	Albert Avenue	C1	Waterloo Street
C4	Albert Road	C1	West Street
D2	Alexandra Parade	D4	Whitecross Road
D2	Alfred Street	C3	Wilton Gardens
D2	Alma Street	D1	Worthy Lane
C4	Beach Road	D1	Worthy Place
D3	Beaconsfield Road	C2	York Street
D1	Boulevard		
D2	Burlington Street		
C3	Carlton Street		
C4	Clevedon Road		
D1	Connaught Place		
D4	Ellenborough Crescent		
C4	Ellenborough Park North		
D4	Ellenborough Park Road		
C4	Ellenborough Park South		
C2	Gloucester Street		
D3	Graham Road		
C1	Grove Road		
C1	High Street		
D2	Hopkins Street		
B1	Knightstone Road		
D2	Locking Road		
D1	Longton Grove Road		
D1	Lower Bristol Road		
C3	Marine Parade		
C1	Market Lane		
D2	Meadow Street		
D3	Neva Road		
D2	North Street		
D2	Orchard Street		
C2	Oxford Street		
D1	Palmer Row		
D2	Palmer Street		
D1	Prospect Place		
C2	Regent Street		
D4	Ridgeway Avenue		
C1	Royal Parade		
C2	St James Street		
C1	South Parade		
C1	South Terrace		
D1	Southside		
D3	Station Road		
D4	Sunnyside Road North		
D1	Victoria Quadrant		
C2	Victoria Square		
C1	Wadham Street		
C4	Walliscote Road		

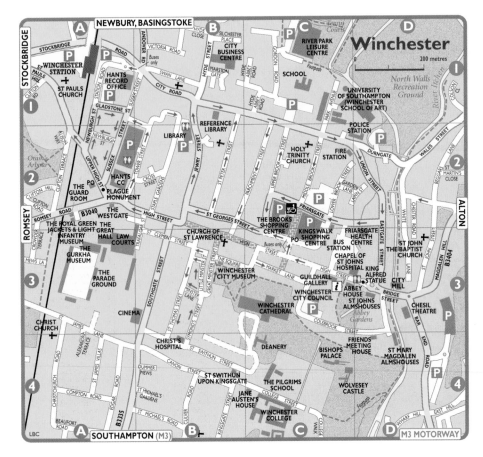

Winchester

A4	Alexandra Terrace	A2	Newburgh Street
A2	Alison Way	C2	Parchment Street
B1	Andover Road	C1	Park Avenue
D3	Bar End Road	A2	Romsey Road
A4	Beaufort Road	B3	St Clement Street
D2	Beggars Lane	B2	St Georges Street
D3	Bridge Street	A3	St James Lane
B4	Canon Street	A4	St James Villas
D2	Chester Road	D3	St John Street
A4	Christchurch Road	D2	St Martin's Close
B1	City Road	B4	St Michael's Gardens
A2	Clifton Hill	B4	St Michael's Road
A2	Clifton Road	A1	St Pauls Hill
A1	Clifton Road	B2	St Peter Street
A2	Clifton Terrace	B4	St Swithun Street
C3	Colebrook Street	B3	St Thomas Street
C4	College Street	B3	Southgate Street
C4	College Walk	B2	Staple Gardens
D1	Colson Close	A1	Station Road
A4	Compton Road	A1	Stockbridge Road
B2	Cross Street	A2	Sussex Street
A3	Crowder Terrace	B1	Swan Lane
B4	Culver Road	B3	Symond's Street
B4	Dummer Mews	B3	The Square
D2	Durngate	B2	Tower Street
D4	East Hill	B3	Trafalgar Street
D3	Eastgate Street	D2	Union Street
A4	Edgar Road	C2	Upper Brook Street
C2	Friarsgate	A2	Upper High Street
C2	Garden Lane	B1	Victoria Road
A1	Gladstone Street	D2	Wales Street
C1	Gordon Road	D4	Wharf Hill
B3	Great Minster Street	D2	White Lane
B2	High Street		
C1	Hyde Abbey Road		
B1	Hyde Close		
B1	Hyde Street		
B2	Jewry Street		
B4	Kingsgate Street		
D2	Lawn Street		
B3	Little Minster Street		
C2	Lower Brook Street		
D3	Magdalen Hill		
C3	Market Lane		
B1	Marston Gate		
A3	Mews Lane		
C2	Middle Brook Street		
B3	Minster Lane		

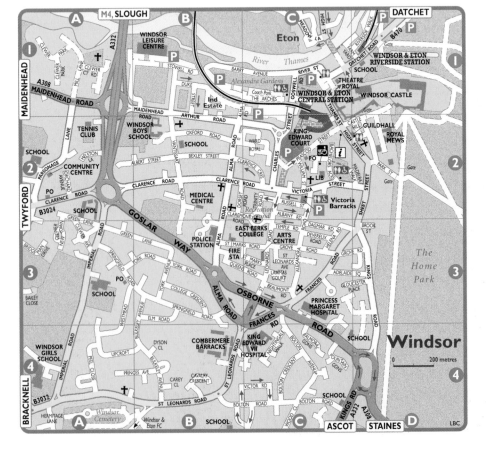

Windsor

C3	Adelaide Square	C1	High Street, Eton
C2	Albany Road	C2	High Street, Windsor
B2	Albert Street	A4	Imperial Road
C3	Alexandra Road	C4	Kings Road
B2	Alma Road	C3	Lammas Court
B2	Arthur Road	D2	Madeira Walk
C2	Bachelors Acre	A1	Maidenhead Road
A3	Bailey Close	C1	Meadow Lane
C4	Balmoral Gardens	A1	Mill Lane
B1	Barry Avenue	C4	Nightingale Walk
C3	Beaumont Road	A2	Orchard Avenue
B2	Bexley Street	C3	Osborne Road
C4	Bolton Avenue	B2	Oxford Road
C4	Bolton Crescent	D2	Park Street
C4	Bolton Road	A2	Parsonage Lane
A3	Bridgeman Drive	C2	Peascod Street
D3	Brook Street	A4	Peel Close
B4	Bulkeley Avenue	A4	Princes Avenue
B4	Carey Close	B3	Queens Road
D2	Castle Hill	C1	River Street
B4	Cavalry Crescent	D1	Riverside Walk
C2	Charles Street	C2	Russell Street
B2	Claremont Road	C3	St Leonards Avenue
C2	Clarence Crescent	B4	St Leonards Road
A2	Clarence Road	C3	St Marks Place
A3	Clewer Avenue	B3	St Marks Road
A1	Clewer Court Road	D2	Sheet Street
A3	Clewer New Town	A3	Springfield Road
A1	Clewer Park	B1	Stowell Road
B3	College Crescent	C3	Temple Road
C3	Dagmar Road	C1	Thames Street
D1	Datchet Road	C1	The Arches
C3	Devereux Road	C2	Trinity Road
B2	Dorset Road	A4	Upcroft
B1	Duke Street	B2	Vantissart Road
B4	Dyson Close	C4	Victor Road
B3	Elm Road	C2	Victoria Street
D1	Farm Yard	C2	Ward Royal
C4	Fountain Gardens	A3	Westmead
C3	Frances Road	C2	William Street
D3	Gloucester Place	C4	Wood Close
B3	Goslar Way	B3	York Avenue
C1	Goswell Road	B3	York Road
A3	Green Lane		
C3	Grove Road		
C3	Helena Road		
A2	Helston Lane		
A4	Hermitage Lane		

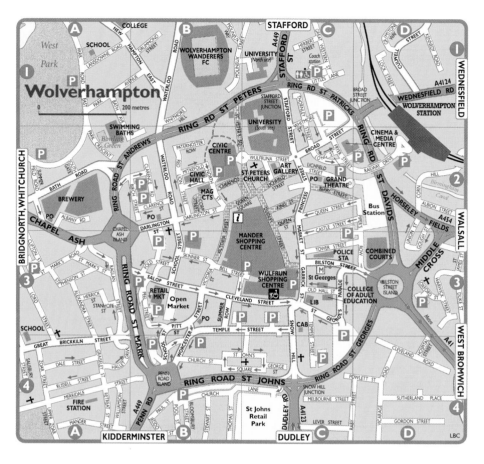

Wolverhampton

A3	Alexandra Street	B3	Peel Street
A1	Bath Avenue	B4	Penn Road
A2	Bath Road	D2	Piper's Row
B3	Bell Street	B3	Pitt Street
C2	Berry Street	C2	Princess Street
C3	Bilston Street	C2	Queen Square
B2	Birch Street	C2	Queen Street
C2	Broad Street	C4	Raby Street
C2	Castle Street	A3	Raglan Street
A2	Chapel Ash	D2	Railway Drive
B2	Cheapside	B2	Red Lion Street
B4	Church Lane	A4	Retreat Street
B4	Church Street	A2	Ring Road St Andrews
B2	Clarence Road	D2	Ring Road St Davids
B2	Clarence Street	C4	Ring Road St Georges
D4	Cleveland Road	B4	Ring Road St Johns
B3	Cleveland Street	A3	Ring Road St Mark
D2	Corn Hill	C1	Ring Road St Patricks
B2	Corporation Street	B1	Ring Road St Peters
D1	Culwell Street	A4	Russell Street
A4	Dale Street	C3	St George's Parade
B2	Darlington Street	C4	St John's Square
C4	Dudley Road	A3	St Mark's Road
C2	Dudley Street	A3	St Mark's Street
B3	Fold Street	B1	St Peter's Square
C2	Fryer Street	B3	Salop Street
C3	Garrick Street	B4	School Street
A4	Graisley Street	B3	Skinner Street
A4	Great Brickkiln Street	C3	Snow Hill
C1	Great Western Street	C1	Stafford Street
A4	Hallet Drive	A3	Stephenson Street
D2	Horseley Fields	B4	Stewart Street
C2	King Street	B3	Summer Row
C2	Lichfield Street	D4	Sutherland Place
C1	Littles Lane	C3	Tempest Street
C2	Long Street	B3	Temple Street
A3	Lord Street	B4	Thomas Street
C3	Market Street	C1	Thornley Street
A4	Merridale Street	C3	Tower Street
D3	Middle Cross	D4	Vicarage Road
B2	Mitrefold	B3	Victoria Street
B1	Molineux Street	B1	Waterloo Road
A1	New Hampton East	D1	Wednesfield Road
B2	North Street	B1	Whitmore Hill
C3	Old Hall Street	C1	Whitmore Street
A1	Park Avenue	B4	Worcester Street
A1	Park Road East	C2	Wulfruna Street
B2	Paternoster Row	A4	Zoar Street

Worcester

A2	All Saints Road	A3	New Road
B2	Angel Place	C3	New Street
B2	Angel Row	A3	North Parade
B2	Angel Street	A2	North Quay
B1	Arboretum Road	C3	Park Street
C4	Bath Road	C2	Pheasant Street
A3	Bridge Street	B1	Pierpoint Street
B1	Britannia Road	C3	Providence Street
B2	Broad Street	B3	Pump Street
D2	Byfield Rise	C2	Queen Street
A1	Castle Street	D4	Richmond Hill
D3	Cecil Road	D4	Richmond Road
C3	Charles Street	D4	Rose Terrace
A1	Charter Place	C2	St James Close
B2	Church Street	C2	St Martin's Gate
C2	City Walls Road	B1	St Mary Street
D4	Cole Hill	B2	St Nicholas Street
B4	College Green	C3	St Paul's Street
B3	College Street	B2	St Swithuns Street
C4	Commandery Road	D4	St Wulstan's Crescent
B3	Copenhagen Street	C1	Sansome Place
A2	Croft Road	B2	Sansome Street
D2	Cromwell Street	B1	Sansome Walk
B3	Deans Way	B4	Severn Street
D3	Dent Close	A1	Severn Terrace
A2	Dolday	B2	Shaw Street
A1	Easy Row	D2	Shrub Hill Road
B1	Farrier Street	C4	Sidbury
B1	Foregate Street	A3	South Parade
D4	Fort Royal Hill	C1	Southfield Street
C3	Friar Street	C3	Spring Gardens
C3	Garden Street	D2	Spring Hill
C4	Green Hill	D2	Spring Lane
C4	Hamilton Road	D3	Stanley Road
B3	High Street	D2	Tallow Hill
D2	Hill Street	B1	Taylors Lane
A2	Hylton Road	A2	The Butts
A1	Infirmary Walk	B2	The Cross
C4	King Street	B2	The Foregate
B1	Little Southfield Street	C3	The Shambles
C4	London Road	B1	The Tything
A1	Love's Grove	D1	Tolladine
C2	Lowesmoor	B2	Trinity Street
C1	Lowesmoor Place	C3	Union Street
C1	Lowesmoor Terrace	D4	Upper Park Street
B1	Middle Street	D3	Vincent Road
D3	Midland Road	C3	Wellington Close
A1	Moor Street	C4	Wylde Lane

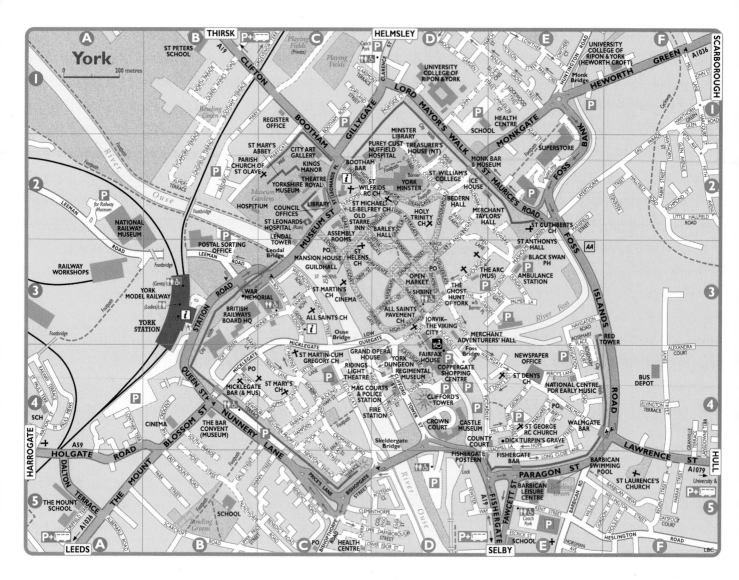

York

Ports

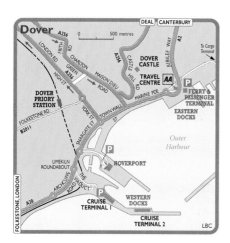

Pay-on-return parking is available at the Dover Eastern Docks and Cruise Terminal 1. Pay and display parking is also available at the Hoverport Terminal.
For charge details tel: 01304 241427

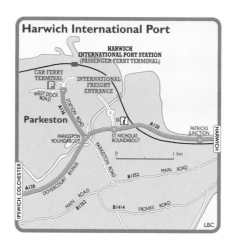

Open-air parking is available at the terminal.
For charge details tel: 01255 242000

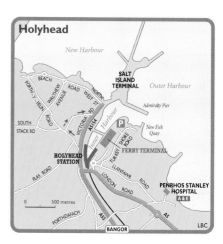

Open-air 'Park and Ride' car park is available close to the Ferry Terminal.
For charge details tel: 01407 762304 or 606732

Free open-air parking is available at King George Dock (left at owners' risk).
Tel: 01482 795141

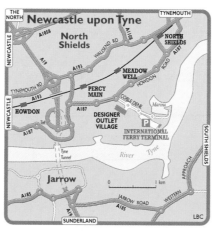

Open-air secure parking is available at the International Ferry Terminal, Royal Quays.
For charge details tel: 0191 296 0202

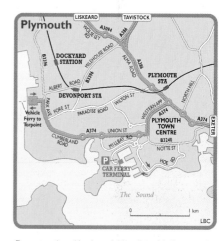

Free open-air parking is available adjacent to the terminal building.
Tel: 08705 360360

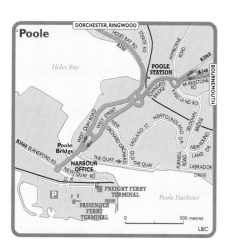

Open-air parking for 600 vehicles is available adjacent to the Ferry Terminal.
For charge details tel: 01202 440220 ext. 343

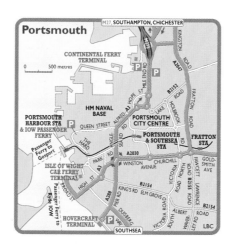

Secure parking facilities are available at the Continental Ferry Terminal and long-stay parking off Mile End Rd.
For charge details tel: 023 9275 1261
Pay-and-display parking is available opposite the Hovercraft Terminal.
Multi-storey parking is available close to the Isle of Wight Passenger Ferry Terminal.
For charge details tel: 023 9282 3153

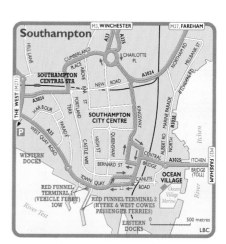

Covered or fenced compound parking for 2,000 vehicles is available within the Western Docks with a collection and delivery service.
For charge details tel: 023 8022 8001
Fax: 023 8063 5699

Major airports

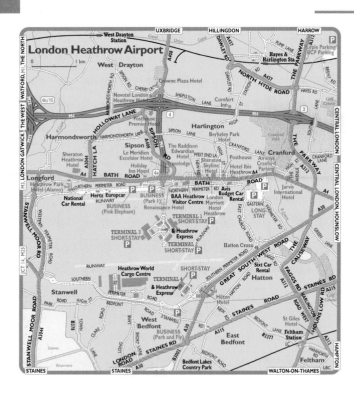

London Heathrow Airport – 16 miles west of London

Telephone: 0870 0000 123 or visit www.baa.com
Parking: short-stay, long-stay and business parking is available.
For charge details tel: 0870 000 1000
Public Transport: coach, bus, rail and London Underground.
There are several 4-star and 3-star hotels within easy reach of the airport.
Car hire facilities are available.

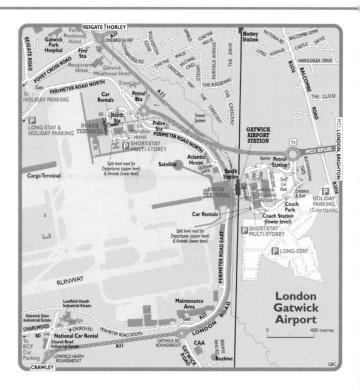

London Gatwick Airport – 35 miles south of London

Telephone: 0870 000 2468 or visit www.baa.com
Parking: short and long-stay parking is available at both the North and South terminals.
For charge details tel: 0870 000 1000
Public Transport: coach, bus and rail.
There are several 4-star and 3-star hotels within easy reach of the airport.
Car hire facilities are available.

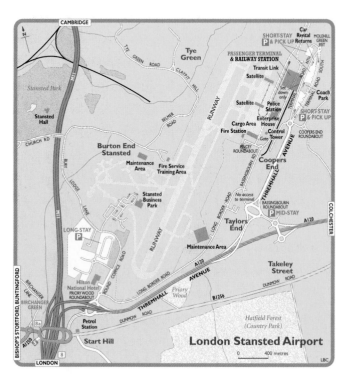

London Stansted Airport – 36 miles north east of London

Telephone: 0870 0000 303 or visit www.baa.com
Parking: short, mid and long-stay open-air parking is available.
For charge details tel: 01279 681192
Public Transport: coach, bus and direct rail link to London on the Stansted Express.
There is one 3-star hotel within easy reach of the airport.
Car hire facilities are available.

London Luton Airport – 33 miles north of London

Telephone: 01582 405100 or visit www.london-luton.com
Parking: short and long-stay open-air parking is available.
For charge details tel: 01582 395580
Public Transport: coach, bus and rail.
There are several hotels within easy reach of the airport.
Car hire facilities are available.

Major airports

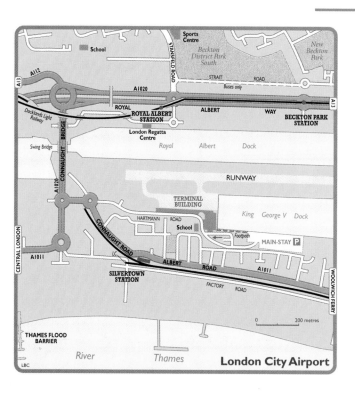

London City Airport – 7 miles east of London

Telephone: 020 7646 0088 or visit www.londoncityairport.com
Parking: open-air parking is available.
For charge details tel: 020 7646 0088
Public Transport: shuttle-bus service into London (Liverpool Street). Easy access to the rail network, Docklands Light Railway and the London Underground.
There are 5-star, 4-star and 3-star hotels within easy reach of the airport.
Car hire facilities are available.

Birmingham International Airport – 8 miles east of Birmingham

Telephone: 0121 767 5511 or visit www.bhx.co.uk
Parking: short and long-stay parking is available. For charge details tel: 0121 767 5511
Public Transport: shuttle-bus service to Birmingham International railway station and the NEC.
There is one 3-star hotel adjacent to the airport and several 4 and 3-star hotels within easy reach of the airport. Car hire facilities are available.

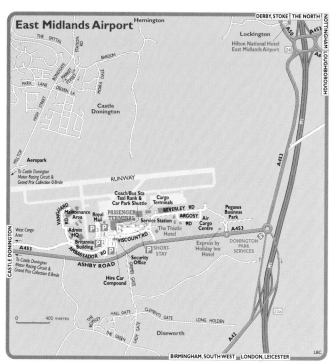

East Midlands Airport – 15 miles south west of Nottingham, next to the M1 at junctions 23A and 24

Telephone: 01332 852852 or visit www.eastmidlandsairport.com
Parking: short and long-stay parking is available.
For charge details tel: 01332 852852
Public Transport: bus and coach services to major towns and cities in the East Midlands.
There are several 3-star hotels within easy reach of the airport.
Car hire facilities are available.

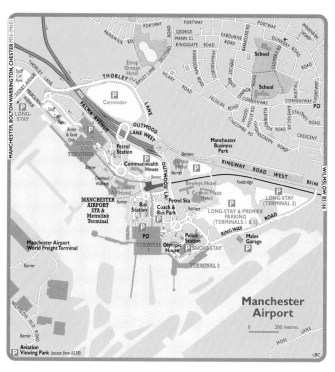

Manchester Airport – 10 miles south of Manchester

Telephone: 0161 489 3000 or visit www.manchesterairport.co.uk
Parking: short and long-stay parking is available.
For charge details tel: 0161 489 3723
Public Transport: bus, coach and rail.
There are several 4-star and 3-star hotels within easy reach of the airport.
Car hire facilities are available.

Major airports

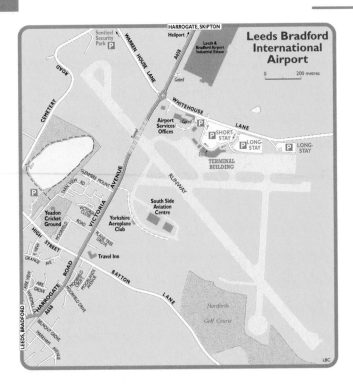

Leeds Bradford International Airport – 7 miles north east of Bradford and 9 miles north west of Leeds

Telephone: 0113 250 9696 or visit www.lbia.co.uk
Parking: short and long-stay parking is available.
For charge details tel: 0113 250 9696
Public Transport: regular bus and coach services operate from Bradford and Leeds.
There are several 4-star and 3-star hotels within easy reach of the airport.
Car hire facilities are available.

Aberdeen Airport – 7 miles north west of Aberdeen

Telephone: 01224 722331 or visit www.baa.com
Parking: short and long-stay parking is available.
For charge details tel: 01224 722331 ext 5142
Public Transport: regular bus service to central Aberdeen.
There are several 4-star and 3-star hotels within easy reach of the airport.
Car hire facilities are available.

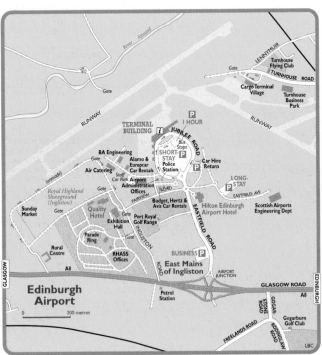

Edinburgh Airport – 7 miles west of Edinburgh

Telephone: 0131 333 1000 or visit www.baa.com
Parking: short and long-stay parking is available.
For charge details tel: 0131 317 1351
Public Transport: regular bus services to central Edinburgh.
There are several 4-star and 3-star hotels within easy reach of the airport.
Car hire facilities are available.

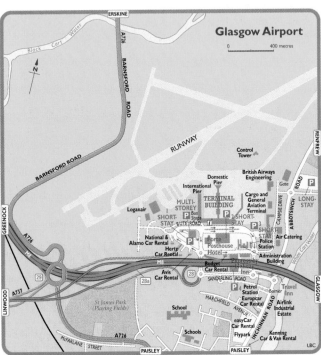

Glasgow Airport – 8 miles west of Glasgow

Telephone: 0141 887 1111 or visit www.baa.com
Parking: short and long-stay parking is available.
For charge details tel: 0141 887 1111
Public Transport: regular coach services operate direct to central Glasgow and Edinburgh.
There are several 3-star hotels within easy reach of the airport.
Car hire facilities are available.

Channel Tunnel and Calais

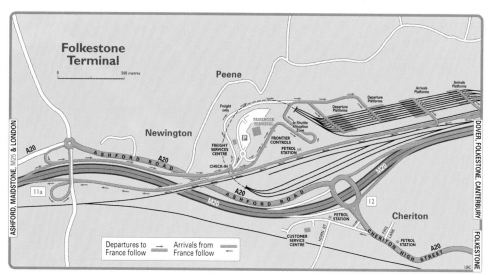

Services to Europe

The Eurotunnel shuttle service for cars, cars towing caravans and trailers, motorcycles, coaches and HGV vehicles runs between terminals at Folkestone and Calais/Coquelles. It takes just over one hour to travel from the M20 motorway in Kent, via the Channel Tunnel, to the A16 autoroute in France.

The service runs 24 hours a day, every day of the year.

Call the Eurotunnel Call Centre (tel: 08705 353535) or visit www.eurotunnel.com for the latest ticket and travel information.

There are up to four departures per hour at peak times, with the journey in the tunnel from platform to platform taking just 35 minutes (45 minutes at night). Travellers pass through British and French frontier controls on departure, saving time on the other side of the Channel.

Each terminal has bureaux de change, restaurants and a variety of shops. In Calais/Coquelles, the Cité de l'Europe contains numerous shops, restaurants and a hypermarket.

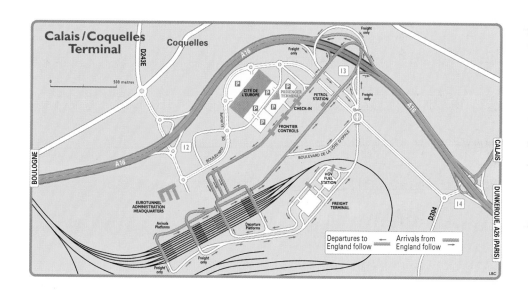

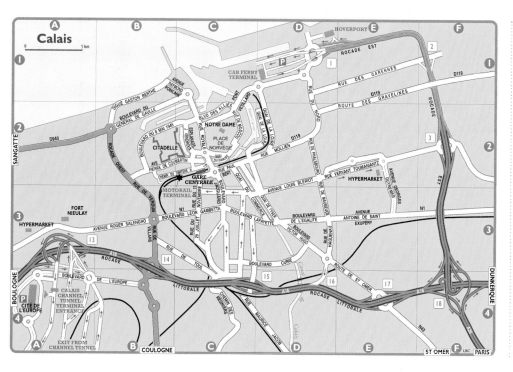

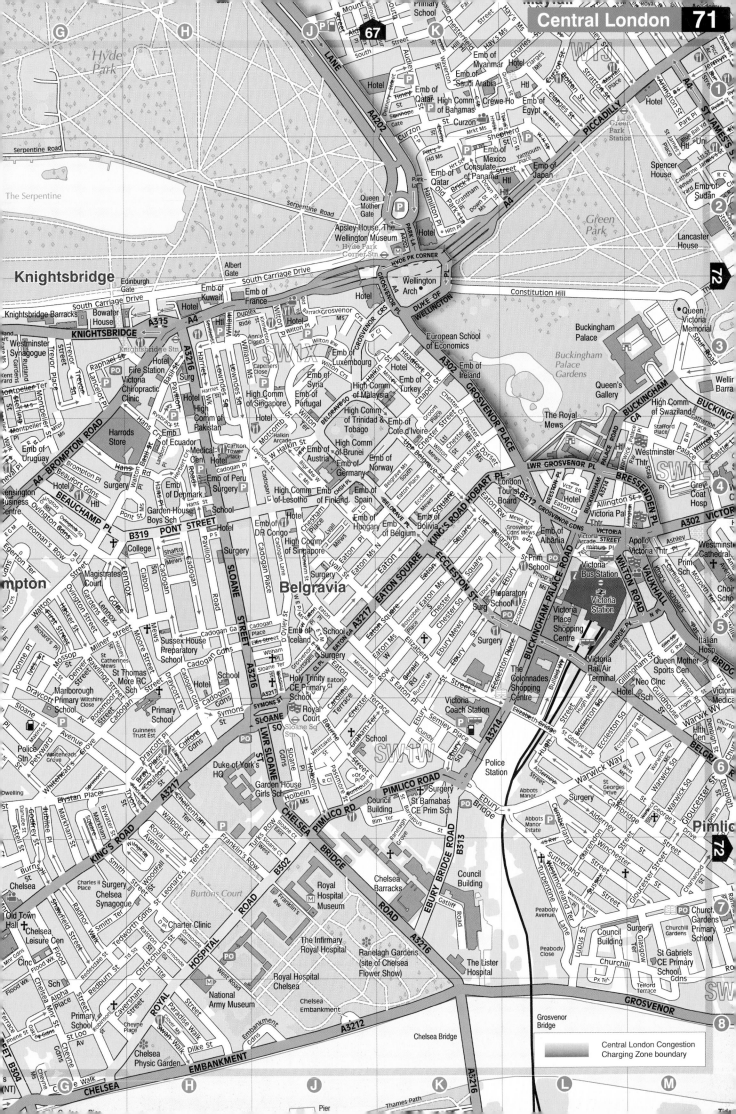

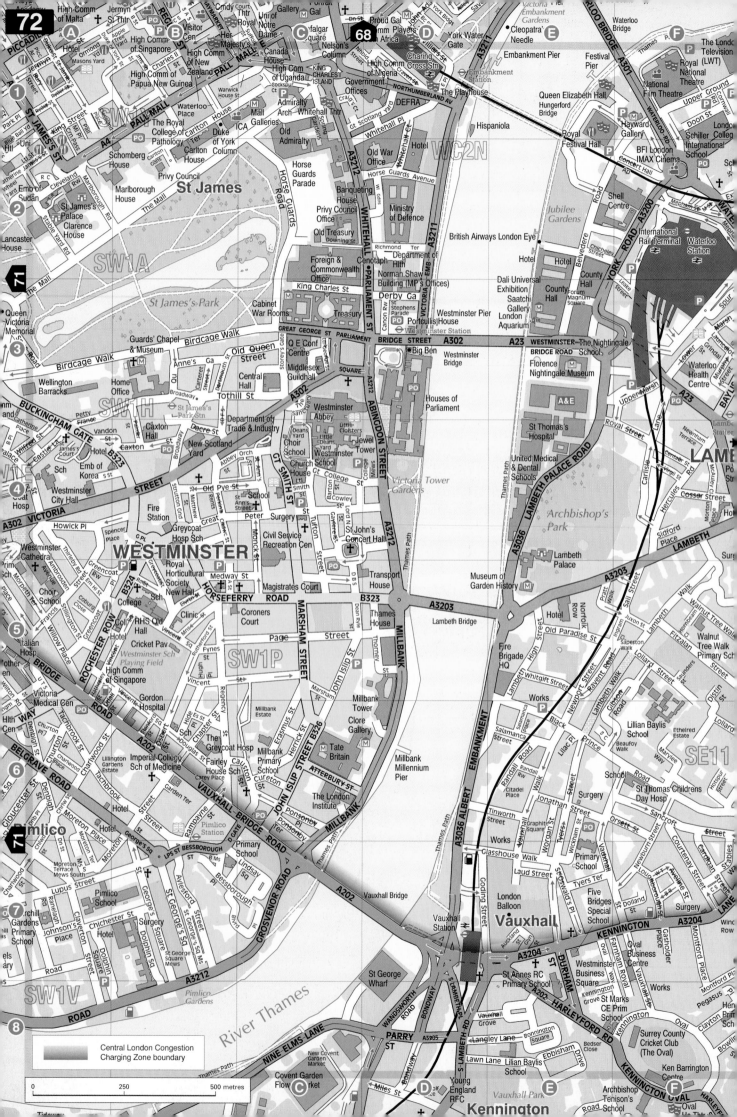

Central London street index

In the index street names are listed in alphabetical order and written in full, but may be abbreviated on the map. Each entry is followed by its Postcode District and each street name is preceded by the page number and the grid reference to the square in which the name is found. Names are asterisked (*) in the index where there is insufficient space to show them on the map.

A

66 C1 **Abbey Gardens** NW8
72 B4 **Abbey Orchard Street** SW1P
74 B7 **Abbey Street** SE1
75 J5 **Abbotshade Road** SE16
74 A6 **Abbots Lane** SE1
71 L6 **Abbots Manor** SW1V
71 L6 **Abbots Manor Estate** SW1V
70 B4 **Abbots Walk** * W8
69 L7 **Abchurch Lane** EC4N
66 C1 **Abercorn Close** NW8
66 C1 **Abercorn Place** NW8
66 E3 **Aberdeen Place** NW8
73 M5 **Aberdour Street** SE1
70 A4 **Abingdon Road** W8
72 D3 **Abingdon Street** SW1P
70 A4 **Abingdon Villas** W8
68 E7 **Acton Street** WC1X
66 D3 **Ada Court** NW8
70 A4 **Adam & Eve Mews** W8
67 K8 **Adam's Row** W1K
68 D8 **Adam Street** WC2R
69 J7 **Addle Hill** EC4V
69 K5 **Addle Street** * EC2V
68 D8 **Adelaide Street** * WC2N
74 F1 **Adelina Grove** E1
68 C5 **Adeline Place** WC1B
68 D8 **Adelphi Terrace** WC2N
74 D2 **Adler Street** E1
75 K5 **Admiral Place** SE16
76 B3 **Admirals Way** E14
66 A4 **Admiral Walk** W9
66 E4 **Adpar Street** W2
70 B8 **Adrian Mews** SW10
68 E1 **Affleck Street** * N1
68 D8 **Agar Street** WC2N
74 F4 **Agatha Close** E1W
69 H3 **Agdon Street** EC1V
75 L2 **Agnes Street** E14
75 G6 **Ainsty Street** * SE16
68 A7 **Air Street** W1B
72 F2 **Alaska Street** SE1
68 A8 **Albany Courtyard** W1J
73 K8 **Albany Mews** SE17
73 M8 **Albany Road** SE5
67 L1 **Albany Street** NW1
67 M8 **Albemarle Street** W1S
69 H4 **Albemarle Way** EC1M
73 H6 **Alberta Estate** SE17
73 H7 **Alberta Street** SE17
74 D1 **Albert Cottages** * E1
72 D6 **Albert Embankment** SE11
75 H3 **Albert Gardens** E1
71 H2 **Albert Gate** SW1X
70 C4 **Albert Mews** W8
75 K4 **Albert Mews** * E14
70 C3 **Albert Place** W8
66 F7 **Albion Close** W2
67 G7 **Albion Gate** W2
67 G7 **Albion Mews** W2
69 H4 **Albion Place** EC1M
67 G7 **Albion Street** W2
75 G7 **Albion Street** SE16
69 J5 **Albion Way** EC1A
68 D1 **Albion Yard** N1
67 K6 **Aldburgh Mews** W1U
68 B1 **Aldenham Street** NW1
69 K6 **Aldermanbury** * EC2V
69 K5 **Aldermanbury Square** EC2V
73 K4 **Alderney Mews** SE1
71 L6 **Alderney Street** SW1V
69 J4 **Aldersgate Street** EC1A
67 J8 **Aldford Street** W1K
74 B3 **Aldgate** EC3M
74 C2 **Aldgate Barrs** * E1
74 B3 **Aldgate High Street** EC3N
66 B4 **Aldsworth Close** W9
68 E7 **Aldwych** WC2R
66 A6 **Alexander Mews** W2
70 F5 **Alexander Place** SW7
70 F5 **Alexander Square** SW3
66 A6 **Alexander Street** W2
70 E3 **Alexandra Gate** SW7
69 K1 **Alford Place** * N1
68 B4 **Alfred Mews** W1T
68 B5 **Alfred Place** W1T
66 A5 **Alfred Road** W2
73 M4 **Alice Street** SE1
74 C3 **Alie Street** E1
70 A4 **Allen Street** W8
69 L8 **Allhallows Lane** EC4R
71 M4 **Allington Street** SW1E
66 F1 **Allitsen Road** NW8
66 F1 **Allitson Road** NW8
75 H1 **Allport Mews** E1
67 H4 **Allsop Place** NW1
67 L5 **All Souls' Place** W1B
66 D1 **Alma Square** NW8
70 A5 **Alma Terrace** W8
67 G3 **Alpha Close** NW1
76 B3 **Alpha Grove** E14
71 G8 **Alpha Place** SW3
73 M7 **Alsace Road** SE17
74 C8 **Alscot Road** SE16
73 M6 **Alvey Street** SE17
74 E2 **Amazon Street** * E1
76 C6 **Ambassador Square** E14
73 H7 **Ambergate Street** SE17
66 A4 **Amberley Road** W9
72 A5 **Ambrosden Avenue** SW1P
73 J6 **Amelia Street** SE17
69 H6 **Amen Corner** EC4M
69 H6 **Amen Court** EC4M
74 B3 **America Square** * EC3N
73 J2 **America Street** SE1
75 K2 **Ames Cottages** * E14
74 D8 **Amina Way** SE16
67 M1 **Ampthill Estate** NW1
68 A1 **Ampthill Square** NW1
68 E2 **Ampton Street** WC1X
76 E5 **Amsterdam Road** E14
68 F2 **Amwell Street** EC1R
69 K3 **Anchor Yard** * EC1V
71 H6 **Anderson Street** SW3
66 B1 **Andover Place** NW6
68 C6 **Andrew Borde Street** * WC2H
69 L6 **Angel Court** EC2R
74 F3 **Angel Mews** E1
69 L8 **Angel Passage** EC4R
69 G1 **Angel Square** * EC1V
69 J6 **Angel Street** EC1A
74 B1 **Annexe Market** * E1
75 G8 **Ann Moss Way** SE16
71 H3 **Ann's Close** SW1X
70 B4 **Ansdell Street** W8
70 B3 **Ansdell Terrace** W8
74 D5 **Anthony's Close** E1W
74 F2 **Anthony Street** * E1
75 H2 **Antill Terrace** E1
69 H7 **Apothecary Street** * EC4V
68 B8 **Apple Tree Yard** SW1Y
69 M4 **Appold Street** EC2A
71 K2 **Apsley Way** * W1J
73 G1 **Aquinas Street** SE1
75 H2 **Arbour Square** E1
69 M5 **The Arcade** * EC2M
75 J7 **Archangel Street** SE16
68 B7 **Archer Street** W1D
67 G6 **Archery Close** W2
68 D8 **The Arches** * WC2N
67 K8 **Archibald Mews** W1J
73 J4 **Arch Street** SE1
76 B5 **Arden Crescent** E14
69 M1 **Arden Estate** N1
68 D2 **Argyle Square** WC1H
68 D2 **Argyle Street** NW1
68 D2 **Argyle Walk** * WC1H
70 A3 **Argyll Road** W8
67 M6 **Argyll Street** W1B
71 M1 **Arlington Street** W1J
69 G2 **Arlington Way** EC1R
68 D6 **Arne Street** WC2H
72 B5 **Arneway Street** SW1P
76 A5 **Arnheim Place** E14
74 C7 **Arnold Estate** SE1
73 K8 **Arnside Street** SE17
69 L7 **Arthur Street** EC4R
74 E4 **Artichoke Hill** E1W
74 A1 **Artillery Lane** EC2M
74 B1 **Artillery Passage** * E1
74 B2 **Artizan Street** E1
68 F7 **Arundel Street** WC2R
66 F4 **Ashbridge Street** NW8
70 C5 **Ashburn Gardens** SW7
70 C6 **Ashburn Place** SW7
69 H2 **Ashby Street** EC1V
74 E4 **Asher Way** E1W
74 F2 **Ashfield Street** E1
75 G2 **Ashfield Yard** * E1
69 M2 **Ashford Street** N1
67 J5 **Ashland Place** W1U
71 M4 **Ashley Place** SW1P
66 F4 **Ashmill Street** NW8
66 B2 **Ashworth Road** W9
69 M1 **Aske Street** N1
73 K6 **Asolando Drive** SE17
76 B1 **Aspen Way** E14
74 D2 **Assam Street** E1
71 G6 **Astell Street** SW3
75 K2 **Aston Street** E14
70 C5 **Astwood Mews** SW7
70 D5 **Atherstone Mews** SW7
72 C6 **Atterbury Street** SW1P
68 F3 **Attneave Street** WC1X
66 C1 **Aubrey Place** NW8
72 E7 **Auckland Street** SE11
71 K1 **Audley Square** * W1K
67 L1 **Augustus Street** NW1
73 G7 **Aulton Place** SE11
69 M6 **Austin Friars** EC2N
69 M6 **Austin Friars Square** * EC2N
73 H5 **Austral Street** SE11
72 F7 **Aveline Street** SE11
71 K6 **Avery Farm Row** * SW1W
67 L7 **Avery Row** W1K
75 H2 **Avis Square** E1
73 J4 **Avonmouth Street** SE1
67 J5 **Aybrook Street** W1U
73 M7 **Aylesbury Estate** SE17
73 L7 **Aylesbury Road** SE17
69 H4 **Aylesbury Street** EC1R
72 B7 **Aylesford Street** SW1V
75 H2 **Aylward Street** E1
73 K2 **Ayres Street** SE1
70 D4 **Ayrton Road** SW7

B

68 B8 **Babmaes Street** SW1Y
69 L2 **Bache's Street** N1
74 D3 **Back Church Lane** E1
69 G4 **Back Hill** EC1R
73 L3 **Baden Place** SE1
75 K2 **Bailey Cottages** * E14
68 C6 **Bainbridge Street** WC1A
69 K3 **Baird Street** EC1Y
67 J6 **Baker's Mews** W1U
69 G4 **Baker's Row** EC1R
67 H4 **Baker Street** NW1
68 F3 **Baker's Yard** EC1R
67 G3 **Balcombe Street** NW1
67 J7 **Balderton Street** W1K
68 F5 **Baldwin's Gardens** WC1X
69 L2 **Baldwin Street** EC1V
75 J1 **Bale Road** E1
68 D1 **Balfe Street** N1
67 K8 **Balfour Mews** W1K
67 J8 **Balfour Place** W1K
73 L5 **Balfour Street** SE1
74 E4 **Balkan Walk** E1W
69 J3 **Baltic Street East** EC1Y
69 J4 **Baltic Street West** EC1M
72 B7 **Balvaird Place** SW1V
68 C7 **Banbury Court** * WC2E
73 K1 **Bank End** SE1
69 J8 **Bankside** SE1
69 K3 **Banner Street** EC1Y
74 F8 **Banyard Road** SE16
69 K5 **Barbican** EC2Y
68 D4 **Barbon Close** WC1N
69 G8 **Barge House Street** SE1
66 B7 **Bark Place** W2
70 B6 **Barkston Gardens** SW5
75 L4 **Barleycorn Estate** E14
67 L7 **Barlow Place** W1J
73 L5 **Barlow Street** SE17
70 E6 **Barnaby Place** SW7
75 H3 **Barnardo Gardens** * E1
75 H3 **Barnardo Street** E1
68 A1 **Barnby Street** NW1
75 K3 **Barnes Street** E14
74 E2 **Barnett Street** * E1
74 A6 **Barnham Street** SE1
76 B6 **Barnsdale Avenue** E14
66 B4 **Barnwood Close** W9
69 G1 **Barons Close** * N1
73 G3 **Baron's Place** SE1
69 G1 **Baron Street** N1
76 A8 **Barque Mews** SE8
67 K6 **Barrett Street** W1H
66 F1 **Barrow Hill Estate** NW8
66 F1 **Barrow Hill Road** NW8
68 D5 **Barter Street** WC1A
69 J5 **Bartholomew Close** EC1A
69 L6 **Bartholomew Lane** EC2R
69 K3 **Bartholomew Square** EC1V
73 L5 **Bartholomew Street** SE1
69 G6 **Bartlett Court** * EC4A
72 C4 **Barton Street** SW1P
71 H4 **Basil Street** SW3
75 K3 **Basin Approach** E14
69 K5 **Basinghall Avenue** EC2V
69 K6 **Basinghall Street** EC2V
69 J3 **Bastwick Street** EC1V
68 B6 **Bateman Street** W1D
75 M3 **Bate Street** E14
69 M2 **Bath Place** N1
69 K2 **Bath Street** EC1V
73 K4 **Bath Terrace** SE1
66 E7 **Bathurst Mews** W2
66 E7 **Bathurst Street** W2
75 K2 **Batten Cottages** * E14
73 M1 **Battle Bridge Lane** SE1
68 C1 **Battle Bridge Road** NW1
74 D3 **Batty Street** E1
68 B5 **Bayley Street** W1T
72 F3 **Baylis Road** SE1
66 C8 **Bayswater Road** W2
75 M1 **Baythorne Street** E3
73 M7 **Beaconsfield Road** SE17
68 A7 **Beak Street** W1B
73 K1 **Bear Gardens** SE1
73 H1 **Bear Lane** SE1
68 C7 **Bear Street** WC2H
70 B5 **Beatrice Place** W8
71 G4 **Beauchamp Place** SW3
69 G5 **Beauchamp Street** EC1N
71 G4 **Beaufort Gardens** SW3
70 D7 **Beaufort Street** SW3
72 F6 **Beaufoy Walk** SE11
67 K4 **Beaumont Mews** * W1U
68 A3 **Beaumont Place** W1T
67 K4 **Beaumont Street** W1U
75 M3 **Beccles Street** E14
73 L4 **Becket Street** SE1
73 K7 **Beckford Place** * SE17
73 M6 **Beckway Street** SE17
73 L1 **Bedale Street** * SE1
68 C5 **Bedford Avenue** WC1B
68 D7 **Bedfordbury** WC2N
68 D7 **Bedford Court** WC2N
68 D4 **Bedford Place** WC1B
68 E4 **Bedford Row** WC1X
68 B5 **Bedford Square** WC1B
68 D7 **Bedford Street** WC2E
68 C3 **Bedford Way** WC1H
66 E3 **Bedlow Close** NW8
72 E8 **Bedser Close** SE11
69 J4 **Beech Street (Below)** EC2Y
71 L4 **Beeston Place** SW1W
75 J3 **Bekesbourne Street** E14
71 K4 **Belgrave Mews South** SW1X
71 J4 **Belgrave Mews West** SW1X
71 K4 **Belgrave Place** SW1X
71 M6 **Belgrave Road** SW1V
71 J4 **Belgrave Square** SW1X
75 J3 **Belgrave Street** E1
68 D2 **Belgrove Street** NW1
76 A3 **Bellamy Close** E14
74 B1 **Bell Lane** E1
66 F5 **Bell Street** W2
69 K7 **Bell Wharf Lane** EC4R
68 F6 **Bell Yard** WC2A
73 J3 **Belvedere Buildings** SE1
72 E2 **Belvedere Road** SE1
76 A8 **Benbow Street** SE8
67 G4 **Bendall Mews** NW1
69 H4 **Benjamin Street** EC1M
75 J1 **Ben Jonson Road** E1
69 J7 **Bennet's Hill** EC4V
71 M1 **Bennett Street** SW1A
74 D7 **Ben Smith Way** SE16
75 G4 **Benson Quay** E1W
67 K5 **Bentinck Mews** W1U
67 K6 **Bentinck Street** W1U
75 J3 **Bere Street** E1W
67 H6 **Berkeley Mews** W1H
67 L8 **Berkeley Square** W1J
67 L8 **Berkeley Street** W1J
74 A6 **Bermondsey Street** SE1
74 E7 **Bermondsey Wall East** SE16
74 C6 **Bermondsey Wall West** SE16
68 D4 **Bernard Street** WC1N
68 A5 **Berners Mews** W1T
68 A5 **Berners Place** W1T
68 A5 **Berners Street** W1T
74 D3 **Berner Terrace** * E1
75 K2 **Berry Cottages** * E14
73 J7 **Berryfield Road** SE17
69 H2 **Berry Place** EC1V
69 H3 **Berry Street** EC1V
68 B6 **Berwick Street** W1F
72 B7 **Bessborough Place** SW1V
72 B7 **Bessborough Street** SW1V
68 D6 **Betterton Street** WC2H
74 E4 **Betts Street** E1
69 L2 **Bevenden Street** N1
67 H5 **Beverston Mews** W1H
75 J5 **Bevin Close** SE16
74 D7 **Bevington Street** SE16
68 F1 **Bevin Way** N1
74 B2 **Bevis Marks** EC3A
74 F3 **Bewley Street** E1
67 H4 **Bickenhall Street** W1U
68 C2 **Bidborough Street** WC1H
66 B2 **Biddulph Road** W9
74 E3 **Bigland Street** E1
74 A3 **Billiter Square** * EC3M
74 A3 **Billiter Street** EC3M
76 E6 **Billson Street** E14
70 C6 **Bina Gardens** SW5
67 J4 **Bingham Place** W1U
67 K7 **Binney Street** W1K
69 L7 **Birchen Lane** EC3V
75 M3 **Birchfield Street** E14
72 A3 **Birdcage Walk** SW1H
67 K6 **Bird Street** W1U
68 D1 **Birkenhead Street** N1
66 C6 **Bishop's Bridge Road** W2
69 H6 **Bishop's Court** EC4M
74 A2 **Bishopsgate** EC2M
74 A1 **Bishopsgate Arcade** EC2M
73 G5 **Bishop's Terrace** SE11
73 J3 **Bittern Street** SE1
69 M3 **Blackall Street** EC2A
67 J7 **Blackburne's Mews** W1K
69 H8 **Blackfriars Bridge** SE1
69 H7 **Black Friars Lane** EC4V
69 H7 **Blackfriars Passage** EC4V
73 H1 **Blackfriars Road** SE1
69 H7 **Blackfriars Underpass** EC4V
73 L4 **Black Horse Court** * SE1
71 H6 **Blacklands Terrace** SW3
66 B8 **Black Lion Gate** W8
72 E6 **Black Prince Road** SE11
74 A6 **Black Swan Yard** SE1
76 E1 **Blackwall Way** E14
73 K6 **Blackwood Street** SE17
67 G4 **Blandford Square** NW1
67 H5 **Blandford Street** W1U
69 G5 **Bleeding Heart Yard** * EC1N
67 L6 **Blenheim Street** W1K
69 K1 **Bletchley Street** N1
70 A4 **Blithfield Street** W8
66 C4 **Blomfield Road** W2
69 M5 **Blomfield Street** EC2M
66 C5 **Blomfield Villas** W2
67 L7 **Bloomfield Place** W1K
71 J6 **Bloomfield Terrace** SW1W
68 D5 **Bloomsbury Place** WC1A
68 D5 **Bloomsbury Square** WC1A
68 C5 **Bloomsbury Street** WC1B
68 D5 **Bloomsbury Way** WC1A
75 K2 **Blount Street** E14
74 C4 **Blue Anchor Yard** E1
71 M2 **Blue Ball Yard** SW1A
67 K1 **Blue Bridge** NW1
75 K4 **Blyth's Wharf** * E14
76 D2 **Boardwalk Place** E14
75 J1 **Bohn Road** E1
66 F3 **Boldero Place** * NW8
70 F3 **Bolney Gate** SW7
67 L4 **Bolsover Street** W1W
69 G6 **Bolt Court** * EC4A
70 B6 **Bolton Gardens** SW5
70 C7 **Bolton Gardens Mews** SW10
70 C7 **The Boltons** SW10
71 L1 **Bolton Street** W1J
72 B7 **Bonaparte Mews** SW1V
72 D8 **Bondway** SW8
69 L4 **Bonhill Street** EC2A
72 E8 **Bonnington Square** SW8
69 J7 **Booth Lane** EC4V
69 M2 **Boot Street** N1
69 H1 **Boreas Walk** N1
73 K3 **Borough High Street** SE1
73 H4 **Borough Road** SE1
73 J3 **Borough Square** SE1
73 J7 **Borrett Close** SE17
76 A8 **Borthwick Street** SE8
71 K5 **Boscobel Place** SW1W
66 E4 **Boscobel Street** W2
74 B6 **Boss Street** * SE1
67 G3 **Boston Place** NW1
68 E4 **Boswell Court** WC1N
68 D4 **Boswell Street** WC1N
69 M7 **Botolph Alley** EC3R
69 M7 **Botolph Lane** EC3R
66 A6 **Bott's Mews** W2
75 J3 **Boulcott Street** E1
73 K8 **Boundary Lane** SE17
73 H2 **Boundary Row** SE1
68 B7 **Bourchier Street** W1F
67 L7 **Bourdon Place** W1K
67 L7 **Bourdon Street** W1K
67 M5 **Bourlet Close** W1T
68 F4 **Bourne Estate** * EC1N
71 J6 **Bourne Street** SW1W
66 B5 **Bourne Terrace** W2
66 E6 **Bouverie Place** W2
69 G6 **Bouverie Street** EC4Y
69 K6 **Bow Churchyard** * EC4M
73 G7 **Bowden Street** SE11
75 H3 **Bower Street** E1
71 H3 **Bowland Yard** * SW1X
69 K7 **Bow Lane** EC4M
75 M4 **Bowley Street** E14
69 G3 **Bowling Green Lane** EC1R
73 L2 **Bowling Green Place** * SE1
72 F8 **Bowling Green Street** SE11
69 M2 **Bowling Green Walk** N1
74 D3 **Bowmans Mews** E1
68 D6 **Bow Street** WC2E
74 D3 **Boyd Street** E1
73 H3 **Boyfield Street** SE1
73 K8 **Boyson Road** SE17
69 K4 **Brackley Street** EC2Y
73 L8 **Bradenham Close** SE17
66 B4 **Braden Street** * W9
69 G1 **Bradley's Close** N1
75 K2 **Bradshaw Cottages** * E14
73 G2 **Brad Street** SE1
73 H7 **Braganza Street** SE17
74 C3 **Braham Street** E1
70 F8 **Bramerton Street** SW3
70 B6 **Bramham Gardens** SW5
75 K3 **Branch Road** E14
73 H8 **Brandon Estate** SE17
69 K5 **Brandon Mews** * EC2Y
73 K6 **Brandon Street** SE17
72 F7 **Brangton Road** SE11
75 H6 **Bray Crescent** SE16
75 G2 **Brayford Square** E1
71 H6 **Bray Place** SW3
69 K7 **Bread Street** EC4V
68 F6 **Bream's Buildings** WC2A
70 D6 **Brechin Place** SW7
74 E4 **Breezer's Hill** E1W
70 D3 **Bremner Road** SW7
67 G5 **Brendon Street** W1H
75 K2 **Brenton Street** E14
71 L4 **Bressenden Place** SW1E
73 L7 **Brettell Street** SE17
68 A7 **Brewer Street** W1B
74 B6 **Brewery Square** SE1
74 F6 **Brewhouse Lane** E1W
75 K5 **Brewhouse Walk** SE16
69 H3 **Brewhouse Yard** EC1V
68 F7 **Brick Court** * EC4Y
71 K2 **Brick Street** W1J
69 H6 **Bride Court** * EC4V
69 H6 **Bride Lane** EC4Y
69 H1 **Bridel Mews** EC1V
74 C8 **Bridewain Street** SE1
69 H7 **Bridewell Place** EC4V
74 F5 **Bridewell Place** E1W
67 L4 **Bridford Mews** W1B
76 E2 **Bridge House Quay** E14
66 F1 **Bridgeman Street** NW8
71 L5 **Bridge Place** SW1V
74 D5 **Bridgeport Place** * E1W
72 C3 **Bridge Street** SW1P
69 J4 **Bridgewater Square** * EC2Y
69 K4 **Bridgewater Street** EC2Y
68 B1 **Bridgeway Street** NW1
68 A7 **Bridle Lane** W1F
66 A6 **Bridstow Place** W2
75 L4 **Brightlingsea Place** E14
68 C1 **Brill Place** NW1
74 F3 **Brinsley Street** * E1
73 H2 **Brinton Walk** SE1
69 H4 **Briset Street** EC1M
66 C4 **Bristol Gardens** W9
66 C4 **Bristol Mews** W9
76 B6 **Britannia Road** E14
68 E2 **Britannia Street** WC1X
69 L2 **Britannia Walk** N1
70 F7 **Britten Street** SW3
69 H4 **Britton Street** EC1M
67 L7 **Broadbent Street** * W1K
68 D6 **Broad Court** * WC2E
66 F4 **Broadley Street** NW8
66 F4 **Broadley Terrace** NW8
67 J5 **Broadstone Place** W1U
69 M5 **Broad Street Avenue** EC2M
69 M5 **Broad Street Place** EC2M
70 C1 **The Broad Walk** W8
73 G1 **Broadwall** SE1
72 B4 **Broadway** SW1H
68 A7 **Broadwick Street** W1F
69 G4 **Broad Yard** EC1M
73 K4 **Brockham Street** SE1
75 H3 **Brodlove Lane** E1W
74 F2 **Bromehead Street** * E1
75 J2 **Bromley Street** E1
71 H3 **Brompton Arcade** * SW1X
70 A8 **Brompton Park Crescent** SW6
71 G4 **Brompton Place** SW3
70 F5 **Brompton Road** SW3
70 F4 **Brompton Square** SW3
73 K7 **Bronti Close** SE17
73 G5 **Brook Drive** SE1
69 G5 **Brooke's Market** * EC1N
69 G5 **Brooke Street** EC1N
67 H7 **Brook Gate** W2
66 D7 **Brook Mews North** W2
67 L7 **Brook's Mews** W1K
66 E7 **Brook Street** W2
67 K7 **Brook Street** W1K
67 K7 **Brown Hart Gardens** W1K
66 D3 **Browning Close** * W9
67 K5 **Browning Mews** * W1G
73 K6 **Browning Street** SE17
68 E3 **Brownlow Mews** WC1X
68 F5 **Brownlow Street** WC1R
67 G5 **Brown Street** W1H
66 A5 **Brunel Estate** * W2
75 G7 **Brunel Road** SE16
74 B1 **Brune Street** E1
74 B6 **Brunswick Court** SE1
70 A2 **Brunswick Gardens** W8
67 H6 **Brunswick Mews** W1H
67 K4 **Brunswick Place** NW1
69 L2 **Brunswick Place** N1
75 J8 **Brunswick Quay** SE16
68 D3 **Brunswick Square** WC1N
75 K3 **Brunton Place** E14
74 B1 **Brushfield Street** E1
67 L7 **Bruton Lane** W1J
67 L7 **Bruton Place** W1K
67 L7 **Bruton Street** W1J
75 L6 **Bryan Road** SE16
67 H5 **Bryanston Mews East** W1H
67 G5 **Bryanston Mews West** W1H
67 G5 **Bryanston Place** W1H
67 H5 **Bryanston Square** W1H
67 H7 **Bryanston Street** W1H
68 C8 **Brydges Place** WC2N
71 M4 **Buckingham Gate** SW1E
71 M3 **Buckingham Mews** * SW1E
71 K6 **Buckingham Palace Road** SW1W
71 M4 **Buckingham Place** SW1E
68 D8 **Buckingham Street** WC2N
69 M1 **Buckland Street** N1

Dorset Square - Harley Place 79

67 H4 Dorset Square NW1
67 H5 Dorset Street W1U
68 E3 Doughty Mews WC1N
68 E3 Doughty Street WC1N
76 D7 Douglas Place E14
72 B6 Douglas Street SW1P
70 C4 Douro Place W8
74 E5 Douthwaite Square E1W
69 L6 Dove Court * EC2R
70 F7 Dovehouse Street SW3
70 C6 Dove Mews SW5
67 L8 Dover Street W1J
69 L7 Dowgate Hill EC4R
66 B4 Downfield Close W9
72 C2 Downing Street SW1A
71 K2 Down Street W1J
71 K2 Down Street Mews W1J
75 K6 Downtown Road SE16
73 J2 Doyce Street * SE1
71 J5 D'oyley Street SW1X
73 J8 Draco Street SE17
75 J6 Drake Close SE16
68 E5 Drake Street WC1N
73 J5 Draper Estate SE17
71 G5 Draycott Avenue SW3
71 H6 Draycott Place SW3
71 H5 Draycott Terrace SW3
70 A3 Drayson Mews W8
70 D7 Drayton Gardens SW10
74 B7 Druid Street SE1
68 B2 Drummond Crescent NW1
72 B7 Drummond Gate SW1V
74 E8 Drummond Road SE16
67 M3 Drummond Street NW1
74 C2 Drum Street E1
68 D6 Drury Lane WC2B
68 D6 Dryden Street WC2E
67 L5 Duchess Mews W1G
67 L5 Duchess Street W1B
73 G1 Duchy Street SE1
68 B6 Duck Lane W1F
66 D5 Dudley Street * W2
70 E7 Dudmaston Mews SW3
69 K3 Dufferin Avenue EC1Y
69 K4 Dufferin Street EC1Y
67 A7 Dufour's Place W1F
71 K3 Duke of Wellington Place SW1A
68 A8 Duke of York Street SW1Y
70 A2 Dukes Lane W8
67 J6 Duke's Mews W1U
74 B3 Duke's Place EC3A
68 C2 Duke's Road NW1
67 J6 Duke Street W1H
73 M1 Duke Street Hill SE1
68 A8 Duke Street St James's W1J
67 K7 Duke's Yard W1K
68 C8 Duncannon Street WC2N
69 H1 Duncan Terrace N1
74 F3 Dunch Street E1
74 E6 Dundee Street E1W
75 H2 Dunelm Street E1
74 C8 Dunlop Place SE16
67 H7 Dunraven Street W1K
67 K4 Dunstable Mews W1G
75 H1 Dunstan Houses * E1
74 A3 Dunster Court EC3M
73 L3 Dunsterville Way SE1
71 H3 Duplex Ride SW1X
75 J2 Dupont Street E14
68 D8 Durham House Street * WC2N
71 H7 Durham Place SW3
75 J1 Durham Row E1
72 E7 Durham Street SE11
66 A6 Durham Terrace W2
74 E1 Durward Street E1
67 H5 Durweston Mews * W1U
76 E1 Duthie Street E14
69 G5 Dyer's Buildings EC4A
68 C6 Dyott Street WC1A
69 M4 Dysart Street EC2A

E

69 H4 Eagle Court EC1M
70 D6 Eagle Place SW10
68 E5 Eagle Street WC1R
70 A7 Eardley Crescent SW5
68 C7 Earlham Street WC2H
70 B6 Earl's Court Gardens SW5
70 A5 Earl's Court Road SW5
70 A7 Earl's Court Square SW5
69 H2 Earlstoke Estate EC1V
69 H2 Earlstoke Street EC1V
69 M4 Earl Street EC2A
68 C6 Earnshaw Street WC1A
72 B4 East Arbour Street E1
66 D6 Eastbourne Mews W2
66 D6 Eastbourne Terrace W2
67 M6 Eastcastle Street W1W
69 M7 Eastcheap EC3M
76 C6 East Ferry Road E14
75 K1 Eastfield Street E14
69 G6 East Harding Street EC4A
74 F1 East Mount Street * E1
76 F8 Eastney Street SE10
72 F3 Easton Street WC1X
69 H5 East Poultry Avenue EC1M
69 L2 East Road N1
74 C4 East Smithfield E1W
73 K7 East Street SE17
74 C3 East Tenter Street E1
71 J5 Eaton Close SW1W
71 J5 Eaton Gate SW1W
71 L4 Eaton Lane SW1W
71 J5 Eaton Mews North SW1X
71 K5 Eaton Mews South SW1W
71 J5 Eaton Mews West SW1W
71 J5 Eaton Place SW1X
71 K4 Eaton Row SW1W
71 K5 Eaton Square SW1W
71 J5 Eaton Terrace SW1W
71 J5 Eaton Terrace Mews SW1X
72 E8 Ebbisham Drive SW8
69 L2 Ebenezer Street N1
71 K6 Ebury Bridge SW1W
71 K7 Ebury Bridge Road SW1W
71 K5 Ebury Mews SW1W
71 K5 Ebury Mews East SW1W
71 K6 Ebury Square SW1W
71 K6 Ebury Street SW1W
71 K4 Eccleston Mews SW1X
71 L5 Eccleston Place SW1W
71 L6 Eccleston Square SW1V
71 L6 Eccleston Square Mews SW1V
71 K4 Eccleston Street SW1W
66 A3 Edbrooke Road W9
70 A4 Eden Close W8
70 A1 Edge Street W8
66 E4 Edgware Road W2
71 G3 Edinburgh Gate W2
75 J3 Edward Mann Close East * E1
75 J3 Edward Mann Close West * E1
67 L1 Edward Mews * NW1
67 J6 Edwards Mews W1H
70 F5 Egerton Crescent SW3
70 F5 Egerton Gardens SW3
71 G4 Egerton Gardens Mews SW3
71 G4 Egerton Place * SW3
71 G4 Egerton Terrace SW3
73 K5 Elba Place * SE17
70 B4 Eldon Road W8
69 L5 Eldon Street EC2M
73 J5 Elephant & Castle SE1
74 F6 Elephant Lane SE16
73 J5 Elephant Road SE17
75 H3 Elf Row E1W
75 K7 Elgar Street SE16
66 B2 Elgin Avenue W9
66 C2 Elgin Mews North W9
66 C2 Elgin Mews South W9
69 H1 Elia Mews N1
69 H1 Elia Street N1
73 M4 Elim Street SE1
71 L6 Elizabeth Bridge SW1W
66 D3 Elizabeth Close * W9
75 K4 Elizabeth Square SE16
71 K5 Elizabeth Street SW1W
74 D3 Ellen Street E1
73 H5 Elliott's Row SE11
71 J5 Ellis Street SW1X
70 E7 Elm Park Gardens SW3
70 D7 Elm Park Lane SW3
70 D8 Elm Park Road SW3
70 E7 Elm Place SW7
66 D7 Elms Mews W2
68 F4 Elm Street WC1X
66 E1 Elm Tree Close NW8
66 E2 Elm Tree Road NW8
66 B3 Elnathan Mews W9
75 K1 Elsa Cottages * E14
75 J1 Elsa Street E1
66 A5 Elsie Lane Court W2
73 M6 Elsted Street SE17
70 D4 Elvaston Mews SW7
70 C4 Elvaston Place SW7
72 B5 Elverton Street SW1P
69 G5 Ely Place EC1N
71 G6 Elystan Place SW3
70 F6 Elystan Street SW3
71 H8 Embankment Gardens SW3
72 D1 Embankment Place WC2N
74 E7 Emba Street SE16
68 E4 Emerald Street WC1N
73 J1 Emerson Street SE1
72 A5 Emery Hill Street SW1P
73 G3 Emery Street SE1
70 C5 Emperor's Gate SW7
76 F6 Empire Wharf Road E14
70 A7 Empress Place SW5
73 K8 Empress Street SE17
69 H3 Enclave Court EC1V
68 C6 Endell Street WC2H
68 B3 Endsleigh Gardens WC1H
68 B3 Endsleigh Place WC1H
68 B3 Endsleigh Street WC1H
67 G4 Enford Street W1H
74 C7 Enid Street SE1
70 F4 Ennismore Gardens SW7
70 F3 Ennismore Gardens Mews SW7
70 F3 Ennismore Mews SW7
70 F4 Ennismore Street SW7
74 D3 Ensign Street E1
70 D6 Ensor Mews SW7
76 B6 Epping Close E14
69 L3 Epworth Street EC2A
72 C6 Erasmus Street SW1P
74 F1 Erlich Cottages * E1
69 K4 Errol Street EC1Y
66 A3 Essendine Road W9
68 F7 Essex Court * WC2R
68 F7 Essex Street WC2R
72 B6 Esterbrooke Street SW1P
72 F6 Ethelred Estate SE11
73 K6 Ethel Street * SE17
69 K2 Europa Place EC1V
67 M3 Euston Road NW1
68 B3 Euston Square NW1
68 A3 Euston Street NW1
70 D7 Evelyn Gardens SW10
69 L1 Evelyn Walk N1
68 A1 Eversholt Street NW1
67 M2 Everton Buildings NW1
73 J2 Ewer Street SE1
75 H1 Ewhurst Close E1
68 B8 Excel Court WC2H
74 A1 Exchange Arcade EC2M
68 D7 Exchange Court * WC2E
74 A1 Exchange Square * EC2A
68 D7 Exeter Street WC2E
70 E3 Exhibition Road SW7
69 G3 Exmouth Market EC1R
68 A2 Exmouth Mews * NW1
75 G2 Exmouth Street * E1
73 M6 Exon Street SE17
72 F2 Exton Street SE1
69 G4 Eyre Street Hill EC1R

F

76 D7 Factory Place E14
69 L1 Fairbank Estate N1
74 D3 Fairclough Street E1
71 G4 Fairholt Street SW7
74 B6 Fair Street SE1
68 B6 Falconberg Court * W1D
73 J1 Falcon Close SE1
69 J1 Falcon Court N1
73 K4 Falmouth Road SE1
69 J4 Fann Street EC1M
69 M1 Fanshaw Street N1
68 B6 Fareham Street * W1F
70 A1 Farmer Street W8
70 A8 Farm Lane SW6
67 K8 Farm Street W1J
74 E7 Farncombe Street SE16
70 B7 Farnell Mews SW5
73 J1 Farnham Place SE1
72 E7 Farnham Royal SE11
75 M3 Farrance Street E14
70 C8 Farrier Walk SW10
69 G3 Farringdon Lane EC1R
68 F3 Farringdon Road WC1X
69 H5 Farringdon Street EC1A
75 K5 Farrins Rents SE16
75 J7 Farrow Place SE16
74 C7 Farthing Alley SE1
74 F5 Farthing Fields E1W
74 C1 Fashion Street E1
73 H7 Faunce Street SE17
70 C8 Fawcett Street SW10
76 F8 Feathers Place SE10
69 L3 Featherstone Street EC1Y
74 A3 Fenchurch Avenue EC3M
74 A3 Fenchurch Buildings EC3M
74 B3 Fenchurch Place * EC3M
69 M7 Fenchurch Street EC3M
74 B8 Fendall Street SE1
73 M2 Fenning Street SE1
76 A6 Ferguson's Close E14
72 F2 Fernsbury Street WC1X
76 D7 Ferry Street E14
69 G6 Fetter Lane EC4A
68 F5 Field Court WC1R
74 D2 Fieldgate Street E1
73 J7 Fielding Street SE17
68 E1 Field Street WC1X
70 B8 Finborough Road SW10
69 M6 Finch Lane EC3V
75 K8 Finland Street SE16
69 M5 Finsbury Avenue * EC2M
69 L5 Finsbury Circus EC2M
69 G3 Finsbury Estate EC1R
69 M4 Finsbury Market EC2A
69 L5 Finsbury Pavement EC2A
69 L4 Finsbury Square EC2A
69 L4 Finsbury Street EC1Y
71 G5 First Street SW3
75 K5 Fir Trees Close SE16
75 J6 Fishermans Drive SE16
68 E5 Fisher Street WC1B
66 E3 Fisherton Street NW8
69 L7 Fish Street Hill EC3R
72 F5 Fitzalan Street SE11
67 J6 Fitzhardinge Street W1H
67 L8 Fitzmaurice Place W1J
67 M4 Fitzroy Mews W1W
67 M4 Fitzroy Square W1T
67 M3 Fitzroy Street NW1
75 K3 Flamborough Street E14
74 D4 Flank Street E1
68 C2 Flaxman Terrace WC1H
69 H6 Fleet Place EC4M
68 E2 Fleet Square WC1X
68 F6 Fleet Street WC2R
73 H8 Fleming Road SE17
74 D3 Fletcher Street E1
73 L6 Flint Street SE17
68 C6 Flitcroft Street WC2H
74 D6 Flockton Street SE16
71 G7 Flood Street SW3
71 G8 Flood Walk SW3
68 D7 Floral Street WC2E
74 C1 Flower & Dean Walk E1
67 M5 Foley Street W1W
76 E3 Folly Wall E14
74 D3 Forbes Street E1
74 E2 Fordham Street E1
74 F2 Ford Square E1
69 L5 Fore Street EC2Y
66 C4 Formosa Street W9
67 G6 Forset Street W1H
73 H8 Forsyth Gardens SE17
74 B1 Fort Street * E1
69 K4 Fortune Street EC1Y
72 E3 Forum Magnum Square SE1
66 C8 Fosbury Mews W2
66 A4 Foscote Mews W9
69 J6 Foster Lane EC2V
68 A6 Foubert's Place W1F
70 E6 Foulis Terrace SW7
75 J5 Foundry Close SE16
68 A3 Foundry Mews NW1
74 E7 Fountain Green Square SE16
74 C1 Fournier Street E1
74 E5 Fowey Close E1W
69 J4 Fox & Knot Street * EC1M
66 E4 Frampton Street NW8
72 A5 Francis Street SW1P
70 E4 Frankland Road SW7
71 H6 Franklin's Row SW3
73 G3 Frazier Street SE1
74 D8 Frean Street SE16
67 G7 Frederick Close W2
73 H7 Frederick Road * SE17
69 K6 Frederick's Place * EC2R
75 J4 Frederick Square SE16
69 H1 Frederick's Row EC1V
68 E2 Frederick Street WC1X
71 J3 Frederic Mews * SW1X
73 M6 Freemantle Street SE17
73 H1 Friars Close * SE1
76 D5 Friars Mead E14
69 K7 Friday Street EC4V
69 H2 Friend Street EC1V
76 A8 Frigate Mews SE8
68 B6 Frith Street W1D
69 K4 Frobisher Crescent * EC2Y
74 C1 Frostic Walk E1
74 B1 Frying Pan Alley E1
74 E1 Fulbourne Street E1
74 F7 Fulford Street SE16
70 D8 Fulham Road SW10
69 L1 Fullwood's Mews * N1
66 C7 Fulton Mews W2
68 F5 Fulwood Place WC1R
69 G5 Furnival Street EC4A
69 J7 Fye Foot Lane * EC4V
72 B5 Fynes Street SW1P

G

69 G8 Gabriel's Wharf SE1
74 B6 Gainsford Street SE1
76 D4 Galbraith Street E14
68 D5 Galen Place WC1A
75 H6 Galleon Close SE16
69 K2 Galway Street EC1V
73 H2 Gambia Street SE1
68 A7 Ganton Street * W1F
67 J5 Garbutt Place * W1U
68 F7 Garden Court * WC2R
66 D1 Garden Road NW8
73 H4 Garden Row SE1
75 H1 Garden Street E1
66 C5 Garden Studios * W2
72 B6 Garden Terrace SW1V
69 M3 Garden Walk EC2A
69 J7 Gardners Lane EC4V
69 J2 Gard Street EC1V
76 A1 Garford Street E14
69 K7 Garlick Hill EC4V
69 G2 Garnault Mews EC1R
69 G2 Garnault Place EC1R
74 F4 Garnet Street E1W
69 K3 Garrett Street EC1Y
68 D7 Garrick Street WC2E
68 C7 Garrick Yard WC2N
66 A6 Garway Road W2
76 E1 Gaselee Street E14
72 F7 Gasholder Place SE11
70 C5 Gaspar Close * SW5
70 B5 Gaspar Mews SW5
74 F8 Gataker Street * SE16
66 F3 Gateforth Street NW8
73 K1 Gatehouse Square SE1
71 G3 Gate Mews SW7
68 E5 Gate Street WC1V
73 K8 Gateway SE17
71 K7 Gatliff Road SW1W
73 J4 Gaunt Street SE1
73 M5 Gavel Street * SE17
76 A5 Gaverick Street E14
72 C4 Gayfere Street SW1P
73 H4 Gaywood Street SE1
73 H7 Gaza Street SE17
74 C7 Gedling Place SE1
67 K6 Gees Court W1U
69 J3 Gee Street EC1V
73 H5 George Mathers Road * SE11
68 A2 George Mews NW1
74 D7 George Row SE16
67 H6 George Street W1H
69 L7 George Yard EC3V
67 K7 George Yard W1K
73 H4 Geraldine Street SE11
71 K5 Gerald Road SW1W
68 C7 Gerrard Place * W1D
68 B7 Gerrard Street W1D
73 G3 Gerridge Street SE1
72 E6 Gibson Road SE11
68 D5 Gilbert Place WC1A
73 H5 Gilbert Road SE11
67 K7 Gilbert Street W1K
67 L5 Gildea Street W1B
71 L5 Gillingham Mews SW1V
71 M5 Gillingham Row SW1V
71 M5 Gillingham Street SW1V
74 E8 Gillison Walk SE16
75 M3 Gill Street E14
66 D5 Gilpin Close W2
70 D7 Gilston Road SW10
69 H5 Giltspur Street EC1A
73 H4 Gladstone Street SE1
76 C8 Glaisher Street SE8
75 H4 Glamis Place E1W
75 G4 Glamis Road E1W
71 M7 Glasgow Terrace SW1V
73 H3 Glasshill Street SE1
75 H3 Glasshouse Fields E1W
68 A7 Glasshouse Street W1B
72 D7 Glasshouse Walk SE11
69 J4 Glasshouse Yard EC1A
75 G3 Glastonbury Place E1
70 F7 Glebe Place SW3
70 C6 Gledhow Gardens SW5
76 E6 Glenaffric Avenue E14
76 C4 Glengall Bridge E14
76 D4 Glengall Grove E14
76 E6 Glengarnock Avenue E14
76 D3 Glen Terrace E14
67 H3 Glentworth Street NW1
76 E6 Glenworth Avenue E14
75 J5 Globe Pond Road SE16
73 L3 Globe Street SE1
74 B4 Gloucester Court EC3R
66 C6 Gloucester Gardens W2
66 D6 Gloucester Mews W2
66 C6 Gloucester Mews West W2
67 H5 Gloucester Place W1U
67 H5 Gloucester Place Mews W1H
70 C4 Gloucester Road SW7
66 F7 Gloucester Square W2
71 M7 Gloucester Street SW1V
66 B6 Gloucester Terrace W2
70 A2 Gloucester Walk W8
69 G2 Gloucester Way EC1R
71 G5 Glynde Mews SW3
72 E7 Glyn Street SE11
71 G6 Godfrey Street SW3
72 D7 Goding Street SE11
69 J6 Godliman Street * EC4V
69 K1 Godwin Close N1
69 K3 Golden Lane EC1Y
69 J4 Golden Lane Estate EC1Y
68 A7 Golden Square W1F
74 E3 Golding Street E1
69 K6 Goldsmith Street EC2V
75 G8 Gomm Road SE16
68 A5 Goodge Place W1T
68 A5 Goodge Street W1T
74 D2 Goodman's Stile E1
74 B3 Goodman's Yard EC3N
74 C8 Goodwin Close SE16
68 C7 Goodwins Court WC2N
69 L7 Gophir Lane * EC4R
70 A2 Gordon Place W8
68 B3 Gordon Square WC1H
68 B3 Gordon Street WC1H
70 D4 Gore Street SW7
74 B2 Goring Street EC3A
67 L5 Gosfield Street W1W
68 B6 Goslett Yard W1D
69 H2 Goswell Place EC1V
69 H2 Goswell Road EC1V
69 G6 Gough Square EC4A
68 F3 Gough Street WC1X
74 B2 Goulston Street E1
68 B5 Gower Mews WC1E
68 B3 Gower Place WC1H
68 B3 Gower Street WC1E
74 D2 Gower's Walk E1
69 M7 Gracechurch Street EC3V
74 D4 Grace's Alley E1
66 D1 Graces Mews * NW8
73 M3 Graduate Place SE1
67 M3 Grafton Mews W1T
68 B2 Grafton Place NW1
67 L8 Grafton Street W1J
67 M4 Grafton Way W1W
69 J1 Graham Street N1
71 J6 Graham Terrace SW1W
67 M1 Granby Terrace NW1
69 H5 Grand Avenue EC1M
69 J1 Grand Junction Wharf * N1
66 A4 Grand Union Canal Walk W2
74 A8 Grange Road SE1
74 B8 The Grange SE1
74 A8 Grange Walk SE1
74 B8 Grange Walk Mews SE1
74 B8 Grange Yard SE1
71 K2 Grantham Place W1J
66 B2 Grantully Road W9
67 J6 Granville Place W1H
66 A1 Granville Road NW6
68 F2 Granville Street WC1X
68 C6 Grape Street WC2H
72 E6 Graphite Square SE11
74 E2 Gravel Lane E1
68 D1 Gray's Inn Road WC1X
68 F5 Gray's Inn Square WC1R
73 G3 Gray Street SE1
67 K6 Gray's Yard * W1U
67 M6 Great Castle Street W1B
67 G4 Great Central Street NW1
68 B6 Great Chapel Street W1F
72 C4 Great College Street SW1P
67 H6 Great Cumberland Mews W1H
67 H6 Great Cumberland Place W1H
73 L4 Great Dover Street SE1
69 M3 Great Eastern Street EC2A
72 C3 Great George Street SW1H
73 J2 Great Guildford Street SE1
68 E4 Great James Street WC1N
67 M6 Great Marlborough Street W1F
73 L2 Great Maze Pond SE1
69 G6 Great New Street * EC4A
74 D1 Greatorex Street E1
68 D4 Great Ormond Street WC1N
68 F2 Great Percy Street WC1X
72 B4 Great Peter Street SW1P
67 M5 Great Portland Street W1W
68 A7 Great Pulteney Street W1F
68 E6 Great Queen Street WC2B
68 C5 Great Russell Street W1T
74 A2 Great St Helen's EC3A
69 K7 Great St Thomas Apostle EC4V
72 C1 Great Scotland Yard SW1A
72 C4 Great Smith Street SW1P
73 H2 Great Suffolk Street SE1
69 H4 Great Sutton Street EC1V
69 L6 Great Swan Alley EC2R
67 L4 Great Titchfield Street W1W
74 A4 Great Tower Street EC3R
69 K7 Great Trinity Lane EC4V
68 E5 Great Turnstile * WC1V
69 M6 Great Winchester Street EC2N
68 B7 Great Windmill Street W1D
75 K2 Greaves Cottages * E14
68 B6 Greek Street W1D
75 J6 Greenacre Square SE16
69 H6 Green Arbour Court * EC4M
74 F5 Green Bank E1W
66 F1 Greenberry Street NW8
72 A5 Greencoat Place SW1P
72 A5 Greencoat Row SW1P
74 C2 Green Dragon Yard E1
76 A7 Greenfell Mansions * SE8
74 D2 Greenfield Road E1
73 G3 Greenham Close SE1
69 H5 Greenhill's Rents * EC1M
68 B7 Green's Court W1F
67 J7 Green Street W1K
69 G2 Green Terrace EC1R
73 M4 Green Walk SE1
67 L4 Greenwell Street W1W
76 C4 Greenwich View E14
68 E3 Green Yard WC1X
73 G2 Greet Street SE1
70 B3 Gregory Place W8
73 J8 Greig Terrace SE17
75 L4 Grenade Street E14
66 F3 Grendon Street NW8
70 C5 Grenville Place SW7
68 D3 Grenville Street WC1N
69 J6 Gresham Street EC2V
68 B5 Gresse Street W1T
69 G5 Greville Street EC1N
72 B4 Greycoat Place SW1P
72 B5 Greycoat Street SW1P
74 B8 Grigg's Place SE1
72 F3 Grindal Street SE1
69 L6 Grocers' Hall Court * EC2R
71 K4 Groom Place SW1X
71 L8 Grosvenor Bridge SW1V
71 J5 Grosvenor Cottages SW1X
71 J3 Grosvenor Crescent SW1X
71 J3 Grosvenor Crescent Mews SW1X
71 L4 Grosvenor Gardens SW1W
71 L4 Grosvenor Gardens Mews East * SW1W
71 L4 Grosvenor Gardens Mews North SW1W
67 H8 Grosvenor Gate W2
67 L7 Grosvenor Hill W1K
71 K3 Grosvenor Place SW1X
71 L8 Grosvenor Road SW1V
67 K7 Grosvenor Square W1K
67 K7 Grosvenor Street W1K
76 E6 Grosvenor Wharf Road E14
73 J3 Grotto Court * SE1
67 J5 Grotto Passage W1U
75 G1 Grove Dwellings * E1
66 D2 Grove End Road NW8
66 F2 Grove Gardens NW8
69 K6 Groveland Court EC4M
69 K6 Guildhall Buildings * EC2V
69 K6 Guildhall Yard EC2V
71 M5 Guildhouse Street SW1V
68 E4 Guilford Place WC1N
68 E4 Guilford Street WC1N
74 A8 Guinness Square SE1
71 H6 Guinness Trust Estate SW3
75 L8 Gulliver Street SE16
74 B1 Gun Street E1
74 C2 Gunthorpe Street E1
75 J6 Gunwhale Close SE16
70 F6 Guthrie Street SW3
69 K6 Gutter Lane EC2V
73 L3 Guy Street SE1

H

69 M2 Haberdasher Place N1
69 L2 Haberdasher Street N1
74 F3 Hainton Close E1
74 F1 Halcrow Street * E1
74 C2 Half Moon Passage E1
71 L1 Half Moon Street W1J
70 A8 Halford Road SW6
71 J4 Halkin Arcade SW1X
71 J4 Halkin Mews * SW1X
71 J4 Halkin Place SW1X
71 J3 Halkin Street SW1X
67 L4 Hallam Mews W1B
67 L4 Hallam Street W1W
75 K1 Halley Street E14
66 C6 Hallfield Estate W2
66 D2 Hall Gate NW8
66 E4 Hall Place W2
66 D2 Hall Road NW8
69 H2 Hall Street EC1V
73 M6 Halpin Place SE17
71 G5 Halsey Street SW3
75 K7 Hamilton Close SE16
66 D2 Hamilton Close NW8
66 D2 Hamilton Gardens NW8
71 K2 Hamilton Place W1J
66 C1 Hamilton Terrace NW8
73 L3 Hamlet Way SE1
74 B4 Hammett Street EC3N
68 B1 Hampden Close NW1
67 H6 Hampden Gurney Street W1H
67 M2 Hampstead Road NW1
73 J6 Hampton Street SE17
68 B7 Ham Yard * W1D
74 D1 Hanbury Street E1
68 E5 Hand Court WC1V
68 D3 Handel Street WC1N
73 L3 Hankey Place SE1
75 G1 Hannibal Road E1
68 D7 Hanover Place WC2E
67 L6 Hanover Square W1S
67 G7 Hanover Steps * W2
67 L7 Hanover Street W1S
67 G2 Hanover Terrace NW1
67 G2 Hanover Terrace Mews NW1
71 H4 Hans Crescent SW3
67 M4 Hanson Street W1W
71 H4 Hans Place SW1X
71 G4 Hans Road SW3
71 H4 Hans Street SW1X
68 B5 Hanway Place W1T
68 B6 Hanway Street W1T
66 F5 Harbet Road W2
76 B6 Harbinger Road E14
69 G7 Harcourt Buildings * EC4Y
67 G5 Harcourt Street NW1
70 C7 Harcourt Terrace SW10
73 J8 Harding Close SE17
75 G3 Hardinge Street E1
68 F2 Hardwicke Mews * WC1X
69 G2 Hardwick Street EC1R
73 M2 Hardwidge Street SE1
75 J6 Hardy Close SE16
76 F8 Hardy Cottages * SE10
69 G7 Hare Court * EC4Y
67 G4 Harewood Avenue NW1
67 L6 Harewood Place W1S
67 G4 Harewood Row NW1
72 E8 Harleyford Road SE11
72 F8 Harleyford Street SE11
70 D7 Harley Gardens SW10
67 K5 Harley Place W1G

80 Harley Street - Maple Street

67 K5 Harley Street W1G
73 G5 Harmsworth Mews SE1
73 H7 Harmsworth Street SE17
74 A4 Harp Cross Lane EC3R
73 K4 Harper Road SE1
68 E4 Harpur Street WC1N
71 H3 Harriet Street SW1X
71 H3 Harriet Walk SW1X
70 C6 Harrington Gardens SW7
70 D5 Harrington Road SW7
67 M2 Harrington Street NW1
68 D2 Harrison Street WC1H
67 G6 Harrowby Street W1H
76 D1 Harrow Lane E14
74 B2 Harrow Place E1
66 E5 Harrow Road Flyover W2
66 F4 Harrow Street * NW1
74 A3 Hart Street EC3R
71 G5 Hasker Street SW3
68 C2 Hastings Street WC1H
74 A7 Hatchers Mews SE1
73 G1 Hatfields SE1
66 B6 Hatherley Grove W2
72 A5 Hatherley Street SW1P
69 H4 Hat & Mitre Court EC1M
75 G6 Hatteraick Street SE16
69 G4 Hatton Garden EC1R
69 G4 Hatton Place EC1N
66 E4 Hatton Row * NW8
66 E4 Hatton Street NW8
69 G4 Hatton Wall EC1N
67 L7 Haunch of Venison Yard W1K
76 A3 Havannah Street E14
75 H3 Havering Street E1
69 G1 Haverstock Place N1
69 J1 Haverstock Street N1
75 H6 Hawke Place SE16
74 E3 Hawksmoor Mews * E1
74 B3 Haydon Street EC3N
74 C3 Haydon Walk E1
67 G4 Hayes Place NW1
67 L8 Hay Hill W1J
73 H5 Hayles Street SE11
73 B8 Haymarket SW1Y
69 J4 Hayne Street EC1A
73 M1 Hays Lane SE1
71 K1 Hay's Mews W1J
69 H3 Hayward's Place * EC1R
71 K3 Headfort Place SW1X
75 H3 Head Street E1
73 M6 Hearn's Buildings SE17
68 E3 Heathcote Street WC1N
75 H3 Heckford Street E1W
67 M7 Heddon Street W1S
73 H5 Hedger Street SE11
73 J8 Heiron Street SE17
75 J4 Helena Square SE16
74 D5 Hellings Street E1W
69 K3 Helmet Row EC1V
75 G4 Helsinki Square SE16
73 L5 Hemp Walk SE17
66 E3 Henderson Drive NW8
74 B2 Heneage Lane EC3A
74 C1 Heneage Street E1
70 D8 Henniker Mews SW3
68 D3 Henrietta Mews WC1N
67 K6 Henrietta Place W1G
68 D7 Henrietta Street WC2E
74 D2 Henriques Street E1
73 L5 Henshaw Street SE17
73 G5 Heralds Place SE11
69 G4 Herbal Hill EC1R
71 H4 Herbert Crescent SW1X
68 C3 Herbrand Street WC1N
72 F4 Hercules Road SE1
66 A6 Hereford Mews W2
66 A6 Hereford Road W2
70 D6 Hereford Square SW7
68 F1 Hermes Street N1
66 E5 Hermitage Street W2
74 D5 Hermitage Wall E1W
69 H2 Hermit Street EC1V
76 A2 Heron Quays E14
72 C6 Herrick Street SW1P
71 K1 Hertford Street W1J
76 B1 Hertsmere Road E14
70 B6 Hesper Mews SW5
76 C6 Hesperus Crescent E14
74 E3 Hessel Street E1
73 K5 Heygate Estate SE17
73 J5 Heygate Street SE17
76 D4 Hickin Street E14
72 B6 Hide Place SW1P
68 E5 High Holborn WC1V
69 J7 High Timber Street EC4V
74 E4 The Highway E1
67 G4 Highworth Street * NW1
70 A8 Hildyard Road SW6
73 L6 Hillery Close SE17
66 C7 Hill Gardens Craven * W2
74 F5 Hilliard's Court E1W
66 D1 Hill Road NW8
66 B1 Hillside Close NW6
67 M6 Hills Place W1F
71 K1 Hill Street W1J
69 G6 Hind Court * EC4A
67 K6 Hinde Mews * W1U
67 K6 Hinde Street W1U
74 D4 Hindmarsh Close E1
71 K4 Hobart Place SW1W
74 D1 Hobsons Place E1
70 D8 Hobury Street SW10
69 L2 Hoffman Square * N1
66 D5 Hogan Mews W2
70 A6 Hogarth Place * SW5
70 B6 Hogarth Road SW5
74 F4 Hogshead Passage * E1W
71 J6 Holbein Mews SW1W
71 J6 Holbein Place SW1W
69 G5 Holborn EC1N
69 G5 Holborn Circus EC1N
68 E5 Holborn Place WC1V
69 H5 Holborn Viaduct EC1A
68 E2 Holford Mews * WC1X
68 F2 Holford Street WC1X
68 F1 Holford Yard * N1
70 B2 Holland Place * W8
70 A3 Holland Street W8
69 H8 Holland Street SE1
68 B6 Hollen Street W1F
67 L6 Holles Street W1G
70 D7 Holly Mews SW10
70 C8 Hollywood Mews SW10
70 C8 Hollywood Road SW10
73 G3 Holmes Terrace SE1
68 F4 Holsworthy Square WC1X
75 L6 Holyoake Court SE16
73 H5 Holyoak Road SE11
74 A6 Holyrood Street SE1
69 M4 Holywell Row EC2A
69 M1 Homefield Street * N1
76 A6 Homer Drive E14
67 G5 Homer Row NW1
67 G5 Homer Street NW1
69 J3 Honduras Street EC1V
74 D3 Hooper Street E1
74 C1 Hopetown Street * E1
68 C7 Hop Gardens WC2N
68 B7 Hopkins Street W1F
73 H1 Hoptons Gardens * SE1
69 H8 Hopton Street SE1
73 L8 Hopwood Road SE17
76 E3 Horatio Place E14
72 F5 Hornbeam Close SE11
70 A3 Hornton Place W8
70 A2 Hornton Street W8
75 J3 Horseferry Road E14
72 C5 Horseferry Road SW1P
72 D2 Horse Guards Avenue SW1A
72 C2 Horse Guards Road SW1A
74 B6 Horselydown Lane SE1
76 D7 Horseshoe Close E14
73 K8 Horsley Street SE17
73 K8 Horsman Street SE5
69 H5 Hosier Lane EC1A
76 F7 Hoskins Street SE10
75 G8 Hothfield Place SE16
72 F6 Hotspur Street SE11
68 E6 Houghton Street * WC2B
74 B2 Houndsditch EC3A
73 J6 Howell Walk SE17
72 A4 Howick Place SW1P
68 A4 Howland Mews East W1T
68 A4 Howland Street W1T
75 K7 Howland Way SE16
66 D4 Howley Place W2
69 M2 Hoxton Market N1
69 M2 Hoxton Square N1
75 M1 Huddart Street E3
69 K7 Huggin Hill EC4V
71 L6 Hugh Mews SW1V
72 B5 Hugh Place SW1P
71 L6 Hugh Street SW1V
74 C1 Huguenot Place E1
75 J6 Hull Close SE16
69 J2 Hull Street EC1V
73 K3 Hulme Place SE1
72 E1 Hungerford Bridge SE1
72 F2 Hungerford Street * E1
73 M4 Hunter Close SE1
68 D3 Hunter Street WC1N
68 B4 Huntley Street WC1E
73 M6 Huntsman Street SE17
67 G3 Huntsworth Mews NW1
73 A3 Hutching's Street E14
69 G7 Hutton Street EC4Y
71 K2 Hyde Park Corner W1J
66 F6 Hyde Park Crescent W2
66 E7 Hyde Park Gardens W2
66 F7 Hyde Park Gardens Mews W2
70 C3 Hyde Park Gate W8
70 D3 Hyde Park Gate Mews * SW7
67 G7 Hyde Park Place W2
66 F7 Hyde Park Square W2
66 F7 Hyde Park Street W2

I

74 A4 Idol Lane EC3R
70 B8 Ifield Road SW10
66 B7 Ilchester Gardens W2
73 J6 Iliffe Street SE17
73 J6 Iliffe Yard SE17
70 E4 Imperial College Road SW7
76 B4 Indescon Court E14
74 B3 India Street EC3N
67 A7 Ingestre Place W1F
68 F2 Inglebert Street EC1R
74 F5 Inglefield Square * E1W
76 B5 Inglewood Close E14
72 F5 Ingram Close SE11
67 J2 Inner Circle NW1
66 B6 Inver Court W2
70 A2 Inverness Gardens W8
66 B7 Inverness Mews W2
66 B7 Inverness Place W2
66 B6 Inverness Terrace W2
73 H1 Invicta Plaza SE1
73 L7 Inville Road SE17
69 K6 Ironmonger Lane EC2V
69 K2 Ironmonger Row EC1V
75 H6 Ironside Close SE16
68 C8 Irving Street WC2H
73 H2 Isabella Street SE1
76 E5 Isambard Mews E14
75 G6 Isambard Place SE16
75 L3 Island Row E14
70 A4 Iverna Court W8
70 A4 Iverna Gardens W8
71 G5 Ives Street SW3
67 G4 Ivor Place NW1
70 F6 Ixworth Place SW3

J

74 C6 Jacob Street SE1
67 J5 Jacob's Well Mews W1U
74 B7 Jamaica Road SE1
75 G2 Jamaica Street E1
70 A1 Jameson Street W8
68 D7 James Street WC2E
67 K6 James Street W1U
75 K1 Jamuna Close E14
74 E2 Jane Street E1
76 A4 Janet Street E14
74 E7 Janeway Place SE16
74 E7 Janeway Street SE16
75 J4 Jardine Road E1W
70 D3 Jay Mews SW7
72 A1 Jermyn Street SW1Y
66 F3 Jerome Crescent NW8
69 H3 Jerusalem Passage EC1R
74 B3 Jewry Street EC3N
73 H2 Joan Street SE1
68 E4 Jockey's Fields WC1X
72 F3 Johanna Street * SE1
68 D8 John Adam Street WC2N
66 D5 John Aird Court W2
69 G7 John Carpenter Street EC4Y
74 D7 John Felton Road SE16
74 D4 John Fisher Street E1
72 C6 John Islip Street SW1P
73 L5 John Maurice Close SE17
74 E8 John McKenna Walk SE16
67 L6 John Prince's Street W1G
74 F5 John Rennie Walk E1W
74 D8 John Roll Way SE16
68 E4 John's Mews WC1N
72 A7 Johnson's Place SW1V
75 G3 Johnson Street E1
74 F2 Johns Place E1
68 E4 John Street WC1N
69 J5 John Trundle Highwalk * EC2Y
73 L1 Joiner Street SE1
72 E6 Jonathan Street SE11
69 G2 Joseph Trotter Close EC1R
72 E2 Jubilee Gardens * SE1
68 D7 Jubilee Market * WC2E
71 G6 Jubilee Place SW3
75 G2 Jubilee Street E1
68 D2 Judd Street WC1H
76 C7 Julian Place E14
66 F5 Junction Mews W2
66 F5 Junction Place * W2
75 G4 Juniper Street E1
70 F8 Justice Walk SW3
72 F5 Juxon Street SE11

K

75 H5 Katherine Close SE16
68 E6 Kean Street WC2B
75 J6 Keel Close SE16
68 E6 Keeley Street WC2B
73 L8 Keesey Street SE17
74 E8 Keeton's Road SE16
73 H4 Kell Street SE1
70 B4 Kelso Place W8
68 E6 Kemble Street WC2B
70 A7 Kempsford Gardens SW5
73 G6 Kempsford Road SE11
67 J5 Kendall Place W1U
67 G7 Kendal Steps * W2
67 G6 Kendal Street W2
70 E5 Kendrick Mews SW7
70 E6 Kendrick Place * SW7
73 L6 Kennedy Walk SE17
74 D5 Kennet Street E1W
69 K7 Kennett Wharf Lane EC4V
75 G6 Kenning Street SE16
73 G7 Kennings Way SE11
72 E8 Kennington Grove SE11
72 E7 Kennington Lane SE11
72 F8 Kennington Oval SE11
73 H8 Kennington Park Gardens SE11
73 G7 Kennington Park Place SE17
73 H6 Kennington Park Road SE11
73 G5 Kennington Road SE11
67 J5 Kenrick Place W1U
70 B3 Kensington Church Court W8
70 A1 Kensington Church Street W8
70 A3 Kensington Church Walk * W8
70 C3 Kensington Court W8
70 B4 Kensington Court Gardens * W8
70 B3 Kensington Court Mews * W8
70 B4 Kensington Court Place W8
66 B6 Kensington Gardens Square W2
70 C4 Kensington Gate SW7
70 D3 Kensington Gore SW7
70 A4 Kensington High Street W8
70 B2 Kensington Palace * W8
70 B1 Kensington Palace Gardens W8
70 B3 Kensington Road W8
70 B3 Kensington Square W8
68 D3 Kenton Street WC1H
67 G3 Kent Terrace NW1
71 G3 Kent Yard SW7
70 A6 Kenway Road SW5
68 C4 Keppel Street WC1E
73 K2 Keyse Road SE1
68 D1 Keystone Crescent N1
73 H4 Keyworth Street SE1
66 A1 Kilburn Park Road NW6
66 A6 Kildare Gardens W2
66 A6 Kildare Terrace W2
68 E1 Killick Street N1
75 H6 Kinburn Street SE16
74 E3 Kinder Street E1
73 K6 King and Queen Street SE17
72 C1 King Charles I Island WC2N
72 C3 King Charles Street SW1A
74 F4 King Charles Terrace * E1W
75 G3 King David Lane E1
69 J6 King Edward Street EC1A
74 E7 King Edward the Third Mews SE16
73 G4 King Edward Walk SE1
76 E6 Kingfield Street E14
74 F4 King Henry Terrace * E1W
69 J5 Kinghorn Street * EC1A
73 H3 King James Street SE1
75 J1 King John Street E1
73 M7 Kinglake Estate * SE17
68 A7 Kingly Court * W1B
67 M7 Kingly Street W1B
73 K6 King & Queen Street * SE17
75 J5 King & Queen Wharf * SE16
69 L6 King's Arms Yard EC2R
73 H3 King's Bench Street SE1
69 G7 King's Bench Walk * EC4Y
76 B5 Kingsbridge Court E14
69 H7 Kingscote Street EC4Y
73 J3 King's Court * SE1
68 D1 King's Cross Bridge * WC1X
68 E2 King's Cross Road WC1X
70 B4 Kingsley Mews * W8
74 F4 Kingsley Mews E1W
68 F4 King's Mews WC1N
73 K3 King's Place SE1
69 J2 King Square EC1V
69 G7 Kings Reach * EC4Y
71 J5 King's Road SW1W
71 M5 King's Scholars' Passage SW1P
74 F6 King Stairs Close SE16
69 K6 King Street EC2V
68 D7 King Street WC2E
72 A1 King Street SW1Y
68 E6 Kingsway WC2B
69 G3 Kingsway Place EC1R
69 L8 King William Street EC4R
71 H3 Kinnerton Place North * SW1X
71 J3 Kinnerton Place South * SW1X
71 J3 Kinnerton Street SW1X
71 J3 Kinnerton Yard * SW1X
73 L3 Kipling Estate SE1
73 L3 Kipling Street SE1
74 F7 Kirby Estate SE16
73 M3 Kirby Grove SE1
69 G4 Kirby Street EC1N
75 L1 Kirk's Place E14
70 B5 Knaresborough Place SW5
74 E6 Knighten Street E1W
76 A4 Knighthead Point * E14
69 J7 Knightrider Court * EC4V
69 J7 Knightrider Street EC4V
71 H3 Knightsbridge SW1X
71 H3 Knightsbridge Green * SW1X
73 H6 Knights Walk SE11
67 H4 Knox Street W1H
70 A7 Kramer Mews SW5
70 C4 Kynance Mews W8
70 C4 Kynance Place W8

L

69 L4 Lackington Street EC2A
74 B6 Lafone Street SE1
75 J5 Lagado Mews SE16
69 J4 Lambert Jones Mews * EC2Y
72 D5 Lambeth Bridge SW1P
72 E5 Lambeth High Street SE1
69 J7 Lambeth Hill * EC4V
72 E4 Lambeth Palace Road SE1
72 F4 Lambeth Road SE1
72 E6 Lambeth Walk SE11
68 E4 Lamb's Conduit Passage WC1X
68 E4 Lamb's Conduit Street WC1N
69 K4 Lamb's Passage EC1Y
74 B1 Lamb Street E1
74 A7 Lamb Walk SE1
73 H5 Lamlash Street SE11
70 E8 Lamont Road Passage SW10
66 D3 Lanark Place W9
66 B1 Lanark Road W9
67 L7 Lancashire Court W1K
66 D7 Lancaster Court W2
76 D2 Lancaster Drive E14
66 C7 Lancaster Gate W2
66 D7 Lancaster Mews W2
68 E7 Lancaster Place WC2R
73 H3 Lancaster Street SE1
66 E7 Lancaster Terrace W2
71 G3 Lancelot Place SW7
70 B3 Lancer Square W8
68 B2 Lancing Street NW1
71 H4 Landon Place SW1X
76 D2 Landons Close E14
66 C1 The Lane NW8
73 J8 Langdale Close SE17
74 E3 Langdale Street * E1
66 D1 Langford Place NW8
67 L5 Langham Place W1G
67 M5 Langham Street W1W
68 D7 Langley Court WC2E
68 D8 Langley Lane SW8
68 D7 Langley Street WC2H
69 L5 Langthorn Court * EC2R
68 E3 Langton Close WC1X
70 A7 Langtry Place SW6
73 L4 Lansdowne Place SE1
68 D3 Lansdowne Terrace WC1N
76 B4 Lanterns Court E14
73 J3 Lant Street SE1
66 C5 Lapworth Court W2
73 K6 Larcom Street SE17
73 M6 Larissa Street * SE17
66 B3 Lauderdale Parade * W9
69 K5 Lauderdale Place * EC2Y
66 B3 Lauderdale Road W9
72 E7 Laud Street SE11
72 F3 Launcelot Street SE1
70 C4 Launceston Place W8
76 D4 Launch Street E14
69 L7 Laurence Pountney Hill * EC4R
69 L7 Laurence Pountney Lane EC4R
70 F8 Lavender Close SW3
75 K5 Lavender Road SE16
70 B6 Laverton Mews * SW5
70 B6 Laverton Place SW5
73 J2 Lavington Street SE1
76 D3 Lawn House Close E14
72 D8 Lawn Lane SW8
69 K6 Lawrence Lane EC2V
70 F8 Lawrence Street SW3
73 L4 Law Street SE1
67 L3 Laxton Place NW1
68 F4 Laystall Street WC1X
68 D7 Lazenby Court * WC2E
74 A3 Leadenhall Place EC3M
69 M6 Leadenhall Street EC3V
72 F3 Leake Street SE1
69 G4 Leather Lane EC1R
73 M3 Leathermarket Court SE1
73 M3 Leathermarket Street SE1
70 E7 Lecky Street SW7
69 E2 Leeke Street WC1X
67 J7 Lees Place W1K
68 C7 Leicester Place * WC2H
68 C7 Leicester Square WC2H
68 B7 Leicester Street W1D
68 C3 Leigh Street WC1H
66 C6 Leinster Gardens W2
66 C7 Leinster Mews W2
66 C7 Leinster Place W2
66 C7 Leinster Square W2
66 C7 Leinster Terrace W2
74 C3 Leman Street E1
71 G5 Lennox Gardens SW1X
71 G5 Lennox Gardens Mews SW3
69 M3 Leonard Street EC2A
75 M1 Leopold Estate E3
75 M1 Leopold Street E3
73 M5 Leroy Street SE1
71 G5 Leverett Street SW3
69 J2 Lever Street EC1V
70 A5 Lexham Gardens W8
70 A5 Lexham Mews W8
68 A7 Lexington Street W1F
74 B2 Leyden Street E1
73 H3 Library Street SE1
72 J2 Lighterman Mews E1
76 B3 Lighterman's Road E14
72 E6 Lilac Place SE11
66 F3 Lilestone Street NW8
74 E5 Lilley Close E1W
70 A8 Lillie Yard SW6
72 A6 Lillington Gardens Estate SW1V
69 G4 Lily Place EC1N
69 H6 Limeburner Lane EC4M
74 D5 Lime Close E1W
76 D4 Limeharbour E14
75 M4 Limehouse * E14
75 M4 Limehouse Causeway E14
75 K1 Limehouse Fields Estate E1
75 K3 Limehouse Link E14
75 L3 Limehouse Link (Tunnel) E14
70 D8 Limerston Street SW10
69 M7 Lime Street EC3M
69 M7 Lime Street Passage * EC3V
68 E6 Lincoln's Inn Fields WC2A
71 H6 Lincoln Street SW3
66 A8 Linden Gardens W2
66 A8 Linden Mews W2
74 F1 Lindley Street E1
72 C7 Lindsay Square SW1V
69 J4 Lindsey Street EC1A
67 G3 Linhope Street NW1
74 C1 Links Yard E1
68 B7 Lisle Street W1D
66 F4 Lisson Grove NW8
66 F4 Lisson Street NW8
67 L3 Little Albany Street NW1
67 M6 Little Argyll Street * W1S
70 C7 The Little Boltons SW10
69 J5 Little Britain EC1A
71 K4 Little Chester Street SW1X
72 C4 Little Cloisters SW1P
72 C4 Little Deans Yard SW1P
73 K2 Little Dorrit Court SE1
67 L2 Little Edward Street * NW1
68 F7 Little Essex Street * WC2R
72 C3 Little George Street SW1P
67 M7 Little Marlborough Street * W1B
68 C7 Little Newport Street WC2H
69 G6 Little New Street EC4A
67 L6 Little Portland Street W1B
68 D5 Little Russell Street WC1A
71 M2 Little St James's Street SW1A
72 C4 Little Smith Street SW1P
67 M5 Little Titchfield Street W1W
69 K7 Little Trinity Lane EC4V
68 E5 Little Turnstile WC1V
73 K7 Liverpool Grove SE17
69 M5 Liverpool Street EC2M
69 K2 Lizard Street EC1V
74 D7 Llewellyn Street SE16
68 F2 Lloyd Baker Street WC1X
74 B3 Lloyd's Avenue EC3N
68 F2 Lloyd Square WC1X
69 G2 Lloyd's Row EC1R
68 F2 Lloyd Street WC1X
75 L2 Locksley Estate E14
75 L1 Locksley Street E14
74 E8 Lockwood Square SE16
73 L3 Lockyer Street SE1
66 F2 Lodge Road NW8
74 D7 Loftie Street SE16
74 C1 Lolesworth Close * E1
72 F6 Lollard Street SE11
73 J2 Loman Street SE1
74 E1 Lomas Street E1
69 L7 Lombard Street EC3V
66 B7 Lombardy Place W2
69 L8 London Bridge EC4R
73 L1 London Bridge Walk * SE1
66 E6 London Mews W2
73 H4 London Road SE1
66 E6 London Street W2
74 A3 London Street * EC3M
69 L5 London Wall EC2Y
69 L5 London Wall Buildings EC2M
68 D7 Long Acre WC2E
67 L3 Longford Street NW1
69 J5 Long Lane EC1A
73 L3 Long Lane SE1
71 M6 Longmoore Street SW1V
73 H5 Longville Road SE11
74 B8 Long Walk SE1
68 E4 Long Yard WC1N
66 B4 Lord Hills Road W2
72 C4 Lord North Street SW1P
70 F8 Lordship Place SW3
66 F2 Lords View NW8
68 E1 Lorenzo Street WC1X
67 G2 Lorne Close NW8
73 J8 Lorrimore Road SE17
73 J8 Lorrimore Square SE17
69 L6 Lothbury EC2R
72 F7 Loughborough Street SE11
69 M7 Lovat Lane EC3M
76 D2 Lovegrove Walk E14
69 K5 Love Lane EC2V
75 K7 Lovell Place SE16
75 K2 Lowell Street E14
71 K4 Lower Belgrave Street SW1W
71 L4 Lower Grosvenor Place SW1X
68 A7 Lower James Street * W1F
68 A7 Lower John Street W1F
72 F3 Lower Marsh SE1
75 G7 Lower Road SE16
71 J6 Lower Sloane Street SW1W
74 A4 Lower Thames Street EC3R
71 J4 Lowndes Close SW1X
67 M7 Lowndes Court W1B
71 J4 Lowndes Place * SW1X
71 H3 Lowndes Square SW1X
71 J4 Lowndes Street SW1X
74 F4 Lowood Street E1
68 D2 Loxham Street * WC1H
70 F6 Lucan Place SW3
70 A1 Lucerne Mews * W8
74 D8 Lucey Road SE16
69 H6 Ludgate Broadway * EC4V
69 H6 Ludgate Circus * EC4M
69 H6 Ludgate Hill EC4M
69 H6 Ludgate Square * EC4V
69 J3 Ludlow Street * EC1V
69 M3 Luke Street EC2A
75 G3 Lukin Street E1
67 K6 Lumley Street W1K
71 L7 Lupus Street SW1V
66 E4 Luton Street NW8
67 J4 Luxborough Street W1U
71 J4 Lyall Mews SW1X
71 J5 Lyall Mews West * SW1X
71 J5 Lyall Street SW1X
71 L4 Lygon Place * SW1W
66 E3 Lyons Place NW8
73 L7 Lytham Street SE17

M

68 C2 Mabledon Place NW1
69 J2 Macclesfield Road EC1V
68 B7 Macclesfield Street * W1D
74 E5 Mace Close E1W
67 K4 Mac Farren Place NW1
66 F1 Mackennal Street NW8
68 D6 Macklin Street * WC2B
67 M2 Mackworth Street NW1
73 K7 Macleod Street SE17
76 C7 Maconochies Road E14
76 C6 Macquarie Way E14
73 H8 Maddock Way SE17
67 L7 Maddox Street W1K
71 G1 Magazine Gate * W2
74 A6 Magdalen Street SE1
72 F8 Magee Street SE11
75 G2 Magri Walk E1
74 C6 Maguire Street SE1
75 K6 Mahogany Close SE16
66 D4 Maida Avenue W2
66 B1 Maida Vale W9
68 D7 Maiden Lane WC2E
73 K1 Maiden Lane SE1
73 K2 Maidstone Buildings Mews SE1
74 E7 Major Road SE16
71 G6 Makins Street SW3
76 A4 Malabar Street E14
68 B4 Malet Street WC1E
70 A1 Mall Chambers * W8
70 E8 Mallord Street SW3
66 F3 Mallory Street NW8
69 L3 Mallow Street EC1V
72 A3 The Mall SW1A
69 H3 Malta Street EC1V
74 B7 Maltby Street SE1
74 B6 Maltings Place SE1
68 F7 Maltravers Street WC2R
76 E2 Managers Street E14
76 E6 Manchester Estate E14
76 D7 Manchester Grove E14
67 J5 Manchester Mews W1U
76 D7 Manchester Road E14
67 J6 Manchester Square W1H
67 J5 Manchester Street W1U
73 L3 Manciple Street SE1
67 K6 Mandeville Place W1U
68 C6 Manette Street W1D
76 A3 Manilla Street E14
69 H2 Manningford Close * EC1V
74 D2 Manningtree Street E1
73 J7 Manor Place SE17
70 F7 Manresa Road SW3
74 C4 Mansell Street EC3N
67 L5 Mansfield Mews W1G
67 L5 Mansfield Street W1G
69 L7 Mansion House Place * EC4N
70 D5 Manson Mews SW7
70 D6 Manson Place SW7
75 J6 Maple Leaf Square SE16
68 A4 Maple Place W1T
74 F1 Maples Place E1
67 M4 Maple Street W1T

Marble Quay - Porter Street 81

74 C5 **Marble Quay** E1W
68 D3 **Marchmont Street** WC1N
74 E8 **Marden Square** SE16
67 M6 **Margaret Street** W1W
70 F8 **Margaretta Terrace** SW3
68 F3 **Margery Street** WC1X
69 G8 **Marigold Alley** SE1
74 E7 **Marigold Street** SE16
76 F5 **Mariners Mews** E14
74 D8 **Marine Street** SE16
76 B7 **Maritime Quay** E14
73 J7 **Markara Mews** SE17
71 K1 **Market Mews** W1J
67 M6 **Market Place** W1D
68 D7 **The Market** * WC2E
71 G6 **Markham Place** * SW3
71 G6 **Markham Square** SW3
71 G6 **Markham Street** SW3
74 A4 **Mark Lane** EC3R
69 M3 **Mark Street** EC2A
73 J6 **Marlborough Close** SE17
67 M7 **Marlborough Court** W1B
66 E7 **Marlborough Gate** W2
66 C1 **Marlborough Place** NW8
72 A2 **Marlborough Road** SW1A
71 F6 **Marlborough Street** SW3
70 A4 **Marloes Road** W8
74 E7 **Marlow Way** SE16
75 H6 **Maroon Street** E14
68 A7 **Marshall Street** W1F
73 K2 **Marshalsea Road** SE1
72 C5 **Marsham Street** SW1P
76 D4 **Marshfield Street** E14
76 B6 **Marsh Street** E14
76 B3 **Marsh Wall** E14
73 J7 **Marsland Close** SE17
69 L3 **Martha's Buildings** EC1V
74 F3 **Martha Street** E1
75 G3 **Martineau Street** E1
69 L7 **Martin Lane** EC4R
68 D6 **Martlett Court** WC2B
66 A4 **Maryland Road** W9
66 A3 **Marylands Road** W9
67 K5 **Marylebone High Street** W1U
67 K6 **Marylebone Lane** W1U
67 K5 **Marylebone Mews** W1G
68 A6 **Marylebone Passage** W1W
67 H4 **Marylebone Road** NW1
67 K5 **Marylebone Street** W1U
73 H6 **Marylee Way** SE11
67 L7 **Mason's Arms Mews** * W1S
69 L6 **Mason's Avenue** EC2V
69 H2 **Mason's Place** EC1V
73 M5 **Mason Street** SE17
69 J3 **Masons Yard** EC1V
72 A1 **Masons Yard** SW1Y
73 M6 **Massinger Street** SE17
75 J1 **Master's Street** E1
76 B6 **Mast House Terrace** E14
76 B6 **Masthouse Terrace** E14
76 B3 **Mastmaker Road** E14
68 C6 **Mathews Yard** * WC2H
73 H3 **Mathieson Court** SE1
75 J2 **Matlock Street** E1
72 B5 **Maunsel Street** SW1P
71 L1 **Mayfair Place** W1J
74 F7 **Mayflower Street** SE16
74 E5 **Maynards Quay** E1W
68 C7 **Mays Court** WC2N
72 F4 **McAuley Close** SE1
73 J3 **McCoid Way** SE1
70 C5 **McLeod's Mews** SW7
73 H8 **Meadcroft Road** SE11
73 J5 **Meadow Row** SE1
73 G4 **Mead Row** SE1
68 B7 **Meard Street** W1F
68 E3 **Mecklenburgh Place** WC1N
68 E3 **Mecklenburgh Square** WC1N
68 E3 **Mecklenburgh Street** WC1N
72 B5 **Medway Street** SW1P
74 F5 **Meeting House Alley** * E1W
68 E7 **Melbourne Place** WC2B
67 G4 **Melbury Terrace** NW1
67 G4 **Melcombe Place** NW1
67 H4 **Melcombe Street** NW1
66 D2 **Melina Place** NW8
73 M2 **Melior Place** * SE1
73 M2 **Melior Street** SE1
76 A4 **Mellish Street** E14
70 A2 **Melon Place** * W8
68 B2 **Melton Street** NW1
69 J3 **Memel Street** EC1Y
72 F2 **Mepham Street** SE1
76 B7 **Mercator Place** E14
75 J2 **Mercers Cottages** * E1
68 C7 **Mercer Street** WC2H
69 H2 **Meredith Street** EC1R
69 G2 **Merlin Street** WC1X
73 K2 **Mermaid Court** SE1
73 K4 **Merrick Square** SE1
70 A8 **Merrington Road** SW6
73 L7 **Merrow Street** SE17
73 L6 **Merrow Walk** SE17
67 G5 **Mertoun Terrace** * W1H
73 G7 **Methley Street** SE11
75 G5 **Metropolitan Wharf** * E1W
71 L4 **Mews North** SW1W
72 A7 **Mews South** SW1V
74 C5 **Mews Street** E1W
73 G2 **Meymott Street** SE1
74 D5 **Miah Terrace** * E1W
69 K1 **Micawber Street** N1
74 B1 **Middlesex Street** E1
69 J5 **Middle Street** EC1A
68 F6 **Middle Temple Lane** WC2R
67 M5 **Middleton Buildings** W1W
75 J6 **Middleton Drive** SE16
67 M5 **Middleton Place** W1W
73 M1 **Middle Yard** SE1
68 A4 **Midford Place** * W1T
68 D2 **Midhope Street** WC1H
68 C1 **Midland Road** NW1
75 J6 **Midship Close** SE16
76 A4 **Midship Point** * E14
70 D7 **Milborne Grove** SW10
73 H3 **Milcote Street** SE1
72 D8 **Miles Street** SW8
68 F7 **Milford Lane** WC2R
69 K6 **Milk Street** EC2V
75 G4 **Milk Yard** E1W
72 C6 **Millbank** SW1P
72 C6 **Millbank Estate** SW1P
69 J8 **Millennium Bridge** SE1
76 E5 **Millennium Drive** E14
74 C6 **Millennium Square** SE1
76 E5 **Millennium Wharf** E14
73 G1 **Miller Walk** SE1
76 C4 **Millharbour** E14
75 M4 **Milligan Street** E14
68 E4 **Millman Mews** * WC1N
68 E4 **Millman Place** WC1N
68 E3 **Millman Street** WC1N
75 L3 **Mill Place** E14
74 B7 **Millstream Road** SE1
67 L7 **Mill Street** W1S
74 C7 **Mill Street** SE1
76 A4 **Millwall Dock Road** E14
70 E8 **Milman's Street** SW10
71 G5 **Milner Street** SW3
69 G8 **Milroy Walk** SE1
69 L4 **Milton Court** EC2Y
69 K4 **Milton Street** EC2Y
73 G7 **Milverton Street** SE11
74 F1 **Milward Street** E1
74 A4 **Mincing Lane** EC3R
71 J5 **Minera Mews** SW1W
74 B3 **Minories** EC3N
74 A4 **Minster Court** * EC3M
73 J2 **Mint Street** SE1
74 F2 **Miranda Close** * E1
74 D3 **Mitali Passage** E1
69 J3 **Mitchell Street** EC1V
73 G3 **Mitre Road** SE1
74 B3 **Mitre Square** EC3A
74 B3 **Mitre Street** EC3A
75 L3 **The Mitre** E14
75 M7 **Moiety Road** E14
67 G5 **Molyneux Street** W1H
72 C4 **Monck Street** SW1P
70 F3 **Moncorvo Close** SW7
73 G5 **Monkton Street** SE11
69 K5 **Monkwell Square** EC2Y
66 A6 **Monmouth Place** W2
66 A6 **Monmouth Road** W2
68 D6 **Monmouth Street** WC2H
73 L1 **Montague Close** SE1
68 C5 **Montague Place** WC1E
68 C4 **Montague Street** WC1B
69 J5 **Montague Street** EC1A
67 H5 **Montagu Mansions** W1U
67 H5 **Montagu Mews North** W1H
67 H6 **Montagu Mews South** W1H
67 H5 **Montagu Mews West** W1H
67 H5 **Montagu Place** W1H
67 H5 **Montagu Row** W1U
67 H5 **Montagu Square** W1H
67 H6 **Montagu Street** W1H
72 F8 **Montford Place** SE11
74 D1 **Monthope Road** E1
71 G4 **Montpelier Mews** SW7
71 G4 **Montpelier Place** SW7
75 G3 **Montpelier Place** E1
71 G3 **Montpelier Square** SW7
71 G3 **Montpelier Street** SW7
70 F3 **Montpelier Terrace** SW7
70 F3 **Montpelier Walk** SW7
68 E7 **Montreal Place** WC2B
71 K3 **Montrose Place** SW1X
69 M7 **Monument Street** EC3R
75 G4 **Monza Street** E1W
75 G7 **Moodkee Street** SE16
71 H5 **Moore Street** SW3
69 L5 **Moorfields** EC2M
69 L5 **Moorfields Highwalk** EC2Y
69 L6 **Moorgate** EC2R
69 L5 **Moorgate Place** * EC2R
69 L5 **Moor Lane** EC2Y
68 C7 **Moor Street** W1D
69 K2 **Mora Street** EC1V
73 K6 **Morecambe Street** SE17
75 H1 **Morecambe Close** E1
69 H2 **Moreland Street** EC1V
72 A6 **Moreton Place** SW1V
72 A7 **Moreton Street** SW1V
72 A6 **Moreton Terrace** SW1V
72 A7 **Moreton Terrace Mews South** SW1V
74 A5 **Morgans Lane** SE1
73 G3 **Morley Street** SE1
67 M1 **Mornington Crescent** NW1
67 L1 **Mornington Place** NW1
74 A7 **Morocco Street** SE1
71 M5 **Morpeth Terrace** SW1P
74 F3 **Morris Street** E1
66 A2 **Morshead Road** W9
67 L5 **Mortimer Street** W1B
70 B6 **Morton Mews** * SW5
72 F4 **Morton Place** SE1
68 B5 **Morwell Street** W1T
66 B7 **Moscow Place** W2
66 A7 **Moscow Road** W2
74 D1 **Moss Close** E1
71 G5 **Mossop Street** SW3
71 J4 **Motcomb Street** SW1X
74 D2 **Mountford Street** * E1
69 J3 **Mount Mills** EC1V
68 F4 **Mount Pleasant** WC1X
67 K8 **Mount Row** W1K
67 J8 **Mount Street** W1K
74 E1 **Mount Terrace** E1
67 J5 **Moxon Street** W1U
76 C4 **Muirfield Crescent** E14
74 D2 **Mulberry Street** E1
70 E8 **Mulberry Walk** SW3
66 F4 **Mulready Street** NW8
69 K6 **Mumford Court** EC2V
69 M2 **Mundy Street** N1
67 L3 **Munster Square** NW1
73 K5 **Munton Road** SE17
72 F3 **Murphy Street** SE1
69 K1 **Murray Grove** N1
75 G2 **Musbury Street** E1
74 B4 **Muscovy Street** EC3N
68 D5 **Museum Street** WC1A
69 G2 **Myddelton Passage** EC1R
69 G2 **Myddelton Square** EC1R
69 G2 **Myddelton Street** EC1R
69 G1 **Mylne Street** EC1R
74 E2 **Myrdle Street** E1
69 M1 **Myrtle Street** N1
69 M1 **Myrtle Walk** N1

N

68 F2 **Naoroji Street** WC1X
76 B7 **Napier Avenue** E14
69 K1 **Napier Grove** N1
75 K4 **Narrow Street** E14
67 L2 **Nash Street** NW1
67 M5 **Nassau Street** W1W
74 C2 **Nathaniel Close** E1
68 C6 **Neal Street** WC2H
68 C6 **Neal Yard** WC2H
73 M8 **Neate Street** SE5
71 M5 **Neathouse Place** SW1V
74 C7 **Neckinger** SE1
74 C8 **Neckinger Estate** SE16
74 C7 **Neckinger Street** SE1
75 H7 **Needleman Street** SE16
68 C6 **Neils Yard** * WC2H
66 A1 **Nelson Close** NW6
69 H1 **Nelson Place** N1
73 H2 **Nelson Square** SE1
74 F2 **Nelson Street** E1
69 H1 **Nelson Terrace** EC1V
75 G7 **Neptune Street** SE16
74 D4 **Nesham Street** E1W
74 D8 **Ness Street** SE16
70 D8 **Netherton Grove** SW10
67 M2 **Netley Street** NW1
70 A6 **Nevern Place** SW5
70 A6 **Nevern Square** SW5
70 E6 **Neville Street** SW7
70 E6 **Neville Terrace** * SW7
74 F1 **Newark Street** E1
74 F2 **Newbold Cottages** * E1
67 L7 **New Bond Street** W1J
69 H6 **New Bridge Street** EC4M
69 M5 **New Broad Street** EC2M
68 A7 **Newburgh Street** W1F
67 M7 **New Burlington Mews** W1S
67 M7 **New Burlington Place** W1S
67 M7 **New Burlington Street** W1S
72 F7 **Newburn Street** SE11
69 J5 **Newbury Street** EC1A
69 H6 **Newcastle Close** EC4M
66 E5 **Newcastle Place** W2
69 G3 **Newcastle Row** EC1R
67 K5 **New Cavendish Street** W1U
69 J6 **New Change** EC4M
69 H2 **New Charles Street** EC1V
70 A1 **Newcombe Street** * W8
73 L2 **Newcomen Street** SE1
68 C6 **New Compton Street** * WC2H
67 F7 **New Court** * WC2R
66 F1 **Newcourt Street** NW8
72 C8 **New Covent Garden Market** SW8
75 G5 **New Crane Place** E1W
75 L3 **Newell Street** E14
69 G6 **New Fetter Lane** EC4A
69 H6 **Newgate Street** EC1A
73 J1 **New Globe Walk** SE1
74 B2 **New Goulston Street** E1
74 A7 **Newham's Row** SE1
73 H6 **Newington Butts** SE11
73 J4 **Newington Causeway** SE1
73 K5 **New Kent Road** SE1
75 G4 **Newlands Quay** E1W
74 B3 **New London Street** * EC3R
68 F5 **Newman's Row** WC2A
68 A5 **Newman Street** W1T
72 F4 **Newnham Terrace** SE1
69 M3 **New North Place** EC2A
69 L1 **New North Road** N1
68 E4 **New North Street** WC1N
68 C6 **New Oxford Street** WC1A
74 E7 **New Place Square** SE16
68 C7 **Newport Court** W1D
68 C7 **Newport Place** * W1D
72 E6 **Newport Street** SE11
67 H6 **New Quebec Street** W1H
74 E2 **New Road** E1
68 C7 **New Row** WC2N
72 D7 **New Spring Gardens Walk** * SE11
68 F6 **New Square** WC2A
74 A2 **New Street** EC2M
69 G6 **New Street Square** EC4A
66 A6 **Newton Road** W2
68 D5 **Newton Street** WC2B
74 F6 **New Tower Buildings** * E1W
76 E4 **New Union Close** E14
69 L5 **New Union Street** EC2Y
69 L7 **Nicholas Lane** EC4N
73 H2 **Nicholson Street** SE1
73 G5 **Nightingale Mews** SE11
70 D8 **Nightingale Place** SW10
69 K2 **Nile Street** N1
72 C8 **Nine Elms Lane** SW8
69 K6 **Noble Street** EC2V
68 A6 **Noel Street** * W1F
75 L2 **Norbiton Road** E14
66 F6 **Norfolk Crescent** W2
66 E6 **Norfolk Place** W2
72 E5 **Norfolk Row** SE1
66 E6 **Norfolk Square** W2
66 E6 **Norfolk Square Mews** W2
69 J3 **Norman Street** EC1V
68 B8 **Norris Street** SW1Y
69 G3 **Northampton Road** EC1R
69 G3 **Northampton Row** * EC1R
69 H2 **Northampton Square** EC1V
67 J7 **North Audley Street** W1K
66 F2 **North Bank** NW8
69 H3 **Northburgh Street** EC1V
67 G7 **North Carriage Drive** W2
76 B2 **North Colonnade** E14
68 B4 **North Crescent** W1T
68 E1 **Northdown Street** N1
75 K4 **Northey Street** E14
68 A2 **North Gower Street** NW1
68 E4 **Northington Street** WC1N
68 F4 **North Mews** WC1N
67 G6 **North Rise** * W2
67 J7 **North Row** W1K
74 C3 **North Tenter Street** E1
70 F5 **North Terrace** SW3
74 B3 **Northumberland Alley** * EC3N
72 D1 **Northumberland Avenue** WC2N
66 A6 **Northumberland Place** W2
72 C1 **Northumberland Street** WC2N
66 E5 **North Wharf Road** W2
66 E3 **Northwick Close** NW8
66 D3 **Northwick Terrace** NW8
75 K7 **Norway Gate** SE16
75 L3 **Norway Place** E14
69 G5 **Norwich Street** EC4A
68 D6 **Nottingham Court** * WC2H
67 J4 **Nottingham Place** W1U
67 J4 **Nottingham Street** W1U
67 J4 **Nottingham Terrace** NW1
66 A8 **Notting Hill Gate** W8
66 D1 **Nugent Terrace** NW8
73 L6 **Nursery Row** SE17
67 G6 **Nutford Place** W2

O

73 G5 **Oakden Street** SE11
73 G4 **Oakey Lane** SE1
70 C8 **Oakfield Street** SW10
66 A3 **Oakington Road** W9
75 L3 **Oak Lane** E14
69 H1 **Oakley Crescent** * EC1V
71 G8 **Oakley Gardens** SW3
70 F8 **Oakley Street** SW3
66 F2 **Oak Tree Road** NW8
69 K5 **Oat Lane** EC2V
70 A2 **Observatory Gardens** W8
70 E4 **Observatory Road** SW7
73 J6 **Occupation Road** SE17
75 J1 **Ocean Estate** E1
75 J1 **Ocean Street** E1
69 M5 **Octagon Arcade** * EC2M
75 L7 **Odessa Street** SE16
68 D6 **Odhams Walk** * WC2H
67 M4 **Ogle Street** W1W
69 H6 **Old Bailey** EC4M
71 J3 **Old Barrack Yard** SW1X
67 M8 **Old Bond Street** W1S
69 M5 **Old Broad Street** EC2M
70 A7 **Old Brompton Road** SW5
68 F6 **Old Buildings** WC2A
67 M7 **Old Burlington Street** W1S
67 J4 **Oldbury Place** W1U
74 C2 **Old Castle Street** E1
67 L6 **Old Cavendish Street** W1G
75 H2 **Old Church Road** E1
70 E7 **Old Church Street** SW3
68 B7 **Old Compton Street** W1D
70 B3 **Old Court Place** W8
69 J7 **Old Fish Street Hill** * EC4V
69 H6 **Old Fleet Lane** EC4M
68 D4 **Old Gloucester Street** WC1N
74 C7 **Old Jamaica Road** SE16
69 L6 **Old Jewry** * EC2R
70 A6 **Old Manor Yard** SW5
67 G5 **Old Marylebone Road** NW1
69 G6 **Old Mitre Court** * EC4Y
74 D1 **Old Montague Street** E1
68 E5 **Old North Street** * WC1X
72 E5 **Old Paradise Street** SE11
71 K2 **Old Park Lane** W1J
72 B4 **Old Pye Street** SW1P
67 H6 **Old Quebec Street** W1H
72 B3 **Old Queen Street** SW1H
69 H6 **Old Seacoal Lane** * EC4M
68 F5 **Old Square** WC2A
69 L3 **Old Street** EC1V
76 F8 **Old Woolwich Road** SE10
74 F3 **O'Leary Square** E1
69 L3 **Oliver's Yard** EC1Y
75 L5 **Olliffe Street** E14
73 J8 **Olney Road** SE17
73 K2 **O'Meara Street** SE1
68 D1 **Omega Place** N1
73 K8 **Onega Gate** SE16
70 A8 **Ongar Road** SW6
70 E6 **Onslow Gardens** SW7
70 E6 **Onslow Mews East** SW7
70 E6 **Onslow Mews West** SW7
70 E6 **Onslow Square** SW7
69 G4 **Onslow Street** EC1M
73 J4 **Ontario Street** SE1
75 M4 **Ontario Way** E14
73 H6 **Opal Street** SE11
75 G8 **Orange Place** SE16
68 C8 **Orange Street** WC2H
74 D5 **Orange Street** E1W
70 F6 **Oratory Lane** * SW3
73 L6 **Orb Street** SE17
66 E4 **Orchardson Street** NW8
67 J6 **Orchard Street** W1H
68 E4 **Orde Hall Street** * WC1N
73 H5 **Orient Street** SE11
66 B8 **Orme Court** W2
66 B8 **Orme Court Mews** * W2
66 B8 **Orme Lane** W2
66 B8 **Orme Square** W2
66 B8 **Orme Square Gate** W8
68 D4 **Ormond Close** WC1N
71 H7 **Ormonde Gate** SW3
71 J6 **Ormonde Place** SW1W
72 A1 **Ormond Yard** SW1Y
66 C6 **Orsett Mews** W2
72 E6 **Orsett Street** SE11
66 C6 **Orsett Terrace** W2
74 D5 **Orton Street** E1W
72 B6 **Osbert Street** SW1P
74 C2 **Osborn Street** E1
67 L3 **Osnaburgh Street** NW1
67 L3 **Osnaburgh Terrace** NW1
67 J5 **Ossington Buildings** * W1U
66 A7 **Ossington Close** * W2
66 A7 **Ossington Street** W2
68 B1 **Ossulston Street** NW1
70 C5 **Osten Mews** SW7
73 H5 **Oswin Street** SE11
73 H6 **Othello Close** SE11
73 H8 **Otto Street** SE17
67 H3 **Outer Circle** NW1
74 A2 **Outwich Street** * EC3A
72 F7 **Oval Way** SE11
76 E4 **Ovex Close** E14
71 G4 **Ovington Gardens** SW3
71 G4 **Ovington Mews** SW3
71 G4 **Ovington Square** SW3
71 G5 **Ovington Street** SW3
69 H1 **Owen's Row** EC1V
69 G1 **Owen Street** EC1V
68 B8 **Oxendon Street** * W1D
69 L7 **Oxford Court** EC4N
66 F6 **Oxford Square** W2
67 J7 **Oxford Street** W1K
75 G3 **Oyster Row** E1

P

74 F3 **Pace Place** E1
66 E5 **Paddington Green** W2
67 J5 **Paddington Street** W1U
75 L5 **Pageant Crescent** SE16
72 C5 **Page Street** SW1P
69 H2 **Paget Street** EC1V
68 F3 **Pakenham Street** WC1X
70 B2 **Palace Avenue** W8
66 A7 **Palace Court** W2
70 A1 **Palace Garden Mews** W8
70 A1 **Palace Gardens Terrace** W8
66 A8 **Palace Gardens Terrace** W11
70 C3 **Palace Gate** W8
70 B2 **Palace Green** W8
71 M4 **Palace Place** SW1E
71 M4 **Palace Street** SW1E
67 G3 **Palgrave Gardens** NW1
72 B1 **Pall Mall** SW1Y
72 B1 **Pall Mall East** SW1Y
72 A1 **Pall Mall Place** SW1Y
72 B4 **Palmer Street** SW1H
69 K6 **Pancras Lane** EC4N
68 B8 **Panton Street** WC2H
69 G7 **Paper Buildings** * EC4Y
74 E7 **Paradise Street** SE16
71 H8 **Paradise Walk** SW3
73 M5 **Paragon Mews** SE17
73 L4 **Pardoner Street** SE1
69 J3 **Pardon Street** EC1V
74 E2 **Parfett Street** E1
73 G1 **Paris Garden** SE1
74 F8 **Park Approach** SE16
73 G3 **Park Close** * SW7
67 L4 **Park Crescent** W1B
67 L4 **Park Crescent Mews East** W1B
67 K4 **Park Crescent Mews West** W1G
68 D6 **Parker Mews** * WC2B
74 C7 **Parkers Row** SE1
68 D6 **Parker Street** WC2B
67 H7 **Park Lane** W1H
71 K2 **Park Lane** W1J
76 A2 **Park Place** E14
71 M1 **Park Place** SW1A
66 D4 **Park Place Villas** W2
67 G2 **Park Road** NW8
76 F8 **Park Row** SE10
67 L3 **Park Square East** NW1
67 K3 **Park Square Mews** NW1
67 K3 **Park Square West** NW1
67 G7 **Park Steps** * W2
67 J8 **Park Street** W1K
73 J1 **Park Street** SE1
70 D8 **Park Walk** SW10
67 G6 **Park West** W2
67 G6 **Park West Place** W2
74 B1 **Parliament Court** * E1
72 C3 **Parliament Square** SW1P
72 D2 **Parliament Street** SW1A
75 K2 **Parnham Street** E14
72 D8 **Parry Street** SW8
76 E6 **Parsonage Street** E14
73 J7 **Pasley Close** SE17
71 J6 **Passmore Street** SW1W
73 H5 **Pastor Street** SE11
69 J6 **Paternoster Row** EC4M
70 A4 **Pater Street** W8
75 L5 **Pattina Walk** SE16
76 E1 **Paul Julius Close** E14
69 M3 **Paul Street** EC2A
70 E8 **Paultons Square** SW3
70 E8 **Paultons Street** SW3
66 F2 **Paveley Street** NW8
71 H3 **Pavilion Road** SW1X
71 H4 **Pavilion Street** SW1X
71 L8 **Paxton Terrace** SW1V
71 L7 **Peabody Avenue** SW1V
71 L7 **Peabody Close** SW1V
69 G3 **Peabody Estate** * EC1R
73 G1 **Peabody Estate** * SE1
73 K1 **Peabody Estate** * SE1
69 K3 **Peabody Estate** * EC1Y
69 G4 **Peabody Terrace** * EC1R
73 J6 **Peacock Street** SE17
73 J6 **Peacock Yard** SE17
74 F5 **Pearl Street** E1W
73 G3 **Pearman Street** SE1
73 G3 **Pear Place** SE1
69 G3 **Pear Tree Court** EC1R
75 G4 **Peartree Lane** E1W
69 J3 **Peartree Street** EC1V
74 C1 **Pecks Yard** * E1
70 A2 **Peel Passage** * W8
69 K2 **Peerless Street** EC1V
72 F8 **Pegasus Place** SE11
70 F6 **Pelham Crescent** SW7
70 F5 **Pelham Place** SW7
70 F5 **Pelham Street** SW7
73 K8 **Pelier Street** SE17
75 M3 **Pelling Street** E14
69 G6 **Pemberton Row** EC4A
66 A8 **Pembridge Gardens** W2
66 A7 **Pembridge Place** W2
66 A7 **Pembridge Square** W2
71 J3 **Pembroke Close** SW1X
74 F5 **Penang Street** E1W
66 F5 **Penfold Place** W2
66 F4 **Penfold Street** NW8
70 B5 **Pennant Mews** W8
74 E4 **Pennington Street** E1W
73 J7 **Penrose Grove** SE17
73 J7 **Penrose Street** SE17
68 F1 **Penton Grove** N1
73 H6 **Penton Place** SE17
68 E2 **Penton Rise** WC1X
68 F1 **Penton Street** N1
68 F1 **Pentonville Road** N1
70 A7 **Penywern Road** SW5
76 C4 **Pepper Street** E14
73 J2 **Pepper Street** SE1
74 B4 **Pepys Street** EC3N
69 H3 **Percival Street** EC1V
68 B5 **Percy Mews** W1T
68 B5 **Percy Street** W1T
72 B4 **Perkin's Rents** SW1P
73 K1 **Perkins Square** SE1
74 E7 **Perryn Road** SE16
70 C4 **Petersham Lane** SW7
70 C4 **Petersham Mews** SW7
70 C4 **Petersham Place** SW7
69 J7 **Peter's Hill** EC4V
68 B7 **Peter Street** W1F
67 L3 **Peto Place** NW1
74 B2 **Petticoat Square** E1
74 B2 **Petticoat Tower** * E1
72 A3 **Petty France** SW1H
71 G6 **Petyward** SW3
73 L7 **Phelp Street** SE17
71 G8 **Phene Street** SW3
74 D3 **Philchurch Place** E1
69 M7 **Philpot Lane** EC3M
74 F2 **Philpot Street** E1
71 L5 **Phipp's Mews** SW1W
69 M3 **Phipp Street** EC2A
76 B6 **Phoenix Court** E14
68 F3 **Phoenix Place** WC1X
68 B2 **Phoenix Road** NW1
68 C6 **Phoenix Street** WC2H
74 C7 **Phoenix Wharf Road** SE1
71 L1 **Piccadilly** W1J
72 A1 **Piccadilly Arcade** W1J
68 B8 **Piccadilly Circus** W1J
69 J2 **Pickard Street** EC1V
72 A2 **Pickering Place** * SW1Y
69 J1 **Pickfords Wharf** * N1
73 J3 **Pickwick Street** SE1
67 K6 **Picton Place** W1H
74 E6 **Pier Head** E1W
76 E6 **Pier Street** E14
75 M3 **Pigott Street** E14
73 L3 **Pilgrimage Street** SE1
69 H6 **Pilgrim Street** * EC4V
73 K6 **Pilton Place** SE17
71 K6 **Pimlico Road** SW1W
74 E3 **Pinchin & Johnsons Yard** E1
74 D3 **Pinchin Street** E1
69 M4 **Pindar Street** EC2A
66 B3 **Pindock Mews** W9
72 A4 **Pine Apple Court** * SW1E
69 G3 **Pine Street** EC1R
69 M2 **Pitfield Street** N1
75 J3 **Pitsea Place** E1
75 J3 **Pitsea Street** E1
71 K2 **Pitt's Head Mews** W1K
70 A3 **Pitt Street** W8
75 L2 **Pixley Street** E14
73 L3 **Plantain Place** SE1
69 L3 **Platina Street** EC2A
69 H7 **Playhouse Yard** EC4V
76 D4 **Plevna Street** E14
69 K2 **Pleydell Estate** * EC1V
69 G6 **Pleydell Street** EC4Y
69 G6 **Plough Place** EC4A
74 C2 **Plough Street** * E1
75 K8 **Plover Way** SE16
68 F7 **Plowden Buildings** * EC4Y
74 D2 **Plumbers Row** E1
69 G5 **Plumtree Court** EC4A
76 E6 **Plymouth Wharf** E14
66 F4 **Plympton Place** * NW8
66 F4 **Plympton Street** NW8
73 H3 **Pocock Street** SE1
76 C7 **Pointers Close** E14
68 A6 **Poland Street** W1F
67 L7 **Pollen Street** W1S
66 E3 **Pollitt Drive** NW8
73 G5 **Polperro Mews** SE11
68 B1 **Polygon Road** NW1
74 C2 **Pomell Way** E1
70 F6 **Pond Place** SW3
74 E3 **Ponler Street** E1
72 C6 **Ponsonby Place** SW1P
72 C6 **Ponsonby Terrace** SW1P
71 H4 **Pont Street** SW1X
71 G4 **Pont Street Mews** SW3
68 F4 **Pooles Buildings** WC1X
75 H6 **Poolmans Street** SE16
75 G3 **Poonah Street** E1
74 B7 **Pope Street** SE1
66 B7 **Poplar Place** W2
69 H6 **Poppins Court** EC4A
66 C7 **Porchester Garden Mews** * W2
66 B7 **Porchester Gardens** W2
66 C8 **Porchester Gate** * W2
67 G7 **Porchester Place** W2
66 B6 **Porchester Road** W2
66 B6 **Porchester Square** W2
66 B6 **Porchester Square Mews** W2
66 C7 **Porchester Terrace** W2
66 C6 **Porchester Terrace North** W2
73 L3 **Porlock Street** SE1
66 C8 **Portchester Gate** W2
67 H4 **Porter Street** W1U
73 K1 **Porter Street** SE1

Starcross Street - Zoar Street 83

68 A2 Starcross Street NW1
74 C4 Star Place E1W
66 F6 Star Street W2
68 F6 Star Yard WC2A
67 J4 Station Approach * NW1
67 L4 Station Arcade * W1W
69 H6 Stationers Hall Court * EC4M
75 J5 Stave Yard Road SE16
73 K6 Stead Street SE17
76 F7 Stebondale Street E14
73 J6 Steedman Street SE17
69 K8 Steelyard Passage EC4R
75 K7 Steers Way SE16
68 B5 Stephen Mews W1T
68 A3 Stephenson Way NW1
68 B5 Stephen Street W1T
75 H3 Stepney Causeway E1
75 H1 Stepney Green E1
75 J1 Stepney High Street E1
74 E1 Stepney Way E1
71 G3 Sterling Street SW7
73 L3 Sterry Street SE1
74 E5 Stevedore Street E1W
74 B7 Stevens Street SE1
74 B1 Steward Street E1
70 F6 Stewart's Grove SW3
76 E3 Stewart Street E14
69 K7 Stew Lane EC4V
72 A5 Stillington Street SW1P
74 D5 Stockholm Way E1W
75 M3 Stocks Place E14
68 F5 Stone Buildings WC2A
69 H6 Stonecutter Street EC4A
70 B4 Stone Hall Gardens * W8
70 B4 Stone Hall Place * W8
74 A2 Stone House Court EC3A
73 J3 Stones End Street SE1
74 B2 Stoney Lane EC3A
73 K1 Stoney Street SE1
73 J7 Stopford Road * SE17
76 F6 Storers Quay E14
68 B5 Store Street WC1E
72 C3 Storey's Gate SW1H
68 E8 Storks Road SE16
67 G6 Stourcliffe Street W2
76 A3 Strafford Street E14
68 D8 Strand WC2R
67 K6 Stratford Place W1U
70 A5 Stratford Road W8
66 F7 Strathearn Place W2
76 D4 Strattondale Street E14
71 L1 Stratton Street W1J
68 C5 Streatham Street WC1A
72 E6 Stroughton Close SE11
72 B4 Strutton Ground SW1P
74 B2 Strype Street E1
71 H3 Studio Place * SW1X
68 D6 Stukeley Street WC2B
73 J7 Sturgeon Road SE17
73 J3 Sturge Street SE1
69 K1 Sturt Street N1
74 D3 Stutfield Street E1
69 H1 Sudeley Street N1
73 J3 Sudrey Street SE1
69 L7 Suffolk Lane EC4R
68 C8 Suffolk Street SW1Y
73 G5 Sullivan Road SE11
73 G2 Summercourt Road E1
69 G4 Summers Street EC1R
70 E6 Sumner Place SW7
70 E6 Sumner Place Mews SW7
73 J1 Sumner Street SE1
66 A6 Sunderland Terrace W2
70 A5 Sunningdale Gardens W8
74 D8 Sun Passage SE16
69 M4 Sun Street EC2A
66 A4 Surrendale Place W9
75 M7 Surrey Grove SE17
75 G8 Surrey Quays Road SE16
73 H2 Surrey Row SE1
73 M6 Surrey Square SE17
68 F7 Surrey Street WC2R
75 J6 Surrey Water Road SE16
66 E7 Sussex Gardens W2
66 E7 Sussex Mews East * W2
66 E7 Sussex Mews West W2
66 E6 Sussex Place W2
67 H3 Sussex Place NW1
66 E7 Sussex Square W2
71 L7 Sussex Street SW1V
66 A4 Sutherland Avenue W9
71 L7 Sutherland Row SW1V
73 J7 Sutherland Square SE17
71 L7 Sutherland Street SW1V
73 K7 Sutherland Walk SE17
70 F6 Sutton Dwelling Estate SW3
68 B6 Sutton Row W1D
75 G3 Sutton Street E1
66 F3 Swain Street NW8
67 L6 Swallow Place W1B
68 A8 Swallow Street W1S
69 L8 Swan Lane EC4R
74 A8 Swan Mead SE1
74 C4 Swan Passage E1
75 G6 Swan Road SE16
73 K3 Swan Street SE1
71 H8 Swan Walk SW3
74 C7 Sweeney Crescent SE1
68 E2 Swinton Place WC1X
68 E2 Swinton Street WC1X
69 J3 Sycamore Street EC1V
70 E6 Sydney Close SW7
70 E6 Sydney Mews SW7
70 F6 Sydney Place SW7
70 F6 Sydney Street SW3
69 M2 Symister Mews * N1
71 H6 Symons Street SW3

T

73 L3 Tabard Garden Estate SE1
73 K3 Tabard Street SE1
69 L4 Tabernacle Street EC2A
72 A6 Tachbrook Street SW1V
76 C6 Taeping Street E14
69 M7 Talbot Court EC3V
66 A6 Talbot Road W2
66 E6 Talbot Square W2
73 L2 Talbot Yard SE1
69 G7 Tallis Street EC4Y
74 D5 Tamarind Yard E1W
68 D2 Tankerton Houses * WC1H
68 D2 Tankerton Street WC1H
74 B7 Tanner Street SE1
73 G3 Tanswell Street * SE1
69 K1 Taplow Street N1
75 G3 Tarbert Walk E1
74 F3 Tarling Street E1
74 F3 Tarling Street Estate E1
73 J4 Tarn Street SE1
67 G5 Tarrant Place W1H
73 J7 Tarver Road SE17
73 M6 Tatum Street SE17
67 H4 Taunton Mews NW1
67 G3 Taunton Place NW1
68 D7 Tavistock Court * WC2E
68 D3 Tavistock Place WC1H
68 C3 Tavistock Square WC1H
68 D7 Tavistock Street WC2E
68 B3 Taviton Street WC1H
73 G6 Tavy Close SE11
75 K6 Teak Close SE16
71 G7 Tedworth Gardens SW3
71 H7 Tedworth Square SW3
76 C6 Telegraph Place E14
69 L6 Telegraph Street EC2R
74 D4 Telfords Yard E1W
71 M8 Telford Terrace SW1V
69 G7 Temple Avenue EC4Y
69 G7 Temple Gardens * EC4Y
69 G7 Temple Lane EC4Y
68 F7 Temple Place WC2R
70 A6 Templeton Place SW5
74 E5 Tench Street E1W
66 C7 Tenniel Close W2
73 L3 Tennis Street SE1
67 L6 Tenterden Street W1S
74 B1 Tenter Ground * E1
71 L5 Terminus Place SW1V
70 B3 Thackeray Street W8
76 F8 Thalia Close SE10
75 J6 Thame Road SE16
76 B6 Thames Circle E14
75 L8 Thames Path SE16
71 K8 Thames Path SW11
76 E8 Thames Path SE10
74 B4 Thames Path EC3N
72 D5 Thames Path SW1P
76 D8 Thames Street SE10
68 C2 Thanet Street WC1H
67 K5 Thayer Street W1U
73 G2 Theed Street SE1
68 E4 Theobald's Road WC1X
73 L5 Theobald Street SE1
76 C6 Thermopylae Gate E14
69 J1 Theseus Walk N1
72 A4 Thirleby Road SW1P
70 D7 Thistle Grove SW10
73 H4 Thomas Doyle Street SE1
74 D4 Thomas Moore Square E1W
74 D4 Thomas More Street E1W
70 B4 Thomas Place W8
75 M2 Thomas Road E14
69 K1 Thoresby Street N1
72 B6 Thorndike Street * SW1V
72 D5 Thorney Street SW1P
66 A3 Thorngate Road W9
68 C4 Thornhaugh Street WC1H
67 H4 Thornton Place W1H
73 K2 Thrale Street SE1
74 C1 Thrawl Street E1
69 L6 Threadneedle Street EC2R
75 M4 Three Colt Street E14
67 K7 Three Kings Yard W1K
74 B6 Three Oak Lane SE1
69 L6 Throgmorton Avenue EC2N
69 L6 Throgmorton Street EC2R
73 J6 Thrush Street SE17
74 D8 Thurland Road SE16
70 F5 Thurloe Close SW7
70 F5 Thurloe Place SW7
70 E5 Thurloe Place Mews * SW7
70 F5 Thurloe Square SW7
70 E5 Thurloe Street SW7
73 M7 Thurlow Street SE17
73 M7 Thurlow Walk SE17
76 A4 Tiller Road E14
74 F3 Tillman Street E1
71 K1 Tilney Street W1K
74 F3 Timberland Road E1
75 J6 Timber Pond Road SE16
69 J3 Timber Street * EC1V
75 L1 Timothy Road E14
75 H1 Tinsley Road E1
72 E6 Tinworth Street SE11
73 L6 Tisdall Place SE17
66 F6 Titchborne Row W2
71 H7 Tite Street SW3
73 J4 Tiverton Street SE1
76 A3 Tobago Street E14
69 L6 Tokenhouse Yard EC2R
68 A3 Tolmer's Square NW1
75 L2 Tomlin's Terrace E14
69 H2 Tompion Street EC1V
68 D2 Tonbridge Street WC1H
68 F5 Took's Court EC4A
73 L1 Tooley Street SE1
69 G3 Topham Street * EC1R
76 A3 Topmast Point * E14
66 A5 Torquay Street W2
69 G1 Torrens Street EC1V
68 B4 Torrington Place W1T
74 E5 Torrington Place E1W
68 B4 Torrington Square WC1E
72 B3 Tothill Street SW1H
75 J2 Tottan Terrace * E1
68 A4 Tottenham Court Road W1T
68 A5 Tottenham Mews * W1T
68 A5 Tottenham Street W1W
73 J3 Toulmin Street SE1
74 D8 Toussaint Walk SE16
74 C5 Tower Bridge EC3N
74 C5 Tower Bridge Approach EC3N
73 M5 Tower Bridge Road SE1
74 F5 Tower Buildings * E1W
68 C7 Tower Court * WC2H
74 B4 Tower Hill EC3N
74 B4 Tower Hill Terrace EC3R
74 A4 Tower Place EC3R
69 K7 Tower Royal * EC4N
68 C7 Tower Street * WC2H
73 L6 Townley Street SE17
73 M5 Townsend Street SE17
74 B1 Toynbee Street E1
75 J1 Trafalgar Gardens E1
76 F8 Trafalgar Grove SE10
68 C8 Trafalgar Square * WC2N
73 L7 Trafalgar Street SE17
76 D2 Trafalgar Way E14
66 F5 Transept Street NW1
76 C7 Transom Square E14
74 E8 Tranton Road SE16
71 L1 Trebeck Street W1J
70 A6 Trebovir Road SW5
70 C7 Tregunter Road SW10
66 F3 Tresham Crescent NW8
73 H1 Treveris Street SE1
76 A8 Trevithick Street SE8
71 G3 Trevor Place SW7
71 G3 Trevor Square SW7
71 G3 Trevor Street SW7
69 J7 Trig Lane EC4V
75 M4 Trinidad Street E14
73 K3 Trinity Church Square SE1
74 F1 Trinity Green * E1
74 B4 Trinity Square EC3N
73 K3 Trinity Street SE1
73 K3 Trio Place SE1
67 M3 Triton Square NW1
75 J2 Troon Street E1
69 K6 Trump Street EC2V
73 J3 Trundle Street SE1
71 G6 Tryon Street SW3
69 G7 Tudor Street EC4Y
72 C4 Tufton Street SW1P
75 G6 Tunnel Road SE16
71 J7 Turks Row SW3
69 H5 Turnagain Lane * EC4M
75 L2 Turner's Road E14
74 E2 Turner Street E1
69 G4 Turnmill Street EC1M
71 L7 Turpentine Lane SW1V
73 K6 Turquand Street SE17
75 G3 Twine Court E1
67 H7 Tyburn Way W1H
74 A7 Tyers Gate SE1
72 E7 Tyers Street SE11
72 E7 Tyers Terrace SE11
74 C2 Tyne Street E1
69 G2 Tysoe Street EC1R

U

72 A6 Udall Street SW1P
73 G3 Ufford Street SE1
67 K4 Ulster Place NW1
74 E2 Umberston Street * E1
74 A3 Undershaft EC3A
69 K2 Underwood Row N1
69 K1 Underwood Street N1
76 C6 Undine Road E14
73 H2 Union Street SE1
68 A4 University Street W1T
70 E4 Unwin Road SW7
66 D6 Upbrook Mews W2
71 K4 Upper Belgrave Street SW1X
67 G6 Upper Berkeley Street W2
67 J7 Upper Brook Street W1K
70 F8 Upper Cheyne Row SW3
67 J8 Upper Grosvenor Street W1K
72 F1 Upper Ground SE1
67 K3 Upper Harley Street NW1
68 A7 Upper John Street W1B
70 B2 Upper Lodge * W8
72 F3 Upper Marsh SE1
67 H4 Upper Montagu Street W1H
68 C6 Upper St Martin's Lane WC2H
69 G1 Upper Street N1
72 A5 Upper Tachbrook Street SW1V
69 J7 Upper Thames Street EC4V
67 K4 Upper Wimpole Street W1G
68 B2 Upper Woburn Place NW1
70 A1 Uxbridge Street * W8

V

66 C2 Vale Close W9
73 H3 Valentine Place SE1
70 E8 The Vale SW3
72 A4 Vandon Street SW1H
69 M4 Vandy Street EC2A
70 A4 Vantage Place W8
74 E2 Varden Street E1
67 M2 Varndell Street NW1
74 C8 Vauban Street SE16
75 L7 Vaughan Street SE16
74 D4 Vaughan Way E1W
72 D7 Vauxhall Bridge SE11
71 M5 Vauxhall Bridge Road SW1V
72 D8 Vauxhall Grove SW8
72 F7 Vauxhall Street SE11
72 F7 Vauxhall Walk SE11
66 E4 Venables Street NW8
67 K6 Vere Street W1U
68 D5 Vernon Place WC1N
68 E2 Vernon Rise WC1X
68 E2 Vernon Square * WC1X
68 F4 Verulam Street WC1X
69 L2 Vestry Street N1
70 A2 Vicarage Gardens * W8
70 B2 Vicarage Gate W8
71 L4 Victoria Arcade SW1V
74 D1 Victoria Cottages * E1
69 G7 Victoria Embankment EC4Y
72 D3 Victoria Embankment SW1A
68 D8 Victoria Embankment Gardens * WC2N
66 F7 Victoria Gate W2
70 C4 Victoria Grove W8
66 A8 Victoria Grove Mews * W11
70 C4 Victoria Road W8
71 L4 Victoria Square SW1W
72 A4 Victoria Street SW1P
74 D3 Victoria Yard * E1
73 K5 Victory Place SE17
75 K7 Victory Way SE16
68 A8 Vigo Street W1J
73 L7 Villa Street SE17
68 D8 Villiers Street WC2N
75 K6 Vincents Close SE16
72 A5 Vincent Square SW1P
72 B5 Vincent Street SW1P
69 H1 Vincent Terrace N1
69 L2 Vince Street EC1V
75 G2 Vine Cottages * E1
74 E1 Vine Court E1
74 E5 Vinegar Street E1W
73 M2 Vinegar Yard SE1
68 F4 Vine Hill EC1R
74 A6 Vine Lane SE1
68 A8 Vine Street W1S
74 B3 Vine Street EC3N
69 G4 Vine Street Bridge EC1M
74 B3 Vine Street Crescent * EC3N
73 K3 Vine Yard SE1
69 G3 Vineyard Mews * EC1R
69 G3 Vineyard Walk EC1R
66 C1 Violet Hill NW8
72 F4 Virgil Street SE1
74 D4 Virginia Street E1W
69 K4 Viscount Street EC1Y

W

73 K6 Wadding Street SE17
68 D3 Wakefield Mews WC1H
68 D3 Wakefield Street WC1N
75 J3 Wakeling Street E1
69 H1 Wakley Street EC1V
69 L7 Walbrook EC4N
74 E3 Walburgh Street E1
73 K6 Walcorde Avenue SE17
73 G5 Walcot Square SE11
72 A5 Walcott Street * SW1P
74 E2 Walden Street E1
70 E8 Waldron Mews SW3
75 J1 Waley Street E1
68 B7 Walker's Court W1F
70 A5 Wallgrave Road SW5
69 K5 Wallside * EC2Y
75 M1 Wallwood Street E14
72 F5 Walnut Tree Walk SE11
71 H6 Walpole Street SW3
75 J2 Walter Terrace E1
71 H4 Walton Place SW3
71 G5 Walton Street SW3
73 K7 Walworth Place SE17
73 J5 Walworth Road SE17
72 D8 Wandsworth Road SW8
73 K6 Wansey Street SE17
74 F5 Wapping Dock Street * E1W
74 D5 Wapping High Street E1W
74 F5 Wapping Lane E1W
74 F4 Wapping Walk E1W
75 G5 Wapping Wall E1W
73 J2 Wardens Grove SE1
68 B6 Wardour Mews W1F
68 A6 Wardour Street W1F
69 H7 Wardrobe Place * EC4V
68 F3 Warner Street EC1R
68 F4 Warner Yard EC1R
67 M4 Warren Mews W1W
67 M4 Warren Street W1T
66 C3 Warrington Crescent W9
66 C4 Warrington Gardens W9
76 E1 Warrington Place E14
66 B3 Warwick Avenue W9
68 F5 Warwick Court WC1V
66 C5 Warwick Crescent W2
72 B1 Warwick House Street SW1Y
69 J6 Warwick Lane EC4M
66 C4 Warwick Place W9
71 M6 Warwick Place North * SW1V
71 L4 Warwick Row SW1E
71 M6 Warwick Square SW1V
69 H6 Warwick Square * EC4M
71 M6 Warwick Square Mews SW1V
68 A7 Warwick Street W1B
71 L6 Warwick Way SW1V
69 K4 Warwick Yard * EC1Y
66 F6 The Water Gardens W2
76 A8 Watergate Street SE8
68 E8 Waterloo Bridge SE1
72 B1 Waterloo Place SW1Y
72 F2 Waterloo Road SE1
74 E5 Waterman Way E1W
74 D7 Waterside Close * SE16
68 F7 Water Street WC2R
69 K6 Watling Court EC4M
69 K6 Watling Street EC4M
74 F3 Watney Market E1
74 F3 Watney Street E1
67 G5 Watson's Mews W1H
74 F5 Watts Street E1W
74 D5 Waveney Close E1W
71 K1 Waverton Street W1J
67 K8 Waverton Street W1K
74 B6 Weaver's Lane SE1
73 G3 Webber Row SE1
73 H3 Webber Street SE1
74 A8 Webb Street SE1
74 E8 Webster Road SE16
67 K7 Weighhouse Street W1K
68 C2 Weirs Passage NW1
67 K6 Welbeck Street W1U
67 K6 Welbeck Way W1U
74 E5 Welland Mews E1W
74 D4 Wellclose Square E1W
74 D4 Wellclose Street E1W
69 K6 Well Court EC4N
68 C1 Wellers Court NW1
73 K3 Weller Street SE1
66 C2 Wellesley Court W9
68 B2 Wellesley Place * NW1
75 H2 Wellesley Street E1
69 K2 Wellesley Terrace N1
66 E2 Wellington Place NW8
66 E1 Wellington Road NW8
71 H7 Wellington Square SW3
68 D7 Wellington Street WC2E
66 A8 Wellington Terrace W2
74 E5 Wellington Terrace E1W
68 A5 Wells Mews * W1T
68 E2 Wells Square WC1X
67 M5 Wells Street W1W
70 D4 Wells Way SW7
69 K1 Wenlock Road N1
69 K1 Wenlock Street N1
74 C2 Wentworth Street E1
68 A1 Werrington Street NW1
73 H6 Wesley Close SE17
67 K5 Wesley Street W1G
75 H2 West Arbour Street E1
66 D7 Westbourne Crescent W2
66 D7 Westbourne Crescent Mews W2
66 B6 Westbourne Gardens W2
66 E7 Westbourne Gate W2
66 A6 Westbourne Grove W2
66 B6 Westbourne Grove Terrace W2
66 A5 Westbourne Park Road W2
66 A5 Westbourne Park Villas W2
66 E7 Westbourne Street W2
66 C5 Westbourne Terrace W2
66 C6 Westbourne Terrace Mews W2
66 C5 Westbourne Terrace Road W2
70 E2 West Carriage Drive W2
68 C5 West Central Street WC1A
73 H8 Westcott Road SE17
71 J5 West Eaton Place SW1X
71 J5 West Eaton Place Mews SW1X
75 M5 Westferry Circus E14
75 M4 Westferry Road E14
74 F4 West Gardens E1W
70 B7 Westgate Terrace SW10
71 J4 West Halkin Street SW1X
69 G6 West Harding Street * EC4A
76 A2 West India Avenue E14
75 M3 West India Dock Road E14
69 K2 Westland Place EC1V
74 E7 West Lane SE16
71 L6 West Mews SW1V
72 D3 Westminster Bridge SW1P
72 F3 Westminster Bridge Road SE1
71 L7 Westmoreland Place SW1V
73 L8 Westmoreland Road SE17
67 K5 Westmoreland Street W1G
71 L7 Westmoreland Terrace SW1V
68 E1 Weston Rise WC1X
73 M3 Weston Street SE1
75 J2 Westport Street E1
69 H5 West Poultry Avenue EC1M
67 G7 West Rise * W2
71 H7 West Road SW3
69 H5 West Smithfield EC1A
73 H5 West Square SE11
74 C3 West Tenter Street E1
71 M6 West Warwick Place * SW1V
70 C6 Wetherby Gardens SW5
70 B6 Wetherby Mews SW5
70 C6 Wetherby Place SW5
74 D2 Weyhill Road E1
67 L5 Weymouth Mews W1G
67 K5 Weymouth Street W1G
70 B7 Wharfedale Street SW10
69 J1 Wharf Road N1
68 F2 Wharton Cottages * WC1X
68 F2 Wharton Street WC1X
67 K5 Wheatley Street W1G
76 B5 Wheat Sheaf Close E14
74 B1 Wheeler Lane E1
68 E5 Whetstone Park WC2A
72 F2 Whichcote Street * SE1
68 D2 Whidborne Street WC1H
69 G2 Whiskin Street EC1R
68 B7 Whitcomb Street W1D
69 G4 White Bear Yard * EC1R
74 C2 Whitechapel High Street E1
74 D2 Whitechapel Road E1
74 D2 White Church Lane E1
69 K3 Whitecross Street EC1Y
69 G6 Whitefriars Street EC4Y
72 C2 Whitehall SW1A
72 D2 Whitehall Court SW1A
72 D2 Whitehall Gardens SW1A
72 D2 Whitehall Place SW1A
73 G6 White Hart Street SE11
73 L2 White Hart Yard SE1
66 F4 Whitehaven Street NW8
71 G6 Whiteheads Grove SW3
75 J1 Whitehorse Road E1
71 L1 White Horse Street W1J
74 B2 White Kennett Street E1
69 M6 White Lion Court EC3V
69 J7 White Lion Hill EC4V
68 F1 White Lion Street N1
69 J4 White Lyon Court EC2Y
74 A6 White's Grounds SE1
74 A6 Whites Grounds Estate SE1
74 B1 White's Row E1
67 M3 Whitfield Place W1T
68 A4 Whitfield Street W1T
72 E5 Whitgift Street SE11
71 J6 Whittaker Street SW1W
69 M6 Whittington Avenue EC3V
73 G2 Whittlesey Street SE1
74 E3 Wicker Street E1
72 E7 Wickham Street SE11
68 E1 Wicklow Street WC1X
74 B1 Widegate Street E1
66 A3 Widley Road W9
67 K5 Wigmore Place * W1G
67 J6 Wigmore Street W1H
73 G7 Wigton Place * SE11
71 J5 Wilbraham Place SW1X
68 E6 Wild Court WC2B
73 M4 Wild's Rents SE1
68 D6 Wild Street WC2B
71 M4 Wilfred Street SW1E
74 C1 Wilkes Street E1
74 D8 William Ellis Way * SE16
68 C8 William IV Street WC2N
71 H3 William Mews SW1X
67 M3 William Road NW1
75 K4 William Square SE16
71 H3 William Street SW1X
72 A5 Willow Place SW1P
69 M3 Willow Street EC2A
68 F3 Wilmington Square WC1X
68 F2 Wilmington Street WC1X
74 E7 Wilson Grove SE16
75 L3 Wilson's Place E14
69 M5 Wilson Street EC2A
71 J3 Wilton Crescent SW1X
71 K4 Wilton Mews SW1X
71 J3 Wilton Place SW1X
71 M5 Wilton Road SW1V
71 J3 Wilton Row SW1X
71 K4 Wilton Street SW1X
71 J3 Wilton Terrace SW1X
71 G6 Wiltshire Close SW3
67 K5 Wimpole Mews W1G
67 K6 Wimpole Street W1G
73 H5 Winchester Close * SE11
73 L1 Winchester Square SE1
71 L7 Winchester Street SW1V
73 K1 Winchester Walk SE1
73 G5 Wincott Street SE11
72 F7 Windmill Row SE11
68 B5 Windmill Street W1T
73 G2 Windmill Walk * SE1
75 H6 Windrose Close SE16
69 K1 Windsor Terrace N1
74 F5 Wine Close E1W
68 B7 Winnett Street W1D
66 E6 Winsland Mews W2
66 E6 Winsland Street W2
68 A6 Winsley Street W1W
70 D8 Winterton Place SW10
74 E1 Winthrop Street E1
68 C3 Woburn Place WC1H
68 C4 Woburn Square WC1H
68 C3 Woburn Walk WC1H
73 J5 Wollaston Close SE17
74 C7 Wolseley Street SE1
74 F1 Wolsey Street E1
69 H3 Woodbridge Street EC1R
66 B4 Woodchester Square W2
71 H7 Woodfall Street SW3
74 C1 Woodseer Street E1
67 H7 Wood's Mews W1K
74 A8 Wood's Place SE1
67 K5 Woodstock Mews W1G
67 K6 Woodstock Street W1K
69 K5 Wood Street EC2Y
76 D8 Wood Wharf SE10
73 L7 Wooler Street SE17
68 C3 Woolf Mews WC1H
74 D8 Woolstaplers Way SE16
73 G2 Wootton Street SE1
72 E7 Worgan Street SE11
69 M5 Wormwood Street EC2M
69 M4 Worship Street EC2A
73 L7 Worth Grove SE17
68 F3 Wren Street WC1X
70 A4 Wright's Lane W8
67 L3 Wybert Street NW1
69 H2 Wyclif Street EC1V
66 A2 Wymering Road W9
76 B7 Wynan Road E14
67 H5 Wyndham Mews W1H
67 H5 Wyndham Place W1H
67 G4 Wyndham Street W1H
70 A4 Wynnstay Gardens W8
72 F7 Wynyard Terrace SE11
69 H2 Wynyatt Street EC1V
67 H6 Wythburn Place W1H

Y

76 E2 Yabsley Street E14
68 F3 Yardley Street WC1X
71 L2 Yarmouth Place W1J
71 G4 Yeoman's Row SW3
67 J3 York Bridge NW1
68 D8 York Buildings WC2N
67 J3 York Gate NW1
70 B2 York House Place W8
72 E3 York Road SE1
68 E5 Yorkshire Grey Yard * WC1V
75 K3 Yorkshire Road E14
75 K2 York Square E14
67 G5 York Street W1H
67 H4 York Street Chambers * W1U
67 K4 York Terrace East NW1
67 J4 York Terrace West NW1
70 B3 Young Street W8

Z

73 J1 Zoar Street SE1

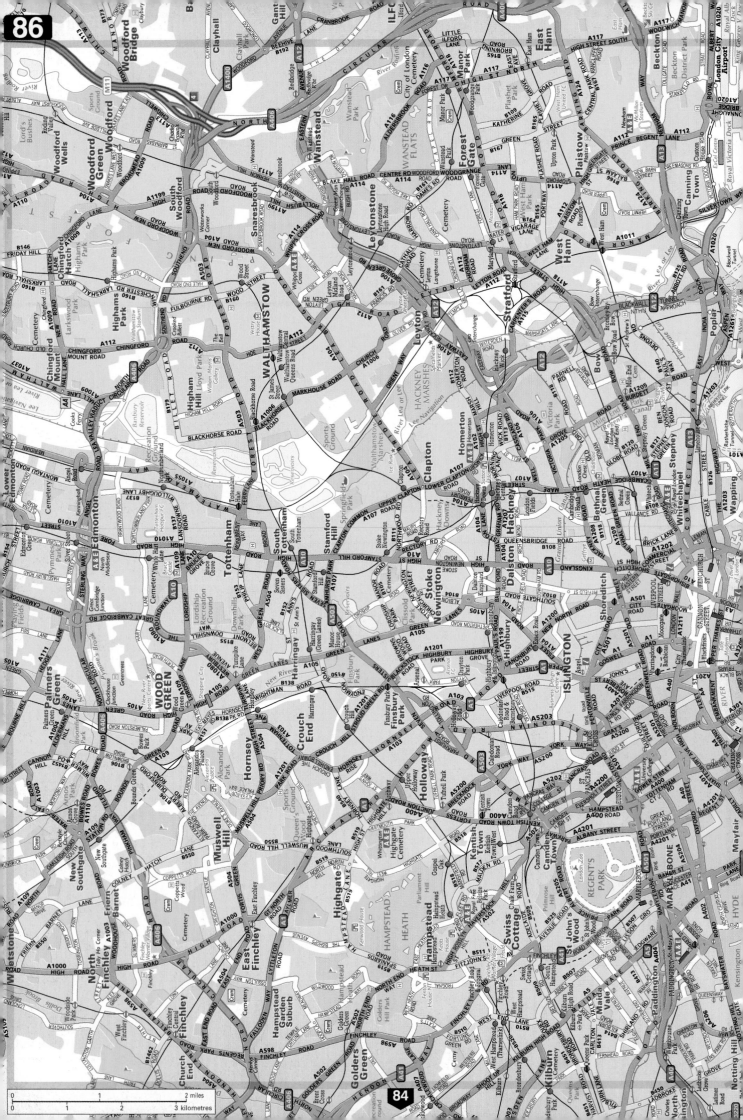

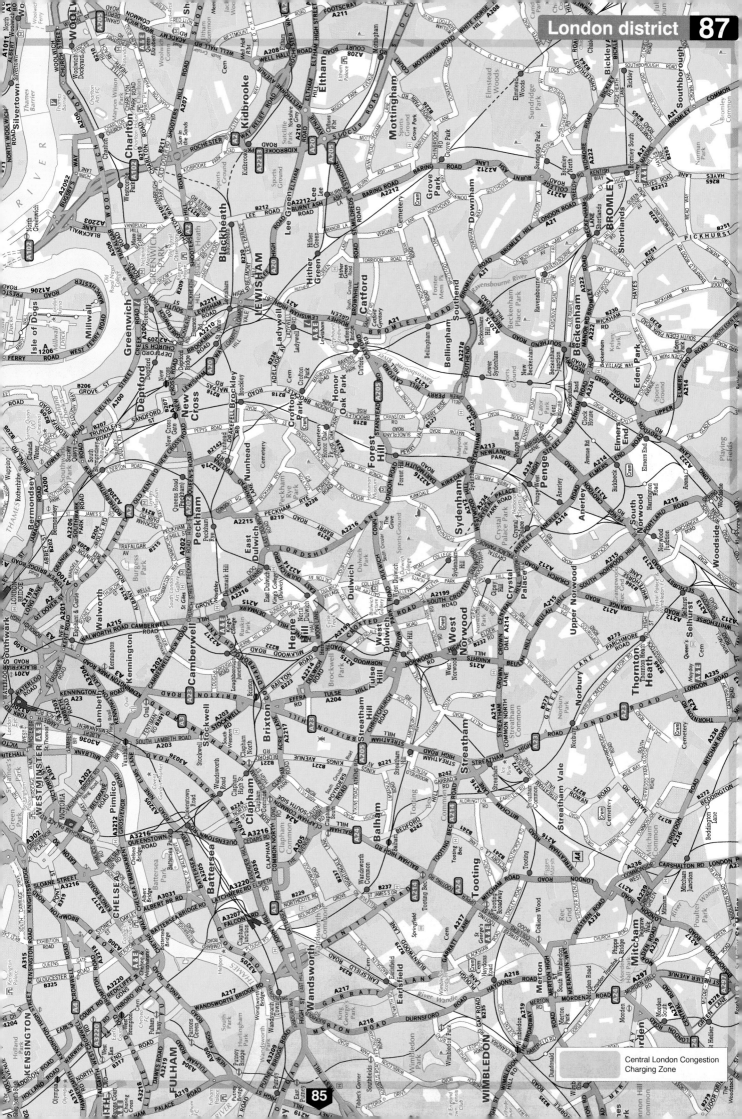

Central London Congestion
Charging Zone

Route planner

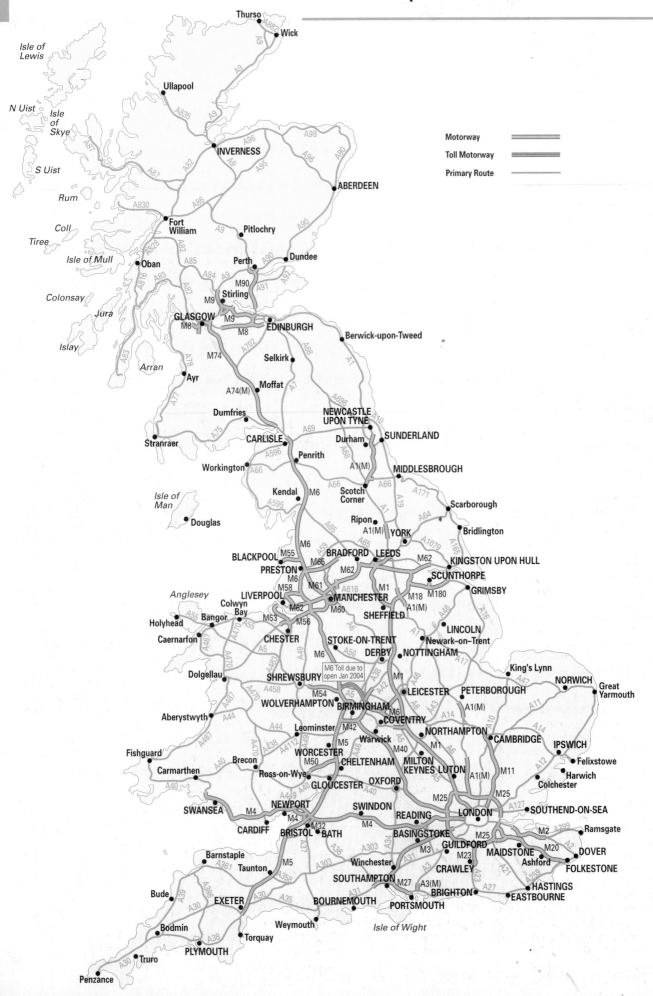